"Creatively conceived, rigorously executed, and critical for anyone interested in the dynamics of labor migration. Will replace the fallacy of the doomed 'unskilled' labor migrant with a nuanced view of the complex ways in which job skills are acquired through lifelong learning and deployed on both sides of the US–Mexico migrant circuit."

—Pierrette Hondagneu-Sotelo, author of *Paradise Transplanted: Migration and the Making of California Gardens*

"*Skills of the 'Unskilled'* challenges stale thinking about migrants and their work by showing how they not only survive but also develop the skills to thrive."

—David FitzGerald, coauthor of *Culling the Masses: The Democratic Origins of Racist Immigration Policy in the Americas*

"*Skills of the 'Unskilled'* is novel, revealing, and transformative. This meticulous, skillful, and profoundly social examination of the intersection of jobs, skills, and knowledge will transform the way we see 'immigrant jobs' and how we talk about 'unskilled' labor. It will recast our images of immigrant workers in multiple consequential ways."

—Cecilia Menjívar, author of *Enduring Violence: Ladina Women's Lives in Guatemala*

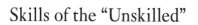

Skills of the "Unskilled"

Skills of the "Unskilled"

*Work and Mobility among
Mexican Migrants*

Jacqueline Maria Hagan,
Rubén Hernández-León, and
Jean-Luc Demonsant

UNIVERSITY OF CALIFORNIA PRESS

University of California Press, one of the most distin-
guished university presses in the United States, enriches
lives around the world by advancing scholarship in the
humanities, social sciences, and natural sciences. Its
activities are supported by the UC Press Foundation and
by philanthropic contributions from individuals and
institutions. For more information, visit www.ucpress.edu.

University of California Press
Oakland, California

©2015 by The Regents of the University of California

Library of Congress Cataloging-in-Publication Data

Hagan, Jacqueline Maria, 1954–.
 Skills of the "unskilled": work and mobility among
Mexican migrants/ Jacqueline Maria Hagan, Rubén
Hernández-León, Jean-Luc Demonsant.
  pages cm.
 Includes bibliographical references and index.
 ISBN 978-0-520-28372-5 (cloth)
 ISBN 978-0-520-28373-2 (pbk. : alk. paper)
 ISBN 978-0-520-95950-7 (ebook)
  1. Foreign workers, Mexican—United States. 2. Labor
market—Emigration and immigration. 3. Guanajuato
(Mexico)—Emigration and immigration—Social
aspects. 4. United States—Emigration and immigra-
tion—Social aspects. I. Hernández-León, Ruben,
author. II. Demonsant, Jean-Luc, author. III. Title.
 HD8081.M6H34 2015
 331.5′440896872073—dc23
                                      2014032691

Manufactured in the United States of America

24 23 22 21 20 19 18 17 16 15
10 9 8 7 6 5 4 3 2 1

Cover image: Top photos by Jacqueline Maria Hagan and
Rubén Hernández-León. Bottom photo by DNY59/
istockphoto.

For the next generation: AnneMarie, Lucas, Olín,
Paloma, Emma, and Léo

CONTENTS

ACKNOWLEDGMENTS

Like many field research projects, ours began as a case study with a particular focus. Over time it expanded in scope and moved in unexpected directions, blossoming into something very different. We are grateful to the many organizations, communities, and individuals who supported and assisted us along this long, sometimes rocky, but always rewarding research road. Initial fieldwork in North Carolina was funded in part by the University of North Carolina (UNC) Office of Economic and Business Development and the UNC Department of Sociology. The fieldwork conducted by Jacqueline Hagan and Jean-Luc Demonsant in Guanajuato, Mexico, was funded by grants from the UNC Carolina Population Center, the UNC Research Council, and the research program of the Mexican Higher Education Secretary (PROMEP-SEP).

Several institutions and fellowships helped us through the writing stages of the book:

The Woodrow Wilson Center awarded Jacqueline Hagan a 2011–12 fellowship, which provided the intellectual environment to develop research ideas and begin analysis and writing. Hagan and Rubén Hernández-León benefited from a summer fellowship from the Institut Méditerranéen de Recherches Avancées (IMéRA) in Marseille, France, in 2011 where they exchanged ideas and wrote on the issue of skills. A 2012 Kenan Fellowship awarded by UNC provided Hagan with the time to draft initial chapters of the book and travel to Mexico to complete the data analysis and to California to work with Hernández-León on drafting the manuscript. A 2012–13 grant from the Chicano Studies Research Center at UCLA provided funds to hire a research assistant to assist with data analysis. A 2012–14 fellowship awarded by the Luxembourg Fond National de Recherche provided Demonsant with a postdoctoral position at CEPS / INSTEAD during which time he completed analysis of the data and assisted with the final stages of the manuscript.

We are very grateful as well to the students and persons in North Carolina, Los Angeles, and Guanajuato, Mexico, who devoted countless hours of their time to interviewing migrants, coding data, and assisting with the final presentation of the book: Andrea Perdoma, Brianna Mullis, Caroline Wood, Carolina Calvillo, Courtney Luedke, Christian Quingla, Jonathan Moreno Gómez, Gabriel Gutiérrez Olvera, Fátima del Rayo Ornelas Ramírez, Rafael Gallegos, Christian Palacios Morales, Erika Rodríguez Ortega, Ruy Valdés Benavides, Angel Alfonso Escamilla Garcia, Holly Straudt-Epsteiner, and Eli Wilson. We also extend a very warm thanks to Joshua Wassink, Annie Lee, Luis Fernando López Ornelas, and Miguel Leboreiro for research provided with data management and analysis.

We thank Cruz, one of the return migrants featured in the manuscript, who escorted us to both family-based and large leather factories where we observed informal learning and on-the-job skills acquisition. A special thanks also goes to our dear friend Miguel Hernandez, who chauffeured us to countless towns and cities to conduct our interviews, all the while entertaining us with lively conversation and warm friendship.

Writing this book would have been extremely difficult without the assistance and support of our editor, our colleagues, and friends. We thank Sergio Chavez and Nichola Lowe, who were fundamental in the data collection and analysis in the exploratory stages of the study. Our appreciation also goes to colleagues and friends who read partial or complete drafts of the manuscript and offered advice and invaluable suggestions that pushed us forward and ultimately took the book one step further, including Harley Browning, Roger Waldinger, David FitzGerald, Douglas Massey, Joshua Wassink, Mike Glatthaar, and Ted Mouw. Our appreciation is also warmly extended to our editor, Naomi Schneider, who believed in the book and pushed it to completion. We would also like to thank the anonymous reviewers for their very useful comments and suggestions.

A very warm and special thanks goes to Leslie Banner, whose intellectual curiosity and exceptional editing skills and critical eye certainly polished the overall style of this book and the presentations of its narratives.

We are indebted to the many migrants from Mexico who shared their time and their migration experiences, their labor market trials and tribulations, but also their many successes. Their stories are what make field research so rich and rewarding. Several migrants requested we use their real names here in the hopes that they can one day share their migration histories with their children.

Who Are the "Unskilled," Really?

Rafael was born in Leon, a large industrial city with a population of over one million in the state of Guanajuato, Mexico, known primarily for its leather, footwear, and textile industries.[1] Typical of many young men in the area, Rafael left school at age 15 and found an entry-level position in a manufacturing firm that produces men's clothing. Through observation and informal training from coworkers, he learned to operate and repair the industrial sewing machines that stitch men's garments. Rafael readily transferred these technical skills to his second job in Leon, where he also worked as a machinist, this time in a factory that manufactured nurses' uniforms. After a year in his second job, he was promoted to supervisor, but without the promised salary increase.

With opportunities for higher earnings limited at the plant, Rafael decided to try his luck in the United States and took the risk of migrating without authorization to Los Angeles, where he had friends and family. He applied for a job as a machinist in a manufacturing firm that produces textile covers for musical instruments. After showing the supervisor that he could operate the machines on the floor, he was hired on the spot. Rafael worked at the plant as a machinist for two years, acquiring new skills and seeing his wages increase from $7 to $14 per hour. In addition to working with industrial sewing machines, Rafael operated and repaired manual sewing equipment, learned new designs, and worked with different types of textiles, from velvet to nylon to canvas. Armed with his new skills and targeted savings, he returned to Leon in 2008 and, once resettled, used his remitted savings to start a small tailoring business, carving a new economic niche for himself in a textile and leather industry that traditionally produces shoes, belts, boots, and purses. Today, Rafael and his two employees stitch men's garments, velvet covers for musical instruments, and nylon backpacks, using tailoring and machinist repair skills that he developed on the job in Los Angeles.

Lalo was born and reared in a small rancho of less than two thousand inhabitants outside of Irapuato, Guanajuato. The community, Alajuela, has an established history of outmigration to the United States and a sizeable number of return migrants who have retired in the community. At the early age of eight he left school to help his father farm their land; at the age of 18, he found an entry-level position at a nearby General Motors auto plant, where he went through a six-month training program before being assigned to the production line. Frustrated with the repetitive nature of the work and seeking adventure, after two years he decided to migrate to the United States, to Georgia, where he had friends working in chicken processing and carpet manufacturing. After trying similarly repetitive work in a line job at the carpet factory, he located an apprentice position with a master carpenter through a friend. Lalo loved this work and admired the craftsmanship of his mentor, whom he calls el Romano (a Mexican American man). El Romano taught Lalo everything about woodworking, and Lalo became a master carpenter in the process. Together they laid floors and designed and built cabinetry and custom-made furniture. Lalo traveled home to Mexico regularly, which enabled him to maintain strong linkages with families and households in his hometown and assess changing economic opportunities in the community.

After four years of working under the guidance of el Romano, Lalo was prepared to return home for good, driving a white Ford truck filled with carpentry tools he had purchased in the United States. Taking advantage of a program launched by the local government to harness the resources and skills of return migrants, Lalo enrolled in a *"programa incubador de empresas"* (a program to incubate new businesses) in order to follow in the entrepreneurial steps of el Romano, who "works hard and is disciplined." Upon completion of the six-month course, Lalo used his savings to open a woodworking business that provides housing and U.S.-style cabinets to the return migrants living in the community. He hired five ex-migrants, choosing them because "they work hard." Like Rafael, Lalo used his new entrepreneurial and technical skills to train his employees and carve a new niche in the local economy, one driven by return migrants who desire U.S. building styles.

Anna, aged 35, grew up in the *municipio* of San Miguel de Allende, a picturesque colonial town and home to tens of thousands of expatriate Americans. At age 15, she left school and found a job cleaning apartments. Several years later, through a friend, she found a job working as a receptionist in a hotel owned and operated by an American. In 1996, after two years on the job, an American woman approached Anna and asked if she would return to Manhattan with her and care for her children. Seeking adventure and opportunity Anna agreed and so worked as a live-in domestic and child caregiver for four years. In 2000, she left her first employer because she no longer wanted a live-in position; she wanted her own apartment and she wanted "freedom." Anna found a day job as a nanny for two small children and increased her salary from $350 to $450 a week. In this job, she learned how to clean with new technology, care for the children, and navigate public transportation; she also improved her English and developed interpersonal skills that she applied when interacting with her employers. By performing these multiple tasks, she developed a set of management skills.

Anna regularly sent her earnings to her mother in San Miguel de Allende, who used them to build a house for her family. When the house was completed, Anna returned home to San Miguel de Allende. Her English skills helped her land her first job upon return as a salesperson at a mailbox company that ships items abroad for the expatriate community. After marrying and giving birth to her first child, she left this job and found part-time work as a sales manager in a high-end store that sells hand-crafted furniture to Americans living in Mexico and tourists. In the shop where one of the authors purchased some patio furniture, she mentioned that she earns 200 pesos more a week than her nonimmigrant counterparts because of her social and management skills and English language proficiency, skill sets she had learned on the job as a domestic and nanny.

Although Rafael, Lalo, and Anna have distinctive migration histories, the three share labor market experiences that are typical of many Mexican return migrants with low levels of education. They leave school at a young age and find entry-level positions in the various industries that characterize the country's local economies. The on-the-job, tacit skills they learn offer some occupational mobility, but for the most part opportunities for job advancement and higher wages are limited. Some migrate to the United States for higher wages, some leave because of economic dislocations, others for occupational advancement, and still others for adventure or to improve their skills. Once in the United States, many migrants achieve these goals by mobilizing the skills they had acquired in Mexico and learning new ones. Rafael was able to apply his machinist skills from the garment factory floor in Leon to his manufacturing job in Los Angeles, and he was rewarded for these skills with higher wages. It is probable that the tactful people skills learned in her job as a receptionist in a San Miguel de Allende hotel made Anna a good candidate for a live-in domestic in Manhattan. Similarly, Lalo's knowledge of how a General Motors assembly line functions would have facilitated his learning an assembly line position in Georgia's carpet industry. Both Lalo and Anna also acquired new skills in the United States, including woodworking and English language proficiency that provided economic gains and advancement.

When they return home, migrants often achieve wage growth and occupational mobility by applying their new skill sets they have acquired abroad, in the process diversifying local economies and introducing new techniques and approaches to work. Some female return migrants, like Anna, are able to bypass domestic work and enter the sales workforce because of the English language and customer service skills they have learned in the United States. As the case of Anna demonstrates, speaking English opens employment prospects in industries such as tourism where this language is the primary language of communication. In the process, these skill transfers introduce new customer-service approaches to the social organization of work. Some, like Rafael and Lalo, optimize their time abroad to achieve specific migration goals, accumulating new skills, work experiences, and enough earnings to start their own businesses. Returnees such as Lalo and Rafael see themselves as innovators, or what Francesco Cerase calls "carriers of change," because their entrepreneurial activities can trigger development and diversify local economies.[2] In the case of Lalo, part of this diversification in his hometown of Alajuela is made possible because of a migrant-driven economy that thrives on transferred skills. Indeed, Lalo's success is in part dependent on the consumer tastes and preferred housing styles of return migrants, but his ability to transfer entrepreneurial skills from the United States also changed his approach to organizing work practices.[3] And, as in the case of Lalo, a migrant-driven economy facilitated the transfer of Anna's skills to Mexico. What makes Anna's case particularly interesting is that the migrants driving the San Miguel de Allende economy and the transfer of her English skills are expatriate Americans, not Mexican return migrants.

As these case narratives show, Rafael, Lalo, and Anna acquired significant skills that they converted into genuine economic gains and opportunities for themselves and the communities to which they returned. In the United States, however, these workers are often perceived as "unskilled" by virtue of the jobs they do because these jobs are shunned by most native workers, who think of them as low in social status—as jobs that only migrants do. The empirical literature on migrant human capital skills and labor market adjustments does not stray very far from this public perception. Most researchers, because of data constraints, rely primarily on the formal institutional settings that produce measurable proxies for human capital, including schooling, professional training, and host country language skills.[4] According to this literature, Anna, Lalo, and Rafael would be most likely classified as "low skilled" by virtue of the low levels of education and formal credentials they brought with them from Mexico or acquired in the United States. Yet, as their labor market and migration histories reveal, their investment in other forms of human capital at home and abroad was substantial, and we can see that obviously far from being unskilled or low skilled, as the literature simplifies, they brought with them to the United States an eagerness and capacity to learn that increased their abilities to earn. Lalo and Anna not only learned English but also other cultural skill sets such as new ways of interacting with customers and approaching work, tacit skills that often go unrecognized by scholars but play a crucial role in the labor process and mobility of migrant workers. Employers need and value these skills although this appreciation does not necessarily translate into higher pay or better working conditions.[5] Rafael and Lalo also reskilled with the mastering of new tools and technologies learned informally in their U.S. jobs, knowledge they then mobilized upon return to introduce new ways of executing job tasks. The valuable technical and interpersonal skills and work habits that they acquired in the United States either broadened their opportunities or empowered them to launch entrepreneurial activities and diversify local economies.

Skills of the "Unskilled" reports the findings of a five-year study launched to test prevalent assumptions about poor migrants with low levels of formal education: that they are a homogeneous group of target earners who neither possess measurable skills nor learn new ones and who, because of their low levels of traditional human capital, face limited prospects for economic, social, and even geographic mobility in their migrant careers. To test these assumptions, we posed the following research questions:

1. What is the *total human capital* that migrants with low levels of education possess?

2. In what institutions and social contexts at home and abroad are these skills acquired? What roles do governments, communities, and families play in creating and maintaining these contexts?

3. How do the skill sets of women and men differ and how do gendered skill transfers shape labor market experiences abroad and upon return?

4. Which skills are better for migrants and return migrants? That is, are certain jobs and skills learned in Mexico better for employment prospects in the United States? Conversely, are some skills learned in the United States more easily transferred to Mexico than others? How are skill transfers related to industrial contexts of arrival and return?

We argue that migration is more than a strategy to earn higher wages, as posited by neoclassical economic theorists, or a means to overcome market failures and diversify household resources through the accumulation of savings, as viewed by the new economics of labor migration.[6] It is also a social process through which migrants learn and develop valuable but often hard-to-measure skills and transfer them across regional and international labor markets to broaden their opportunities abroad and upon return.

Sociologists Susan Star and Anselm Strauss have memorably described the manner in which individuals, especially those working in the service sector, such as janitors, maids, or caregivers, are often viewed as nonpeople despite the value of their work experience and substantial interpersonal skills.[7] The low degree of social recognition of these skills contributes to their low status. Nowhere is this truer than in the perception of "unskilled" migrants in the United States, and in particular, undocumented immigrants with low levels of education, who often learn through on- and off-the-job observation and informal interaction in their home communities and abroad. Because this group of workers is viewed as unskilled by virtue of their low levels of education and formal training, their labor market contributions are overlooked and their mobility pathways are poorly understood.

In this book, we draw on two stages of exploratory fieldwork, one in the United States, the other in Mexico, followed by a survey of a representative sample of 200 return migrants in Leon, Mexico, to identify and measure the *total human capital* that migrants with low levels of education can acquire, transfer, and apply throughout their life courses and migratory careers—before migration, while abroad, and upon return—to further their labor market opportunities. The skills, competences, and knowledge that we identify and describe here include easy-to-measure components of traditional human capital, such as education and language skills, but also incorporate sets of technical, social, and cultural competences that are harder to measure. These harder-to-measure abilities include working knowledge and technical skills learned informally through observation and interaction on and off the job in home communities and abroad, along with interpersonal competences that migrants acquire in new workplace environments, such as customer service, leadership, teamwork, and innovative and culturally specific ways of approaching work. As we demonstrate, these social skills can sometimes translate into entrepreneurial activities. We further conceptualize the learning of skills as a lifelong and gendered process that is not restricted to an individual's time in school or in the workforce.[8] Our perspective emphasizes how and where total human capital is created, recognizing the importance of the social processes, contexts, and locations in which learning takes place, focusing on what people do rather than what their credentials may be.[9]

As the cases of Rafael, Lalo, and Anna demonstrate, migration is a social process through which migrants reskill and transfer new work experiences across borders to facilitate alternative mobility pathways. But the implications of skilling processes extend beyond individual labor market experiences because the acquisition and transfer of skills is also a process embedded in social relations, cultural practices, and distinctive labor markets in Mexico and the United States. Thus, international migration has the potential to change industry techniques, diversify local economies, and introduce new approaches to work, sometimes operating as an engine of social change in the communities to which migrants return. The linkage between individual labor market experiences and social change in local communities is especially characteristic of entrepreneurs in the return stage of the migratory circuit. Along with financial capital and technical skills, migrants return home with a cultural capital of sorts: self-confidence and the ability to deal with new challenges and to adapt to different approaches to work.

Our micro social analysis of human capital formation across the migratory circuit has broad implications for the ways in which migration and labor scholars and economic sociologists conceptualize and measure skills and identify and assess the mobility pathways of migrants. In the migration literature the standard human capital model of socioeconomic attainment sees migration as an investment in which returns are balanced against costs.[10] According to human capital theory, migrants generally earn less than the native born because the human capital acquired in countries of origin is undervalued in destination labor markets. With the acquisition of country-specific human capital such as education, language skills, and professional credentials, however, immigrants can experience occupational mobility and wage growth.[11] Moreover, return migrants who bring back home with them these formal forms of human capital, including English language and additional schooling, may experience economic gains upon return if employers recognize and value these skills.[12] Although the theory recognizes that human capital includes both an individual's stock of observable skills (language, schooling) as well as unobservable skills (innate abilities, pre-labor market experiences), in the empirical literature data constraints compel most researchers to rely primarily on measurable proxies, such as years of education. As Allan Williams points out, this focus on officially recognized and codifiable knowledge privileges the more educated as "skilled" learners and knowledge bearers, encouraging a dichotomy of skilled and unskilled or low skilled based solely on formal qualifications. Ultimately, categories such as unskilled and even low skilled function as a black box: obscuring, instead of revealing, the social processes by which certain workers perform distinct jobs that also require knowledge, competences and tacit skills.[13]

Migration and labor scholars who study the technical and social skills of workers with little formal human capital have more recently recognized that "[w]ork at the bottom of the labor market may require little formal education, but it nonetheless involves job-related proficiencies of significant degree."[14] In other words, the fact that certain jobs require fewer formally acquired skills does not mean that such jobs do not necessitate a measure of skill or working knowledge. These scholars also acknowledge that migrants working on the low-wage and less prestigious rungs of the labor market (in construction, hospitality, landscaping, manufacturing, and agriculture) often acquire job-specific skills and develop them informally on the job, learning by doing, observing, and through interaction and cooperation with others.[15] While our study also focuses on the skills learned in job-specific formal and informal work environments, we go further than prior contributors to this literature as we identify and describe those human capital skills learned through informal interaction and observation *outside* work environments in migrant homes and communities. This process of skill development begins in home and communal settings in the country of origin, when individuals at a young age participate in the building of a family home, or the repairing of a family automobile or household appliance. Following geographers David Beckett and Alan Williams, who recognize the importance of informal learning across the life cycle, we approach learning and skill development as a *lifelong process* that is not limited to an individual's labor market experiences or schooling.[16]

SKILL ACQUISITIONS AND TRANSFERS: INTEGRATING INTERNATIONAL MIGRATION, HUMAN CAPITAL, AND LEARNING APPROACHES

To shed light on how migrant workers with low levels of traditional human capital are able to acquire and mobilize skills across the migratory circuit, we engage different scholarly traditions that thus far have had limited cross-fertilization: studies of knowledge and learning, scholarship on the labor process in industrial and postindustrial capitalism, and the empirical literature on international migration and human capital transfers. We build primarily on the literature on knowledge and learning that recognizes multiple types of knowledge and makes an important distinction between codified and tacit knowledge. The concept of tacit knowledge or tacit knowing was introduced by Michael Polanyi in *Personal Knowledge*[17] and later expanded in *The Tacit Dimension*[18] and *Meaning.*[19] Tacit knowledge refers to all forms of embodied personal knowledge, including the practical skills required to complete a task. According to Polanyi and Prosch, "any practical skill consists in the capacity for carrying out a great number of particular movements with a view to achieving a comprehensive result."[20] All forms of work involve some form of skill, even when those skills have been internalized and routinized and cannot be demonstrated or measured in explicit terms or cannot be adequately articulated by verbal means. It follows from Polanyi's concept of tacit knowing that while there are jobs that require distinct and varied skills, there are no unskilled jobs.

Following Polanyi's seminal contributions on tacit knowledge, sociologists examining the labor process have expanded on the concept of tacit skills, alternatively called working knowledge, competences, social skills, and also "soft" or "people" skills to distinguish them from technical skills.[21] Challenging Harry Braverman's argument that managerial control of the labor process in advanced capitalism requires the absolute deskilling of jobs and workers,[22] Tony Manwaring and Stephen Wood contend that all forms of work entail a series of tacit skills, which are often taken for granted because such skills are subjectively

implications: first, this type of recruitment creates durable relations between the firm and the community where employers find their workers; second, managers use the mutual obligations that characterize social networks to turn the hiring channel into a mechanism for social control within the firm;[28] and third, hiring through the social ties of existing employees and with certain tacit skills in mind brings a degree of closure to the labor markets of particular groups of workers, excluding those who are not members of the social network. While managers have the upper hand in this process, collectively applied tacit skills and shared social characteristics form the basis for workers to claim "membership in the social community of the workplace,"[29] for "workers [to] develop an identity in relation to the labor process,"[30] and particularly for workers with low levels of formal human capital and working in low-wage and less prestigious jobs to obtain a measure of power in the workplace and the larger labor market.[31]

Historically, studies of the labor process, tacit skills, and workplace learning have used native workers in industrial settings as the empirical basis for their analyses. And while it is clear that all workers deploy tacit and variable technical skills in the labor process, it is also clear that not all jobs are regulated in the same way and not all workers receive the same social recognition for their labor. In the early 1970s, economists and sociologists developed the concept of the internal labor market to show how, in different segments of the economy, jobs and labor are governed by different sets of rules. In the primary sector, regulated by government and dominated by large corporations, the internal labor market offers workers (primarily male) job security, higher-than-living wages, collective bargaining, medical and other benefits, and mobility opportunities based on seniority and skill. As Michael

Piore argues, having invested in their workers' skills, employers seek to retain them over the long term.[32]

By contrast, in the secondary sector of the labor market, jobs are not regulated by the government, typically pay low wages, do not require formal skills, do not provide collective bargaining and other group benefits, offer minimal to no mobility opportunities, and quickly disappear when demand shrinks. In the secondary sector, interactions between managers and workers are framed in highly personalistic terms instead of the rational-bureaucratic employer-employee rules of the primary sector. As Peter Doeringer and Michael Piore state, "the secondary sector tends to be associated with the employment of certain social and demographic groups—women, youth, and ethnic and racial minorities,"[33] and as Piore subsequently argued, migrants are a key social group that fits the needs of the industrial society's secondary labor market. Migrants initially think of their presence in the host society as only temporary, an orientation that contributes to a weak attachment to the local labor market. Furthermore, the newcomers' assessment of wages and working conditions in a foreign land are based on the standards of their home country. This dual frame of reference partly explains why migrant workers are willing to take low-paying and low-status jobs otherwise rejected by natives.[34] In fact, as Roger Waldinger and Michael Lichter argued, employers might prefer migrants over native workers because of their status as societal outsiders. In other words, the social distance between employer and employee in terms of nativity, legal status, race, and language makes the foreigner a "natural" candidate for jobs considered too demeaning for natives to take.[35] Dual labor market theory thus is less concerned with the absolute levels of skill newcomers possess and more with the relationship between the migrant and the societal institutions that regulate labor and employment.

Migrants do sustain more than a fleeting presence in the host society, however. As time passes, newcomers become acquainted with the mobility opportunities available in the country of destination. And repeated sojourning allows them to establish long-term connections to employers who, in turn, develop a preference for foreign labor, demanding more of the same. Established foreign-born employees are entrusted by supervisors with the task of supplying new recruits from the country of origin. Pioneer migrants make use of their kinship and friendship networks to satisfy this demand, while creating a powerful "engine of migration"[36] and a de facto extended labor market connecting workers at home with employment opportunities abroad.[37] The labor-market beachheads that migrants first establish become full-blown colonies, or what scholars have called ethnic niches, that is, distinct occupational concentrations and specializations that result from skill, network connections, language, and discrimination.[38] As this process unfolds, the workplaces migrants colonize also become populated with the tacit skills these newcomers have transferred from the home country, applied, and continued to develop at the destination. The self-feeding mechanism behind this social process is transparent: once migrants, with their common language and tacit skills, dominate the occupational niche, employers will be compelled to go to the newcomers' social networks to staff the workplace and get the job done. A byproduct of this process is that the occupations dominated by migrants become associated with the real and imagined characteristics of the newcomers, turning them into "migrant" jobs, that is, jobs only migrants take on.

The scholarship on both knowledge and learning and the labor process recognize that workers with low levels of formal education deploy a variety of skills in the workplace. In contrast, the empirical literature on migration and human capital and skill transfers has focused almost exclusively on the study and measurement of formally acquired, codifiable human capital, often capturing it through a handy but problematic indicator: years of schooling.[39] This limited and limiting understanding of human capital has led some economists working in the human capital tradition to argue that the quality of today's immigrants is declining compared to the newcomers of earlier waves.[40]

There are several additional problems with the empirical literature on human capital investments, migration, and skill transfers. Often neglected in this literature is the learning and transfer of skills from the home country.[41] The economists Harriet Duleep and Martin Regets have recognized this flaw in human capital models and developed a more inclusive theoretical model of human capital investment called the Elusive Concept of Immigrant Quality.[42] One of the things that Duleep and Regets stress in their model is the value of home country skills for learning new skills. They argue that although technologies between source and destination countries may differ, the materials and goals of the skills are comparable. Drawing on the case of a Cambodian carpenter, they illustrate how "his experience with a hand saw comes into use when learning to use an electric saw." To quote from their summary, "People who have learned one set of skills, even if those skills are not valued in the destination country's labor market, have advantages in learning a new set: in learning a previous skill, one learns how to learn."[43]

Sociologists have also documented the skills and working knowledge that migrants acquire in their home countries and mobilize to advance their labor market careers in the United States. Rubén Hernández-León found that immigrant machinists working in Houston's petrochemical industry had transferred machinist skills acquired on the job in Mexico and used them to leverage higher wages and better work conditions in their U.S. occupations.[44] These migrants tapped into social networks composed of workers with similar skill levels to obtain information about employment opportunities and identify companies and jobs that offered higher pay. In this process, workers not only transferred skills but also developed new ones as they learned how to operate more advanced, computer-controlled machines. These machinists were able to reskill because of the trigonometry and drafting lessons they had received in secondary school and the vast on-the-job skills they accumulated in Mexico. In his study of Caribbean and Korean immigrants in the construction and buildings trade in New York City, Roger Waldinger found that premigration experience in the construction work gave immigrant business owners an edge over their native-born counterparts.[45] Similarly, Jacqueline Hagan and colleagues found that undocumented immigrant construction workers laboring in the building and trades industry in the United States had previously acquired many of their construction skills on the job in Mexico and / or the United States. Once in the United States they regularly mobilized these skills to "job jump" to better positions.[46]

Though the technologies used in construction and building trades in the two countries are different, the skills that migrants had acquired in Mexico, nonetheless, had value in their U.S. construction jobs. For example, as Hagan and her colleagues found, many of the construction workers had learned to mold bricks by hand in Mexico. Their familiarity with the brick material proved useful when it came time to lay bricks in their U.S. jobs. The construction workers also learned new on-the-job skills in the United States, which they then mobilized to negotiate higher wages and "job jump," called *brincar* (as the migrants refer to it), an individual labor market strategy that is purposefully and successfully used by both native-born workers and highly skilled immigrants to circumvent discrimination and secure higher wages and better working conditions.[47] Their ability to job jump, however, was also dependent on the workers being able to demonstrate their skills and the employers to recognize them, especially in the case of tacit skills, which are common skill sets in construction work.

Other scholars challenging traditional measures of human capital also recognize the importance of social skills and competences learned informally on the job abroad. In their study of skilled labor migrants who had returned to Slovakia, geographers Allan Williams and Vladimir Baláž find that the value of working abroad extends beyond professional experience and training to gains associated with improved communication skills, along with personal competences, such as self-confidence.[48] There is every reason to assume that the "unskilled" migrant returns home with similarly enhanced social and personal skills acquired in new work environments in the U.S. labor market. As Williams argues, the acquisition of both tacit and technical knowledge is dispersed across local, regional, and national labor markets; across jobs, from the professional to the informally skilled; and across populations whether educated to the doctoral or the third grade level.[49] This is not to say that the distinction between social and technical is always clear. Take the case of English language capital, which as we show is one of the most valued skills acquired abroad among our sample of return migrants. It is both a communication and a technical skill, and while it can be directly rewarded through paid employment, it is also valorized through the generation of self-esteem and social recognition.[50]

Not all knowledge (even that which is codified) is shared or recognized, however, nor is it always valued or rewarded. Successful knowledge transfers are shaped by mobility that is bounded (within intercompany transfers) or unbounded as part of the career of what Williams refers to as "free agent labor migrants" who forge their own mobility pathways.[51] Disadvantaged ethnic groups may also experience blocked mobility in their jobs if their skills are not recognized.[52] Successful transfers also depend on the language of work and whether the migrant is authorized to work. Lack of English language ability can make it more difficult for a migrant to demonstrate skills, and lack of work authorization may impose institutional barriers that block mobility and rewards, even when skills are recognized.[53]

In this book we go further than existing research to explain how migrants and return migrants develop skills in their labor market careers. We identify and describe the cumulative process of formal and informal skill acquisition and transfer across three stages of the migratory circuit, from native work and life experiences to U.S. employment, to life after returning home. Contrary to accounts that focus solely on blocked mobility and exploitation, we contend that migrants mobilize skills across jobs, labor markets, and borders. That is, informal learning and work experience at home and abroad matter for the long-term success and careers of migrants.

The research we present in this book has broad implications not only for how skills are conceptualized and measured, but also for how the mobility pathways of migrants and return migrants are assessed. Studies that look at human capital in the traditional way usually measure economic mobility, be it higher wages (which is almost always the case), occupational change, or self-employment, solely as an outcome of skills acquisition in the more developed country.[54] In contrast, we conceptualize skills acquisition and development as a lifelong process embedded in workplaces, families, and communities throughout the migrant trajectory. We stress that human capital models should not only focus on narrow cross-sectional measures of mobility but also consider skills acquisition as a social process and a mobility pathway in and of itself. Along these lines, we demonstrate the ways in which skills acquired at one stage of the migratory cycle can create individual labor market opportunities at another stage. We further suggest that skill transfers have the potential to extend beyond individual opportunity, sometimes contributing to the generation of entrepreneurial ventures. In this way, skill transfers fuel local development, shape industry techniques, and influence work practices. And because our mixed methodology includes a survey with detailed measures of occupations and skills across the migratory trajectory, case studies, and workplace observations, our research is in a prime position to address the relationship among individual skill transfers, job mobility, and social change in local economies.

RESEARCH DESIGN, STUDY SITES, AND SAMPLE

Skills of the "Unskilled" is based on two stages of exploratory field-work, followed by a survey of a representative sample of return migrants in Leon, Guanajuato, and two case studies. Stage One (2007–09) involved a study of roughly 50 immigrant construction workers in North Carolina.[55] We selected the construction industry for several reasons. First, at the time of our study, 2007–09, it was the fastest growing employer of Mexican immigrants in the state.[56] Second, most jobs in construction depend heavily on learning by observation and interaction rather than formal education and involve a variety of explicit and tacit skills. As such, this industry provides a strategic setting in which to study on-the-job skills acquisition and the social context in which it takes place, and so we conducted a half-dozen worksite observations. From this North Carolina research, we learned that on-the-job skills learning in places of both origin and destination is fundamental to understanding the mobility pathways of immigrants with low levels of traditional human capital.

Based on our initial findings—that many migrants in the construction industry bring some skills with them and return home with additional ones—it was only natural to extend the exploratory stage of the study to examine skill transfers back to Mexico. Stage Two (2009) involved exploratory field research in Guanajuato, Mexico (see Figure 1.1). We selected Guanajuato because we had network connections in the state; because it includes both rural and urban areas that are well-established migrant sending areas; and because of its dynamic yet uneven development and diverse economic structures, features we sought for the variety of skill transfers we might find. Guanajuato has a system of cities of varied size and economic specialization, with some urban areas structured around services and others organized around manufacturing for the international or the internal market. In 2009, a team of researchers traveled to 12 communities in Guanajuato and conducted lengthy interviews with 79 return female and male migrants working in different occupations and industries.

From this second stage of exploratory research, we discovered the importance of off-the-job learning to working-class Mexicans with low levels of traditional human capital. We further found that many migrants reskilled in the United States, learning to work with new technology and approaching work tasks in new

Figure 1.1. State of Guanajuato and principal urban research sites.

ways. We also found that some skills are place specific and cannot be transferred to Mexico (e.g., certain techniques used in roofing, sheetrocking, and some aspects of agriculture and husbandry), while others are easily transferable (e.g., skills in metalworking and automotive repair, and English language skills that often create economic opportunities upon return). We also identified a number of nontechnical skills that migrants are exposed to in their U.S. jobs and bring back with them from the United States, such productive intangibles as customer service, punctuality, and organizational and leadership skills. As expected, we found that the industrial context of return matters. For example, some migrants who returned to their small rural communities were unable to apply their customer service and language skills in these limited arenas and so opted to migrate to tourist towns and international business centers where their new skills could be applied to promote economic opportunity. Recognizing the importance of industrial context for skills transfers, in 2012 we conducted two case studies of skills transferability, one in a rural village in Guanajuato and the other in the Guanajuato tourist town of San Miguel de Allende. These case studies, which involved lengthy interviews with 20 return migrants at each site, along with worksite observations, enabled us to examine further the relevance of local institutions and industrial contexts of return for encouraging and supporting skill transfers.

Stages One and Two revealed the acquisition of skills in Guanajuato and in North Carolina's construction industry, but neither captured the learning careers of migrants nor the entire process of transnational human capital acquisition and its implications for economic mobility. The only way to truly understand these processes was to interview the migrants across the migratory circuit, and identify the skills learned and mobilized at each stage. Thus, in Stage Three we drew on our qualitative findings and developed a survey instrument that would retrospectively capture the skill acquisitions of women and men across the migratory circuit, detailing work experiences, learning techniques, and skill transfers before migration, while abroad, and upon return. Recognizing the importance of industrial context, we selected Leon, Guanajuato, as our strategic research site to interview a random sample of 200 return migrants. The survey's 150 closed-ended answers, which capture detailed job and migration histories and skill acquisition and transfers, were coded into STATA.[57] The responses to an additional 30 open-ended questions were transcribed into a word processing file and organized by theme. Finally, to conclude the interview, each respondent relayed (via a voice recorder) a personal narrative of lifelong work experience and skill development and transfers. These narratives were also transcribed and then organized by gender, occupation, industry, and by additional themes as they emerged from a review of the data.

A BRIEF OVERVIEW OF LEON

Leon, Guanajuato, is a sprawling industrial city with a population of almost 1.3 million, the largest in the state. Known as the shoe capital of Mexico, it produces about two-thirds of the country's leather and almost all of it goes into shoes. Its specialty lines are cowboy boots and men's shoes. Not surprisingly, leather and shoemaking, together with textiles, are the largest employers in Leon, accounting for 20 percent of the city's labor force. The shoe industry is organized in three types of establishments: large manufacturing plants, medium-sized factories, and small, family-owned "*picas*." These different types of establishments are not isolated from each other; they are in fact interconnected through the mobility of labor and subcontracting relations. Skill acquisition begins at an early age in the *picas* (also called *piquitas*) and medium-sized workshops where young men work as apprentices and helpers to fathers and older relatives. *Picas* and workshops employ a handful of workers per establishment and are often unregistered.[58] Men trained in the *picas* and workshops often find jobs in large factories where they apply skills conducting specialized tasks and earn higher wages and benefits. Family-owned *picas* and medium-sized shops are also subcontracted by large manufacturing establishments, which transfer old machinery, supplies, and raw materials to the smaller units. During economic downturns, laid-off factory workers find refuge in the hundreds of family-owned, informal tanneries and *picas* that dot the shoe districts of Leon.[59]

A traditional manufacturing sector largely oriented to the domestic market, the city's leather and shoemaking industries have suffered the effects of Mexico's sweeping economic restructuring. Once a referent of the government's economic development strategy of import-substitution industrialization, the shoe industry has struggled to adapt to the new model of export-oriented industrialization and open markets. In 1986, Mexico became signatory to the General Agreement on Tariffs and Trade (GATT), which removed licenses and taxes that had sheltered domestic production from foreign competition. Lower tariffs and unregulated imports had a direct impact on domestic production, which began a steady decline. In 1988, Mexico produced 245 million pairs of shoes and imported only 5.5 million pairs. The following year, only 200 million pairs of shoes were produced in Mexico, while imports, mostly from the United States, East Asian countries, and Brazil, underwent more than a fourfold growth, reaching 23 million pairs.[60] In response to the lobbying efforts of trade organizations, the Mexican government established dumping penalties on Chinese shoe imports and in 1993 issued a new law to tax foreign shoe and leather products. From a high of nearly 48 million pairs in 1992, shoe imports declined to only 10 million in 1996.[61]

In 1994, Mexico signed the North American Free Trade Agreement (NAFTA) with the United States and Canada. Although NAFTA allowed for a modest growth of Mexican exports and established rules to avoid the importation of Taiwanese-made shoes via the United States, the small firms typical of the Mexican shoe industry were not able to benefit from the newly signed treaty.[62] Efforts to develop the shoe and leather industry in Leon along the lines of the Italian industrial districts and to take advantage of the export opportunities opened by NAFTA appeared to yield limited results.[63] In 2008, Mexico exported only 5 percent of the shoes produced in the country and imported 55 million pairs or 19 percent of the shoes sold domestically.[64]

In addition to a steady process of market liberalization, Mexico's economic restructuring has been punctuated by recessions and crises. The 1995 financial crisis and devaluation of the peso, when more than $8 billion left the country in less than a week, had a mixed effect on the leather and shoe industry.[65] On the one hand, the devaluation lowered the cost of Mexican shoes and made imports more expensive. The dramatic change in the exchange rate of the peso explains the rise in exports from 5.1 million pairs of shoes in 1994 to 11.6 million pairs in 1995. On the other hand, the crisis produced an overall decline in the demand for shoes, leading to a net loss of thousands of jobs and the closing of nearly 150 shoe manufacturing plants in Leon.[66] Because of these economic hardships, many of the city's factories increased the share of routine work outsourced to lower-paid home workers. Small household firms, many of which were kinship based, adopted a risk aversion strategy, shelving specialty lines (e.g., cowboy boots) and concentrating on secure markets (e.g., school shoes) to survive the crisis.[67] Though the industry eventually rebounded somewhat, Mexico's economic liberalization coupled with successive economic crises displaced many urban workers, including those in leather and shoemaking who made their way north in search of work.[68] We revisit some of the most recent challenges faced by the leather and shoe industry in Leon as we analyze the context of return for our survey respondents in chapter 5.

In addition to the industrial context, we selected Leon because international migrants from this city have several characteristics that made them well suited for our project. Unlike the traditional and predominantly rural migration stream that has attracted young men with limited skills, the migrants from Leon and other industrial centers in Mexico acquire diverse skill sets before migration.[69] Furthermore, although these metropolitan districts are important sending areas, they have remained understudied in the Mexico-U.S. migratory circuit. Finally, we wanted a city with a diverse industrial base to capture a range of total human capital so that we could explore various opportunities for skills transfers, economic mobility, and local economic development. In addition to the leather industry, Leon is home to a cluster of textile, automotive, chemical, and transportation industries, as well as a growing service sector. This sectorial diversity was an especially important consideration since we learned from our exploratory research and the literature on Mexico-U.S. migration that migrants often choose not to return to the towns and hamlets they call home. Instead, migrants frequently return to medium and large cities because these urban areas offer diverse and thriving markets to invest accumulated capital and apply skills learned through migration.[70] Still, we know relatively little about how return migrants use savings and skills in urban settings.

We were reluctant at first to choose Leon because of the dominance of the shoe industry; however, we soon realized it would be valuable to examine how many former migrants returned to the shoe industry and in what capacity, considering that the informality and small size of most factories put ownership within reach of an individual or family with sufficient financial means. Further enriching the sample is the fact that shoe industry production is largely driven by workers' experience. Some tasks are simple and routine (cutting leather); others require more developed skills and involve multitasking (operating and repairing industrial machines, assembling shoes); still others are highly skilled and require both talent and years of experience (e.g., designing shoes). Because leather and shoemaking skills are acquired and improve through on-the-job observation, interaction, and informal training, the industry provides a perfect opportunity to better understand the role of on-the-job learning of skills in migrants' mobility pathways.

BRIEF INTRODUCTION
TO DATA AND SAMPLE

This research project has extended over five years during which time the authors interviewed 50 immigrants in the United States; a representative sample of 200 return migrants in Leon, and in greater depth an additional nonrandom sample of 79 return migrants in 12 communities of different sizes and industrial features in the state of Guanajuato. Collectively, these surveys, in-depth interviews, and worksite observations allowed us to identify and measure the lifelong human capital of our study population and make the case for skills acquisition and transfer among the so-called "unskilled." From the survey findings, in-depth interviews, and worksite observations, we developed detailed occupation and skill-level codes, variables to capture learning contexts in home communities in Mexico and labor markets in the United States, and measures of social and technical human capital acquired and transferred across the migratory circuit. These learning contexts and measures of total human capital and skill levels, which we use throughout the book, are presented in Table 1.1.

The descriptive statistics presented in this book come from the Leon random sample of return migrants, while the narratives and quotes in the text are drawn from worksite observations on either side of the border, from the qualitative dimension of the Leon survey, and from labor market experiences described to us in key interviews and community case studies. While all the statistics refer to the experiences of the random sample of return migrants, we do incorporate some selected findings from the exploratory stages of the fieldwork. For example, in chapter 4, "Transferring Skills, Reskilling, and Laboring in the United States," we include narratives from the North Carolina construction worker sample. Similarly, in chapter 5, "Returning Home and Reintegrating into the Local Labor Market," we draw narratives from the in-depth interviews conducted in multiple locations in Guanajuato in 2009 to emphasize the importance of the industrial context of return.

Our Leon sample of 200 return migrants reside in a variety of areas both in the center and the outskirts of town and not in a

TABLE I.I

Skill types and levels and learning contexts created and used
in analysis

Variable	Definition
Formal education	Years of completed schooling.
English	Sufficient knowledge of English such that a migrant recognizes it as a skill and may use it in a job.
On-the-job learning	Technical skills learned through observation, interaction, and other informal learning processes that can be transferred across occupations and industries (cooking, painting, framing, constructing a stone wall, auto body repair, operating and repairing machinery). In a few cases these involved on-the-job training classes, e.g., workplace safety classes.
Off-the-job learning	Technical skills similar to those above that migrants acquire in the home or in nonwork environments in communities of origin (working on a neighbor's home; appliance repair; working on the engine of a family car; specialized domestic activities, including the preparation of regional foods).
Social skills and competences	Customer service skills, new ways of approaching work, new work habits (e.g., punctuality), entrepreneurial skills (e.g., initiative), self-confidence, leadership skills, teamwork, and follow-through. These are skills that migrants reported acquiring in specific occupational settings as a result of occupational change.
Skill level 1	Work that requires little training and involves one repetitive task, e.g. dishwasher, leather cutter, laborer who mows lawns.
Skill level 2	Requires experience and formal or informal training. Involves multitasking or the mastery of a specific skill, e.g., painter, *ayudante* (helper), gardener who can prune trees and build walls.

Skill level 3	Work based on extensive occupational mobility over time and mastering of all skills within an occupation through extensive formal or informal training, e.g., *maestro albañil* (master mason), shoe designer, factory floor supervisor, carpenter, nurse, teacher.
Self-employed	Returned migrants who reported owning their own businesses. This does not include return migrants who were independent contractors, such as *albañiles*, unless they owned a business that was housed in a structure.
Patrón	Returned migrants who reported owning their own business with one or more employees.

single or even a cluster of adjacent neighborhoods. However, because return migrants are rarely present in very high- and very low-income neighborhoods, most of our respondents were residents of low- and low-middle income blocks.[71] Tables 1.2 and 1.3 introduce the sample and provide some basic characteristics of the Leon migrants. Throughout the course of the book, we profile the sample in greater depth, describing relevant characteristics in each of the substantive chapters. As Table 1.2 shows, 86 percent of the return migrants in our sample are male. This sex ratio is consistent with other studies of return migration showing that Mexican women are more likely than men to stay longer or settle permanently in the United States, often migrating to join a spouse or another family member.[72] Because of the small number of females in the sample, we acknowledge that we should interpret gender comparisons with care. Fortunately, we have the findings from in-depth interviews conducted with female return migrants in the exploratory second stage of the project, which we also rely on in our qualitative analysis. The

TABLE I.2

Profile of return migrant sample

Individual Characteristics (at time of interview)	Total (n=200)	Men (n=172)	Women (n=28)
Age (mean)	39.6	39.6	39.3
Married	82%	86%	61%
Education Level			
Less than primary	26%	25%	29%
Completed primary	21%	22%	14%
Some secondary	34%	35%	32%
Completed secondary	12%	11%	18%
More than secondary	7%	7%	7%
Work and Migration History (means)			
Total years worked	21.8	22.4	18.5
Years worked prior to first migration	7.5	7.7	5.7
Years working in U.S.	4.4	4.6	3.2
Years since last return	7.5	7.9	5.6

NOTE: Due to missing values, number of observations for each variable ranges from 191 to 200.

average age of the respondent at the time of the survey was 39 years for both men and women, suggesting that for some their migratory careers may be completed. Eighty-six percent of the men were married compared to 61 percent of the women, and at least half had children at the time of their first migration, factors that would weigh heavily in decisions to return home from the United States.[73]

Although we recognize that some in our sample may remigrate to the United States at some point in their labor market careers, we analyze return migration as a permanent event. The characteristics of our sample suggest a fairly permanent return migrant stream. Most are older (mean = 39) than one would expect from the typical temporary migrant. In contrast to the repeat migration of rural streams from Mexico, more than half of our Leon sample undertook only one trip to the United States and an equal percentage have been home ten years, suggesting a low probability of remigration, and as our analysis in chapter 5 highlights, about 60 percent returned because they were drawn home to be with family or because they had completed their migration objectives.

Table 1.2 also shows that the return migrants possess relatively low levels of traditional human capital as measured by years of formal education, a finding consistent with other studies showing that return migrants have lower levels of education than Mexicans who stay in the United States.[74] Except for a handful of return migrants who had attended a university or a vocational school before migrating and then returned to finish that schooling, the educational levels presented in Table 1.2 refer to completed years of formal schooling before migration. As the table shows, 81 percent of the sample had not finished secondary school (middle school) at the time of the interview, and more than a quarter had not completed primary school. Yet, despite their relatively low levels of formal education, the Leon return migrants possess considerable total human capital as measured by work experience. On average, our respondents entered the labor force 22 years ago, with significant differences between men (22.4 years) and women (18.5 years). Not surprisingly, men (7.7 years) had accumulated more years of work experience than women (5.7 years) before undertaking their first migration to the United States. Men have also spent slightly more time working in the United States than women, 4.6 and 3.2 years respectively. Similarly, men have spent 4.7 years employed since their last return compared to 2.9 years for women. Despite these gender differences, what is clear is that both men and women spent considerable time in the labor force before migration, while abroad, and upon return—providing us with the opportunity to examine and compare skill acquisitions and transferences across the migratory circuit and assess their implications for economic mobility pathways.

We are aware that we cannot attribute some skills acquired by our respondents to the fact that they migrated to the United States. Men and women develop competences and acquire knowledge as they progress through their employment careers and it is possible that at least some of the skills attributed to international migration could also be obtained in the local labor market or by migrating internally. Teasing out with precision the sources of different skills would require comparing similar samples of migrants and nonmigrants. While we also collected a sample of nonmigrants in Leon, we only inject their numbers into our analysis when we compare the experiences of the reintegration of return migrants into the Leon labor market to highlight the distinctive skills acquired abroad. We believe that a larger comparative endeavor would detract from the central goal of this book: to focus specifically on the skills that are transferred, adapted, and learned across stages of the migratory circuit as sojourners negotiate leaving, entering, and navigating labor markets at home and abroad.[75]

We also realize that beyond exposure to particular labor and societal dynamics, migrants' distinct characteristics might predispose them to be rapid learners, apt problem solvers, and innovators. The migration literature has long referenced and sought to understand the mechanisms by which individuals get positively selected into international sojourning, a process that by all means requires the ability to take on and manage risk and uncertainty and deftly adapt to new situations. It is likely that in some

TABLE 1.3

Distribution of Leon return migrants and total working
population of Leon by economic sector (2010)

Industry	Leon Sample	Leon (City)
Agriculture	0.5%	0.4%
Construction	12.4%	6.2%
Shoe, leather, and textile manufacturing	20.0%	20.1%
Other manufacturing	9.7%	9.1%
Automotive and bicycle repair	7.6%	1.3%
Retail and hospitality	36.8%	29.3%
Other services	12.9%	32.4%
Other industries (mining, utilities, and unspecified)	—	1.1%

SOURCE: Leon city population, INEGI, *Censo de Población y Vivienda* 2010, Micro-datos de la Muestra. www.inegi.org.mx/sistemas/microdatos2/default2010.aspx.

of our individual cases, the ability to acquire and mobilize skills is also connected to the traits that selected our respondents into the process of migration. Whatever the individual case may be, migrants themselves tend to believe that there was little hope for the development and mobilization of their talents and abilities on home ground, and hence their decisions to migrate.

Table 1.3 compares the job distribution by industry of the sample at the time of the survey with a 10 percent sample of the Leon labor force from INEGI, the Mexican census, in the same year. To indirectly tap into some of the distinct occupations of return migrants, we developed more detailed categories, such as breaking down manufacturing into three different types of production, including shoe and leather manufacturing, other manufacturing, and automotive and bicycle repair. The table illustrates some similarities and distinctions between our sample and the Leon labor force. Both populations were equally represented in shoe, leather, and textile manufacturing, though as we shall discuss in chapter 5, return migrants were more likely than nonmigrants to be self-employed in this industry (see Table 5.5). The table also shows that return migrants were more likely than nonmigrants to work in retail and hospitality, construction, and automotive and bicycle repair. In chapter 5, where we analyze the labor market incorporation of return migrants, we will demonstrate that the distinct industrial breakdown of the Leon sample compared to the total working population of Leon is in part related to the skills they transferred home from the United States, skills that we argue also help shed light on the much higher self-employed percentage among the return migrants compared to the total Leon population of comparable age (27 percent vs. 15 percent; see Table 5.5).

ROADMAP OF THE BOOK

The next five chapters of the book follow the social processes of learning and transferring skills across the three stages of the migratory circuit: before, during, and after migration. Chapter 2, "Learning Skills in Communities of Origin," reveals that the learning of skills begins early in the life of many migrants. More specifically, the chapter describes the multiple social contexts and institutions in which migrants learn skills before migration in their home communities, from families to schools to workplaces and other community contexts. In Leon, as well as in other cities and rural areas of Guanajuato, learning and skills acquisition take place during late childhood and early adolescence in the context of home-based and family-owned businesses in traditional industries. As we describe in chapter 2, the shoe industry clustered in Leon and its myriad unregistered household-organized *picas* offer the informal training grounds where mostly young men learn basic shoemaking skills from fathers and more experienced workers.

Chapter 3, "Mobilizing Skills and Migrating," focuses on the proximate causes and dynamics of migration to the United States. Even though migration from Guanajuato to *el norte* is a century-old phenomenon, the stream from Leon to the United States emerged largely during the second half of the 1990s, when economic restructuring and liberalization and a financial crisis converged to produce one of the largest waves of outmigration from Mexico to the United States in history. The majority of the return migrants we surveyed in Leon were part and parcel of this great migration. Most of our Leon respondents migrated to the United States without documents and have conducted one or two migratory trips. California and Texas were the most common destinations of these respondents, although a substantial number also migrated to nontraditional destinations. The salience of traditional destinations reflects the fact that, as newcomers to the social process of migration, the residents of Leon rely primarily on established kinship networks, which have long channeled migrants to California and Texas.

Chapter 4, "Transferring Skills, Reskilling, and Laboring in the United States," focuses primarily on the experiences of the migrants in their first and last U.S. jobs. We demonstrate that far from being unskilled, Mexican migrants have working knowledge and skills they first acquired at home and later deployed in the United States. These skills become explicit as migrants encounter new technologies, interact with other workers, and need to solve problems in the workplace. We also discuss which skills are transferable to U.S. jobs and which are not. The chapter highlights the reskilling that takes place on job sites and at workplaces in the United States as migrants learn new techniques and work with different materials and tools. In chapter 4, we also find that the experiences of skills acquisition and mobility are different for men and women and explain how and why occupational and mobility paths are gendered.

In chapter 5, "Returning Home and Reintegrating into the Local Labor Market," we analyze the economic context of departure from the United States as well as the conditions of arrival in Guanajuato during the 2006–10 period, when most of our survey respondents returned home to Mexico. Interestingly, the majority of respondents attributed their return to family reasons and not to economic factors associated with the impact of the great recession in the United States. We interpret this finding with caution as the need to return for family reasons might reflect the difficulty to bring close family members to the United States as well as low levels of social integration. Our respondents returned to a fluid context characterized by modest economic growth, a sharp downturn caused by the U.S. and global financial crises, and then a sustained recovery.

More than half of our respondents said that they transferred skills learned in the United States to Mexico (see Table 5.2). Our data indicate that the skills transferred and applied to jobs upon return are more diverse than the ones our respondents first mobilized when they migrated to the United States. Our findings also indicate that men and women transfer skills differently. Reflecting their incorporation into service jobs that required constant face-to-face interaction with English-speaking supervisors in the United States, women transferred language skills back home at twice the rate of men. Interestingly, many of the skills acquired formally by men in institutional settings, via safety and other state-enforced programs, were not readily transferable to Leon.

In other cases, the technology used in the United States was not available in Mexico. In contrast to the technical skills applied by men, women were more likely to transfer social and interpersonal skills, highly appreciated in service industries that revolve around customer satisfaction.

In the concluding chapter 6, we summarize the findings of the study and consider its policy implications. Our work has implications for the migration policies of both the United States and Mexico. There is a fundamental skills mismatch in current U.S. immigration policy that gives preference to "skilled" immigrants who rank high on traditional human capital attributes and restricts the entry of "low-skilled" migrants, a classification that ignores the high level of informal skills and working knowledge they bring to labor markets, especially to industries like construction that have been partly vacated by the native born but traditionally characterized as very skilled. And while the failure to pass comprehensive immigration reform has temporarily closed some opportunities to bring attention to the skills that so-called "unskilled" migrants import from the home country and deploy in U.S. labor markets, we believe that our work can inform the efforts of migrant advocacy groups, economic and social justice organizations and foundations, and binational institutions dedicated to workforce development and migrant and worker rights.

Mexico also can benefit from our findings. While sizeable return flows are a long and persistent characteristic of the Mexico-U.S. migratory system, the great recession, stepped-up enforcement, and a policy of mass deportations have impacted patterns of return migration to Mexico. From 2005–10, 1.4 million migrants moved back to Mexico, a figure twice the rate of those who returned home from 1995 to 2000.[76] The Mexican government has a long history of building programs to serve

Mexicans abroad and encourage their remittances. In this context, it is notable that the Mexican government has only begun developing policies to reintegrate returning migrants to local and regional labor markets and to harness the skills acquired in the United States and transferred back home. Our research suggests that the Mexican government would be well served by supporting self-employment ventures and reintegration programs that recognize the enhanced skill sets of return migrants, many of whom are able to fill valued positions and start businesses of their own, creating more jobs in their home communities and thus promoting local economic development.

CONCLUSION

Despite the lack of formal credentials to authenticate their skills and despite the many institutional hurdles they faced because of their unauthorized status, Lalo, Anna, and Rafael succeeded in mobilizing their lifelong human capital across the migratory circuit to improve their economic circumstances. In this book, we argue that, contrary to prevailing scholarship, many international migrants with low levels of formal education and training like Lalo, Anna, and Rafael are far from unskilled. In fact, shorthands such as "unskilled" and even "low skilled" obscure a complex social and lifelong process of skill acquisition, development, and mobilization across stages of the migratory circuit. Based on qualitative and quantitative data collected with returnees in Guanajuato, Mexico, we demonstrate that migrants begin to acquire skills early on in the sending country in family, communal, and workplace settings. Active and latent skills acquired through these informal learning experiences are transferred to worksites in the United States where they are made explicit by migrants as they solve problems, seek better working conditions and wages, and interact with coworkers and employers.

Our approach, which involves tracing labor market experiences across the migratory circuit and broadening our notion of how we measure mobility, enables us to overcome many of the methodological shortcomings of earlier studies, moving beyond rather unreliable wage data to identifying both skill improvements and transitions to better-paying and more skilled jobs as measures of mobility. We find that even though migrants face numerous constraints and often encounter exploitative conditions, many of them transfer and acquire skills that facilitate limited but real labor market mobility in the United States. Once in the U.S. labor market, migrants develop new skills, including working with more advanced technologies, using different materials, and becoming familiar with new ways of organizing the labor process. Moreover, migrants often use their personal and employment-based networks to jump between jobs for reasons that include the opportunity to earn higher wages, circumvent abusive conditions, and demonstrate newly acquired skills.

The majority of the respondents in our study report transferring newly acquired skills back to the home country, but the transfer of these skills upon return is not a seamless process. Many of our respondents state that not all skills could be transferred and applied because working materials and technologies are different. Nonetheless, we find that the skills and working knowledge acquired abroad, at times in combination with the capital accumulated through migration, facilitate important transformations in the occupational trajectories of our respondents who are able to secure better-paid and more skilled positions, obtain jobs in services, and initiate entrepreneurial ventures.

Learning Skills in Communities of Origin

We left at noon on Saturday for *El Coecillo,* the Leon neighborhood where the vast majority of manufacturers of shoes and other leather goods in the city are located. As we wound through the narrow streets of the city's leather district and observed men laboring on antique industrial sewing machines, we recalled old photographs from New York City's garment industry at the turn of the twentieth century.[1] Walking through *El Coecillo,* we watched men hunched over machines making girls' shoes and women stitching the colorful flowers that would adorn the front of the shoes. We saw teams of workers producing men's work shoes, cowboy boots, belts, handbags, and virtually any other imaginable leather product. *El Coecillo* is crammed with *piquitas* (or *picas* as some residents refer to them), small family-owned shoe workshops, along with a number of mid-scale manufacturers housed in *talleres* (small-to-medium size businesses), and large-scale operations called *fábricas* (factories). The quantity and concentration of *piquitas* is remarkable. As an owner of one *piquita* told us, "For every 20 *fábricas* in *El Coecillo,* there are 1000 *piquitas.*"

Alongside the family enterprises are stores crammed with piles of brightly colored paper molds and wooden shoe molds, large swathes of dyed leather hanging from metal hooks, and mounds of boxes—block after block of small family-owned shoe factories and stores servicing them. Traffic is heavy in the leather district and streets are regularly blocked off by trucks unloading materials or loading shoeboxes to take to the retail stores in towns and cities throughout central and northern Mexico.

Reminiscent of the tenement housing in some U.S. northeastern cities in the 1900s, typically a *piquita* consists of a small two-room work center located on the first floor, and similarly sized living quarters for the owner and his family located either in the back of the factory or on the second floor. Owners of family-operated factories usually move back and forth between home and factory during the workday, checking on daily progress. As one worker explained, "I worked for the boss. I worked where he lived. He woke up, ate breakfast, and came down to the factory to check on things and later would go back up and watch television and then come down again to inspect things." Unlike early twentieth century immigrant family-home work sites in the United States where piecemeal wares were manufactured for outside owners and businesses, the organization of labor in contemporary home-based shoe factories in Leon is distinctively entrepreneurial and social. Shoe production is under the control of the owner and is very much both a coveted business venture and a craft that relies on experience, social contacts, and capital, but rarely formal education. The social process of learning is also distinctive in these small factories. Workers, often members of the same family, operate as a team in intimate settings where they work and eat alongside one another. They informally learn technical and interpersonal skills from each other through observation, interaction, and practice, and work closely together to assemble all parts of the shoe, from cutting the leather to shining the finished product.

The first *piquita* we visited consisted of two rooms and employed four full-time workers. As is typical in most small family enterprises, the workers and owners are mostly men, although none of the machines are too large or heavy to be operated by a woman. Not only do the smaller family-owned shops and the larger factories employ female workers in much smaller numbers, but there is also a gendered division of labor: while the men operate and repair machinery on the assembly line, the women are restricted to putting the finishing touches on the shoes— cleaning, shining, lacing, and packaging them. Clearly, the possibility of skills development and occupational mobility within the shoe industry is greater for male workers.

Visiting each worker, the owner took us through the stages of shoe production. First, we were introduced to the *cortador* (cutter), who begins the shoe production process by cutting the leather from shiny silver paper patterns. The leather can be cut with a simple handheld instrument or a machine with a blade. In this case, the cutter was standing and using a handheld knife to cut the leather on a drafting board. The leather is then sent to the *pespuntador* (stitcher), who stitches the pieces together with what looks like a large industrial sewing machine. The next person in the assembly line is the *montador* (assembler), who shapes by hand the leather over a wooden mold of the shoe. Meanwhile, the heel is created using a machine called the *máquina de pulir* that inflates the rubber component of the heels by exerting heat. The *pegador* then joins the *talón* and *suela* (heel and sole) of the shoe together. The fifth person in the shop was making small flowers by hand, using scissors and thread, and attaching them to the front of a girl's shoe. All the workers were also machinists in that they were able to both operate and repair the machinery they used. When I asked the assembler where he had learned his skills, he told me that he began to learn the trade *"desde que era un niño de ochos años"* (since I was a young child of eight years). What became clear is that in the local context of Leon, shoemaking is a trade that is learned informally and organically at an early age, long before young men enter the labor force. It is also a trade characteristic of a household economy in which production takes place in the home and often involves unpaid family members and skills that are passed from father to son, which probably explains the concentration of men in shoe manufacturing. None of the workers we interviewed in the *piquita* had attended a vocational school or participated in a formal on-the-job training program.

The learning and skill acquisition that takes place in the small, family-owned, and often informal *picas* also occurs in other traditional industries in Guanajuato that involve a combination of light manufacturing and service and are or have been oriented toward local, regional, and national markets. Guanajuato has had a cluster of garment factories in Leon and the neighboring cities of Moroleon and Uriangato, and learning and skill development in the garment industry also occurs informally at an early age and in the context of home-based firms, medium-sized shops, and big factories. Similarly, the state's large numbers of artisan industries, largely based on ceramics, copper, tin, and metalworking, also depend on skills learned at home and passed from generation to generation. In Leon, welding, mechanic, and auto body repair shops and even restaurants are also common work environments where a wealth of skills are transferred between fathers and sons and mothers and daughters well before a young person joins the paid labor force.

SOCIAL CONTEXTS AND
PROCESSES OF LEARNING SKILLS

When economists describe how migrant labor market skills are developed, they primarily focus on formal contexts of learning for adults—on-the-job training programs, measurable work experiences, and the influence of credentials. In contrast, sociologists of immigration emphasize the importance of social networks and work environments for informal learning and skill development among many newcomer migrants. Migrant social networks encompass personal and informal social and employment contacts,[2] along with more formal community-based and immigrant advocacy supports.[3] Both historical and contemporary accounts of immigrant groups in the United States have further documented the role of ethnic communities and niches in learning that provide a work space in which newcomers, some of whom may lack work authorization, can avoid exploitation or discrimination in the mainstream labor market, find employment, and learn new on-the-job skills while working alongside the linguistic comfort of co-ethnics.[4] These ethnic niches also provide newcomers with time to learn about the U.S. labor market more generally, and as an increasing number of studies are finding, on-the-job learning in the U.S. labor market has consequences for immigrant labor market careers in the long run. The human capital that migrants acquire in this way can serve as the basis for finding alternative jobs that offer opportunities for advancement or higher wages outside the ethnic economy.[5]

The problem with this bourgeoning and important scholarship on learning and skill development among migrants with low levels of education is that, with few exceptions, it assumes that all learning takes place on work sites and in ethnic communities abroad. In essence, it assumes that most migrants arrive with few or no skills. Yet, as our visit to *El Coecillo* demonstrates, the learning of skills and knowledge among many Mexican migrants begins at a young age in their homes, work sites, and other social contexts in the communities in which they were born and often reared. While some of the skills that migrants possess before they migrate are indeed measurable and explicit because they were acquired at schools, vocational institutions, and in structured on-the-job training programs, the locus of learning for other skills is less visible, and thus these skills are more difficult to identify and measure—they have been acquired informally, on and off the job, through social interaction with parents, older siblings, coworkers, close observation, practice, informal mentoring, trial and error—interpersonal rather than institutional experience.

In this chapter, then, we argue that to identify correctly the skills and knowledge that migrants possess when they enter U.S. labor markets and assess how their human capital influences their work trajectories, migration scholars must approach learning and skill development as lifelong processes that begin at early ages in households and home communities, and may include formal schooling and training but also informal learning experiences. Learning is also very much a social process that is acquired through interaction with members of personal and work networks and in the context of businesses that are part of the household economy. Implicit in our view of how learning is acquired by migrants is recognition that the social contexts and types of skills learned can be differentiated by life cycle and gender. This broader sociological perspective on learning recognizes migrants as more than just workers; rather and more importantly, they can be viewed as whole persons embedded in a web of social relations throughout their lives, whose learning processes are organic and not limited to paid employment.[6] In the following pages we identify and describe the social contexts and processes through which migrants acquire skills and working knowledge in their home communities, and then discuss how these skill acquisition processes influence job transitions *before* migration, as well as prepare them for entry into U.S. labor markets later in their work careers.

Table 2.1 lists the learning contexts in which the Leon return migrants in our study acquired skills that applied to their jobs in Mexico before migrating to the United States. Formal learning in institutional contexts refers to skills acquired through a structured set of learning experiences leading to qualifications or credentials that are recognized beyond the workplace and local industry, and often in regional and national labor markets.[7] This form of learning is most readily associated with identifiable and recognizable formal institutional sectors, such as educational sectors and vocational courses or programs that lead to jobs in the regulated sector of the economy. "Skilled" or "professional" migrants acquire their skills through these formal learning processes and the credentials acquired help them gain access to regulated jobs, whether temporary or permanent, in destination labor markets. Because the qualifications and skills delivered through formal learning recognized by industry and government bodies are more easily transferable across local, regional, and national labor markets, these migrants in essence are routed via credentials through a largely regulated global labor market.

Skills acquired in formal workplace contexts refer to those designed by particular workplaces for skill development, such as on-the-job training programs or explicit demonstrations by a supervisor or other experienced worker. Because formal work-

TABLE 2.1

Social context and processes of learning skills in communities
of origin by gender

Learning Process	Total (n=200)	Men (n=172)	Women (n=28)
Formal (institutional)			
Vocational training and other schooling leading to credentials	8%	9%	4%
Formal (workplace)			
On-the-job training program designed by the workplace or explicit instruction from boss or coworker	39%	40%	29%
Informal (work)			
Observation, social interaction with coworkers, experimentation, and practice	55%	56%	50%
Informal (home and community)			
Observation, social interaction with family, friends, and neighbors	53%	54%	43%

NOTE: Totals exceed 100 percent because respondents could report more than one method of learning.

place learning processes are designed and implemented by the specific workplace, they do not lead to qualifications or credentials and, thus, are not readily recognized in other regional, national, or international labor markets. For example, cobbling skills acquired by workers through a training program in one factory in *El Coecillo* might well be transferred to another factory in the local or regional labor market within Mexico, but for a worker to transfer these nonformal skills across national borders, say, to a shoe factory in the United States, that worker must be able to demonstrate the skills and an employer must be able to recognize and valorize them. Limited knowledge of English, unfamiliarity with foreign labor markets, and a host of institutional barriers may further prevent migrants from communicating to employers the sets of skills they possess. We should recall here the skilling narrative of Rafael that opens this book; it was his ability to demonstrate his skills and the recognition of those skills by his factory supervisor that enabled Rafael to land his job at a textile factory in Los Angeles.

Informal learning, as the name suggests, is unstructured and refers to learning that is acquired through everyday work and life. Informal learning is a lifelong process that takes place in homes, neighborhoods, communities, and workplaces. It is the most common way that workers, migrants and nonmigrants alike, acquire their skills and knowledge.[8] Informal learning is very much a social process since knowledge is acquired through interacting with, speaking or listening to, or observing more skilled individuals at work or in the community.[9] The social processes underlying informal learning are especially important to understanding skill development and labor market adjustments for persons employed in work that has few formal educational requirements. Informal learning also contains an individual dimension in that it can be acquired independently through reading (how-to books, magazines, instruction booklets, newspapers, etc.), trial and error strategies, demonstrations, and practice. Unlike formal learning, which leads to widely recognized qualifications, informal learning rarely leads to credentials and so the skills acquired and developed through this arrangement are most difficult to demonstrate and recognize. Once again, recall the case of Rafael, who entered the labor force at the age of 15 and informally accumulated substantial skills in garment manufacturing. Rafael learned these skills in several local shops and factories through observation and interaction with coworkers, long before taking leave for the United States.

How did the migrants in our study sample acquire skills and knowledge in Mexico prior to migrating to the United States? As Table 2.1 shows, most combined various forms of learning, although informal learning clearly dominates. Only a small portion of the migrants in the Leon sample (8 percent) applied skills acquired through formal schooling to their jobs, a low figure that we might expect given that the average years of schooling in the Leon sample is seven years. However, of these 16 persons, more than half reported that either the mathematics or English they had acquired in school proved to be a valuable skill in the labor market. When asked how these skills helped in their jobs, almost all who responded positively to the question remarked on the importance of measurement in the shoe manufacturing and construction industries. As our worksite observations had taught us, measuring a piece of wood or creating a shoe design does require some basic knowledge of mathematics. Similarly, construction workers laying materials or drafting designs need some ability with mathematics to measure accurately. English acquired in school came in handy for persons working in jobs that involved face-to-face interaction with English-speaking people. Workers like Anna, the hotel receptionist featured in chapter 1, relied in her job on English acquired in school and informally in the expatriate community of San Miguel de Allende before migration.

Similarly, some used their English language skills to plow through how-to manuals. A number of respondents who had worked as auto mechanics prior to migration reported relying on the little English they had acquired in school in Mexico to follow installation instructions for a product such as an auto part that had been imported from the United States. Indeed, male return migrants reported learning more English in schools in Mexico than in their U.S. jobs, reflecting the importance of even a few years of schooling in Mexico and the fact that many male Mexican migrants work alongside co-ethnics in jobs in the United States that require little or no English, such as construction or low-wage work in the hospitality industry. Acquiring mathematical and English language skills during the early years of schooling has implications in terms of how we measure formal skills in empirical research, which is usually categorized into broad classifications, such as primary or secondary schooling. But as we demonstrate here, formal education, even if only a few years, can be important in the acquisition and application of particular technical and language skills. After all, from the perspective of the learner, four years of schooling is substantially more valuable than no years of schooling.

Included in the category of formal learning are vocational schools. In the United States and many other developed countries, construction workers, cobblers, carpenters, and other crafts persons learn their trades for the most part in vocational schools or in formal on-the-job training programs taught by licensed experts. In Mexico, these trades operate in traditional industries in which a significant portion of the production takes place in small, informal businesses. In these social contexts, newcomers learn informally through more experienced workers on and off the job. Among our sample, only a handful of migrants reported acquiring and applying skills learned through vocational training. One young migrant attended a technical engineering school to learn how to operate digitized design machines used in a factory that produces high-end and exotic cowboy boots, while another attended an accounting program offered by the municipal government. Yet another respondent studied auto mechanics at a vocational school in Leon. Later, a combination of formal training and practical experience at a European auto dealership allowed him to learn and develop skills in the assembly and repair of the electrical systems of high-end vehicles. During his tenure as an employee of this dealer, he won a competition organized by the company to receive additional training and work temporarily in the United States.

As Table 2.1 shows, 39 percent of the sample acquired skills through formal arrangements at the workplace. On-the-job training programs were reported as provided or required in several industries and workplaces including nursing, real estate, pharmacies, international auto maintenance and manufacturing, and agriculture-related companies with dealers and production facilities in Mexico, sometimes leading to intercompany transfers. The Guanajuato area is home to several auto manufacturing plants, including Volkswagen, Chrysler, and General Motors, and some of the men in the sample worked in these plants, which are located a short bus ride from Leon. On-site training programs, and for some, the machinist skills acquired through workplace training, would later prepare them for their work as auto mechanics in the United States. Lalo, the owner of a woodworking business we introduced in chapter 1, entered a formal six-month training program at the General Motors plant in Silao (a short ride from Leon) at age 18. Although the repetitive nature of the assembly line bored him, Lalo nonetheless learned the principles of auto manufacturing.

One young woman from Leon, Karen, worked for Fresh Select, an Australian company that produces and distributes

vegetables to local and overseas markets. Karen entered the job
as an assistant secretary but through in-house job training in
administrative activities and an English class paid for by the
company, she moved up the ladder to administrative secretary.
After four years on the job, she relocated to the same position in
Santa Maria, California, where the company had a branch. Table
2.1 also shows that roughly 39 percent of workers in the sample
mentioned that at some point on the job they had received on-
the-job training or explicit instruction from a coworker or
supervisor. In some cases, it was difficult to distinguish these
learning arrangements from informal learning.

The social contexts of learning most often reported by
migrants included acquiring skills informally on the job through
observation, trial and error, practice, and off the job in their
communities; and precisely because there are no formal or
explicit guidelines for acquiring skills through informal learning, workers must be quick studies. The capacity, eagerness, and
initiative to learn are important features of successful learning
through informal arrangements. Learning both on and off the
job was fundamental for just about all of the jobs migrants held
before emigrating, but especially for those concentrated in traditional industries such as farming, or associated with artisan
crafts or in trades, such as shoemaking, construction, garment
manufacturing, and brickmaking, work environments that rely
on learning by observation, doing, and practice rather than formal education or training.

The distinction between on-the-job and off-the-job informal
learning can be blurred. Take the case of Christian, who was
born in Leon. He was introduced to shoemaking in his father's
piquita. "I would come home from school and watch my father
make shoes. He would cut the leather pieces, spread them on

wooden molds, and stitch the leather to soles with a sewing machine. Eventually he taught me how to use the machine and let me practice stitching leather pieces." When Christian entered the paid labor force almost ten years later, he possessed considerable cobbling skills, which he had acquired informally through observation and practice at home and in the family-run enterprise. While some of the men and women who worked in the larger factories in the leather and shoe manufacturing sector of Leon's economy did report participating in worksite training programs, learning through observation and interaction was a common narrative among cobblers and machinists working in family-owned and -operated enterprises, many of whom learned their skills from their fathers, in settings in which workplace and home were a few steps from each other.

Off-the-job learning is also associated with the production of artisanal items. If the enterprise is family owned, skills are often learned in the home and passed from one family member to another or from one generation to the next. In San Miguel de Allende, many of the artisanal works for sale in tourist shops and markets or displayed by small ambulatory vendors on street corners are crafted in the home. Take the case of Roberto, who was born and raised in San Miguel de Allende, a colonial town in the heart of Guanajuato, which attracts a large inflow of national and international tourists. From his uncle and father he learned the craft of designing the brilliant cutout aluminum star-shaped lampshades that San Miguel de Allende artisans are known for. Interestingly, having explained that he learned all his skills in the home or in the metalworking room adjacent to the home, he would later tell us that earnings saved through migration would allow him to "escape the family business" and open up a sundry store on the edge of town.

Off-the-job informal learning is also common in the acquisition of construction skills such as brickmaking and tile installation, know-how that many working-class people learn because they would not be able to afford to hire someone with these skills. In his study of Caribbean and Korean construction workers in New York City, Roger Waldinger documented that a number of immigrant workers had acquired their premigration construction skills "naturally" and in the course of "growing up."[10] We also documented many cases in which construction skills were acquired organically in the home and community before migration.

Take the case of Ruy, who grew up in San Antonio, a small town located close to the Guanajuato industrial city of Irapuato. At the early age of 14, Ruy left school as his older brothers had done, to begin tilling the soil of his family's farm. Working alongside his father, he learned through observation and practice to plant and harvest soybeans and alfalfa. While he was still in primary school, his family decided to add a brick room to the back of the house, and Ruy naturally assisted his father and brothers in the construction of this addition to the family home. Both his brothers had worked in construction, and they taught Ruy the skills they had learned. From them and through observation, demonstration, experimentation, and practice, he learned to make red bricks, beginning with "molding them from mud, horse and donkey manure, twigs, and straw, drying them in the hot sun and then firing them in an oven fueled by plastics until they turned red."[11] Ruy also learned the value of teamwork and, through observation, learned the fundamentals of laying tile and framing windows. Thus, these were marketable skills he acquired from his brothers *before* entering the labor force. Workers like Ruy apply and continue to develop their skills in regional labor markets, commuting to Leon and other urban centers, where they work in residential and commercial construction projects. As we note in chapter 3, when the financial crisis paralyzed the Mexican economy in 1995, many of these workers with experience in the building trades migrated to the United States, where they encountered a booming construction industry and were easily able to apply their premigration skills.

Because learning through formal avenues is out of reach for many poor or working-class Mexicans, some depend on books and how-to manuals to develop their technical skill sets. We have no exact figures to assess how common this type of independent learning is among the sample because we did not ask the question directly; rather, it was volunteered in open-ended questions about learning more generally. Nonetheless, we believe it is probably a common learning strategy and one that many return migrants adopt, lugging Home Depot manuals with them, as we shall discuss in a subsequent chapter. A good number of the men stated that they had used how-to manuals to improve their auto mechanic and mathematic skills. Interestingly, these how-to manuals, which are often written in English, provide another avenue for acquiring language skills.

Informal learning is gendered in other occupations held by our respondents in Leon. In addition to the masons and shoemakers we talked to, mechanics, welders, and auto body repair workers were frequently introduced to these jobs by their fathers. Before entering the formal labor force, many of these male workers were unpaid helpers at the family shop, often an independent business that was part of the light manufacturing and service sector economy of Leon. As they observed and helped their fathers in the welding of aluminum windows, fixing transmissions, changing tires, and repairing fender benders, these men acquired valuable skills that were later used in jobs they held in Mexico and in the United States. Some of these men even established their own independent businesses before migration and used their U.S. savings to expand and upgrade their shops back in Leon. Fathers apparently do not recruit daughters as helpers in these jobs, as we found that women were altogether absent from these occupations. As the next chapters demonstrate, the skills acquired by men in these occupations proved highly portable across the binational labor market and not only allowed these migrants to obtain comparable jobs in the United States, but also facilitated their learning to work with new and more advanced technologies abroad.

Women in the study also acquired the majority of their skills through informal learning, and the types of skills were very much shaped by their work experiences. Among those women who labored in the shoemaking industry, there was a distinct gendered division of labor. While the men operate machinery on the assembly line, the women's tasks are limited to putting the finishing touches on the shoes and boots—cleaning, adorning with bows, lacing, and packaging them. In one large shoe factory we visited that produces high-end cowboy boots (selling for upwards of $500) for specialty stores in the United States, the only female among 78 workers was boxing the boots to be shipped abroad. Thus, women's opportunities for skill development and occupational mobility within the shoe industry are very restricted. This is in contrast to many other assembly plants in Mexico and Guanajuato, where women account for a large percentage of the labor force.

Because the women in our study were concentrated in domestic service, retail, and administrative support positions prior to migration, they had acquired substantial technical and interpersonal skills related to these job positions. Several of the women worked as cooks in private homes where they applied cooking skills they had learned off the job in their own homes and acquired new ones through observing the food preparation skills of their employers. Karen, the administrative assistant at Fresh Foods, had developed management and intergroup skills, which then facilitated good working relations with coworkers. Guadalupe, who worked as a domestic for an American family in Leon, reported acquiring English language skills, American-style cooking, and interpersonal skills. Because their positions involved face-to-face interactions, the women were more likely than the men to describe interpersonal competences such as teamwork, customer service, and communication skills. As we shall demonstrate, their jobs as secretaries, domestics, receptionists, and cooks made them good candidates for similar work in the United States.

SKILLS AND JOB TRANSITIONS
BEFORE MIGRATION

As the cases of Ruy, Christian, and many others in our study show, the social contexts and processes through which migrants acquire their skills can shape opportunities in local labor markets. The nuclear and extended family, household-based businesses, and local communities not only provide opportunities to learn and acquire skills but also serve as sources of contacts and information about jobs in Mexico. As Table 2.2. shows, 62 percent of the Leon survey respondents indicated that family members and friends recommended them for, told them about, or directly hired them into their first paid job. Only 30 percent of these respondents said that they had been approached by an employer, had contacted one on their own, or had searched for

TABLE 2.2

Sources of employment information for first and last job in Mexico
before migration

Sources	First Job (n=189)	Last Job[a] (n=97)
Recommended by family/friends	32%	36%
Family/friends told about job	13%	10%
Hired by family/friend	17%	14%
Approached employer	18%	19%
Was approached by employer	5%	3%
Classifieds	7%	10%
Other	8%	8%
Total	*100%*	*100%*

[a]Last Job column includes only persons who had two or more jobs.

job opportunities in the classifieds section of a local newspaper.
Even those respondents who had two or more jobs before migration relied heavily on family and friends to identify employment
opportunities. Sixty percent received recommendations and
information about an employment opportunity or were hired
directly by a family member or friend in the last job they held
before migrating to the United States. Rather than relying on
the institutions of the regulated labor market, workers with low
levels of formal education depended on families and local communities to acquire skills and obtain valuable information and
contacts leading to actual employment opportunities. In the
early stages of an occupational career, family and friends appear
to certify the skills the worker has developed in informal settings and to communicate this information to employers.

Many of our respondents underwent a series of occupational
and industry transitions before migrating to the United States.
These transitions are important because they offer opportuni-

ties to apply skills learned earlier on in the individual's occupational career and to implement newly acquired skills. Needless to say, these skills can also translate into opportunities for occupational mobility. Both men and women in the sample were able to apply the off-the-job skills they learned at a young age to their first jobs in paid employment. Table 2.3 lists the industry transitions from first to last job before emigration. Among those who did change jobs two or more times, most transitions occurred within the two industries that include more than 70 percent of the first jobs: leather manufacturing and services. Persons initially working in construction and manufacturing industries transitioned to different manufacturing and services, and of these most transitioned to jobs in the manufacturing sector where they worked as cobblers or machinists, or to construction where they worked as *ayudantes* (helpers), plumbers, metalworkers, and brickmakers or in services. These transitions were in part facilitated by off-the-job skills acquired in the social spheres of household and community before paid employment. Like Christian who worked in his father's *piquita* before entering paid employment, many of our respondents brought to their first jobs skills learned at home.

For example, four of the respondents who transitioned from agriculture to construction and other manufacturing reported that the skills they acquired informally off the job at home had enabled their mobility across industries and into new jobs. Mariano, one of four men who left farming for construction, learned plumbing skills from his father while building a bathroom in the family home. Jaime learned at a young age how to repair toasters, blenders, televisions, and other appliances, as well as the rudiments of auto mechanics by tinkering with the engine of his father's truck. This off-the-job learning experience in the family

TABLE 2.3

Industry transitions before migration (n=109)

First Industry before Migrating	Last Industry before Migrating (% of total in the first industry)					
	Agriculture	Construction	Leather	Other manufacturing	Service	Total
Agriculture	0	29	29	14	29	*6*
Construction	0	18	9	27	45	*10*
Leather	0	19	46	11	24	*34*
Other manufacturing	0	0	21	36	43	*13*
Service	3	8	18	5	68	*37*
Last industry Distribution	*1*	*13*	*28*	*14*	*45*	*100*

NOTE: Twelve subjects never worked, and 79 single-job holders are distributed as follows: 9 percent in agriculture, 18 percent in construction, 20 percent in leather, 20 percent in other manufacturing, and 33 percent in service. Due to rounding, percentages do not total exactly to 100%.

home enabled his transition from laborer on his father's farm to apprentice and then mechanic in an auto repair shop. Jaime would continue to fix appliances as a sideline to his regular position as an auto mechanic.

Recall Ruy, who learned brickmaking and tile installation from his brothers and father. His off-the-job construction skills acquired while working on the family home allowed him to transition out of farming and land a paid job in the construction industry in Mexico, a much desired occupation among the migrants we interviewed because although it requires no formal educational credentials, it offers a moderately good salary, some autonomy at the top of the ladder, and the opportunity to learn multiple skills that can be easily transferred to other industries. The skill sets of an *albañil* (mason) are recognized and valued across local and regional labor markets and, as we will show, across national labor markets as long as the mason can demonstrate his skills. When asked why he went into *albañilería* (the career of a mason, who primarily works in the residential construction of homes), Ruy told us, "because there's a lot of work in that field, and they don't ask for requirements or documents," that is, because it is a field in which skills are demonstrated practically and not through educational diplomas. He went on to tell us that "a lot of young men in their late teens, say 17 or 18, enter as helpers with the idea of making it a lifelong career, and if they like the work, like I did, they stay; if not, they move on and pursue other things."

A description of the occupational structure of *albañilería* illustrates the skill complexity in the hierarchy of this profession and the centrality of on-the-job learning and its relationship to occupational advancement in Mexico. According to an interview we had with a career mason and conversations with respondents who had worked in construction in Mexico, most young men enter the profession of *albañilería* as *chalanes* (also referred to as *peón* or *ayudante,* though in Guanajuato a distinction is often made between a *chalán* and the more skilled *ayudante),* entry-level workers in any craft trade, and an occupation that we cautiously code as Skill Level 1 (see Table 1.1) in our analysis, despite the demands of the position. In most cases, they come to the job with some knowledge of building from having worked on a project in the family home.

One of the first things a *chalán* learns on the job is how to mix cement with *cal* (limestone), a potentially dangerous task because the limestone can get near or into the eyes. The entry-level worker is also responsible for setting up the scaffolding and clearing the area of nails and construction debris. Physical endurance is also required of the *chalán*, who must haul bricks and other building materials to the work site. A common sight in many hilltop towns in Guanajuato, where access to homes is through narrow passages called *callejones*, is of a young worker hauling dozens of bricks in a cloth sling that is tied to the forehead and strapped around the waist. The tenure of a *chalán* varies from one to two years, depending on how fast the apprentice acquires the skills to transition to the *media cuchara* (a half-filled spoon or person with medium skill and whom we code in our analysis as Skill Level 2), who supervises the *chalán* and is the direct assistant or "right arm" of the *albañil*, the most skilled in the profession. Finally, supervising the *media cuchara* is the *maestro oficial*, who is responsible for the physical construction of the building. After *maestro oficial* comes the *maestro* (similar to a contractor), who is responsible for securing the job and supervising the entire project, though he is not physically involved in the day-to-day construction of it. We code the *maestro oficial*, the *albañil*, and the *maestro* as Skill Level 3.

According to one *maestro albañil*:

An ideal *maestro oficial* is one who knows how to do everything, from construction and installation of adobe and bricklaying, tile and mosaic, all with his hands and simple tools. A good mason can build with bricks quickly—1000 bricks in one day. He can also install a floor in one day and do everything quickly and, most importantly, well. The responsibility of the mason is to see that the house's foundations are good and that there won't be any cracks or damages, or else you have to go back and repair it; therefore, you have to guarantee your work is good. The master mason has to look at the details and fix what is wrong and measure the proportions of the materials, which is very important.

As we described above, Ruy came to the trade of *albañilería* with some skills learned off the job at home. He also acquired a number of technical skills and learned the importance of teamwork in the building trade. Just as his off-the-job-skills acquired informally while building his family home enabled his transition from farming into construction work in Mexico, so these technical and social skills would later help him secure a job and advancement in the construction industry in Nebraska. Key here is that the development of his construction skills set was a process that took place over the course of his life—first, as a boy in his father's home, and later as a young adult in the paid workforce, and still later while abroad in the United States.

A similar narrative explains job transitions from the service to the manufacturing sectors of Leon's economy. Off-the-job skilling in construction and shoemaking also enabled half of those working in low-skilled, low-wage, and often dead-end service jobs as dispatchers, janitors, and stockers to secure manufacturing jobs as construction workers, welders, mechanics, and tailors, where opportunities for skill development and occupational mobility were greater than in the service sector. Take the case of Paco, who labored as a dispatcher for several years before being able to demonstrate the automotive skills he acquired off the job to his current employer. It is not uncommon for men who work repairing cars in the United States to have started learning· the trade by repairing farm vehicles or assisting family members who own small auto and tire repair shops in Mexico's working-class neighborhoods.

As Table 2.3 shows, there was very little movement from services and the shoe and leather industry where workers held jobs as machinists and semiskilled and skilled shoemakers. Several factors explain the low rate of transition from leather manufacturing. Laboring in the shoe and leather industry allows for some flexibility and provides familiarity and social comfort for many workers. Individuals work alongside family and kin and can move back and forth between home and work site. The shoe industry also offers some occupational mobility and skill development as it puts ownership of a *piquita* within reach of an individual or family with modest available funds. Before migrating, one respondent moved from the position of salaried machinist to entrepreneur, establishing his own shoe factory and hiring two workers. However, most of the mobility within this industry is from an entry-level *ayudante* (helper) to skilled cobbler, advanced machinist, or online supervisor or manager. As we briefly pointed out in chapter 1, some of this mobility is achieved through job jumping, moving from laboring at a family-owned enterprise to working at a midsize shop or factory. Job jumping is a strategy to circumvent negative workplace conditions and low salaries, but it is a strategy that is facilitated by the possession of skills. When employers do not agree to raise salaries, workers in the shoe industry often responded by moving laterally to another *pica* or *taller* within the secondary or unregulated sector of the Leon labor market. Workers then job jump because of the lack of institutionally established and recognized mobility ladders that may exist in larger firms in the primary sector of the Mexican economy. At the same time, workers who are laid off from the large factories during a recession or decline of the industry move back and find employment in the family-owned *picas*.[12]

For example, when Marcos left his father's *piquita* and found work in a local factory, he started at the entry level working as a cutter. In his father's shop, he had cut leather with a small hand-held instrument; in the factory, he learned from an experienced coworker how to cut on a large industrial machine. Once he had mastered the cutting machine, he quickly moved up to stitcher, the person who stitches the pieces of leather together, then to the shoe assembler and the person considered the most skilled in the production of shoes because of the time and experience it takes to reach this position. Several years later he moved to a large factory where he earned a higher wage, and because of his proficiency in the trade he is also referred to as a *comodín,* or jack-of-all-trades. The most challenging aspect of his job in the factory was learning to operate and repair the large industrial machines, some of which were computerized. The machinist skills he acquired through learning from more experienced coworkers, observation, and practice would prove valuable many years later when Marcos traveled to the United States and worked in a plastics factory where he maintained and repaired machinery.

The cases of Ruy in construction and Marcos in the shoe industry also illustrate how, as a result of these occupational and industrial transitions, many of our respondents had accumulated and regularly applied a wide variety of skills. In fact, their occupational transitions and the demands of the jobs they held before migration required that Ruy, Marcos, and many others in the sample be multiskilled and multifunctional workers. Not only had Marcos mastered different tasks in the shoemaking process and demonstrated his ability to work with old and new technologies, but he had also learned how to repair the machines he utilized at the small *pica.* Just as Marcos had become a *comodín,* or jack-of-all-trades, at the shoe factory, Guillermo, another respondent in the Leon sample, performed multiple skills at the bakery where he worked. While he had learned basic masonry and painting skills from his father, Guillermo was in charge of repairing the bakery's ovens, conducting general maintenance tasks at the business, and even baking bread.

Almost a quarter of the women did work in the labor force before migration, but those who did were concentrated in three occupational clusters: administration, personal service, and retail. In these industries, they labored as clerks, domestics, receptionists, and food preparation workers. Relative to the men in the sample, who worked in craft and manufacturing industries, the women's prospects for skill development and occupational mobility were limited. Nonetheless, most were able to apply skills they had learned off the job to their paid employment. All the women who worked as domestics or cooks reported applying in their workplaces the cooking and cleaning skills they had acquired in their own kitchens and homes. One woman, Marta, combined the cooking skills she had acquired on and off the job to open a small *taquería* (taco stand) and hire an employee. Another woman, Amelia, was able to use English skills learned in school to her job as a receptionist in the hospitality industry in Leon. In this position, she strengthened her English language ability, a skill that would improve Amelia's marketability for her U.S. job as a live-in nanny.

Despite their more limited labor market experiences in Mexico before migration, some of the women in the sample accumulated varied skills as they transitioned through different jobs in their early occupational careers and learned tasks they were not necessarily required to perform, by observing and interacting with coworkers. Take the case of Camelia, who like other women in the Leon survey began her paid employment career in a small restaurant. In charge of the eatery, Camelia learned basic service and cooking skills, including how to make pizzas. In her last job before moving abroad, she worked as a secretary at a leather jacket factory. At this job, Camelia developed accounting skills but also obtained an understanding of the process of manufacturing this particular piece of clothing.

CONCLUSION

The skills that Christian, Ruy, Guadalupe, and many others developed in their home communities and transferred to their jobs were acquired in an informal learning context in which home and work are not easily distinguishable. Clearly, Ruy learned his masonry skills from his brothers and through observation, and outside of any work site, but what about Christian? He probably spent as much time downstairs in his father's workshop as he did upstairs in the family home. Similarly, Guadalupe probably spent as much time cooking in her own home as she did in her American employer's kitchen. What is clear, however, is that in all these cases, our respondents acquired their skills informally on and off the job through observation, interaction with fathers, mothers, older siblings, and friends, and experimentation and practice long before they entered the formal labor market in Mexico or the United States. Family and friends also play an important role facilitating the entry of these workers into the world of paid employment. Older family members and friends directly hired and provided referrals for the majority of our respondents, de facto certification of the skills that workers had acquired in informal settings.

These findings emphasize the importance of approaching learning as a lifelong process that is not limited to an individual's paid employment history. Once in the labor market, the migrants in our sample, like Ruy, would pick up additional on-the-job skills through observation, practice, and informal training, not through formal schooling or on-the-job training programs, certifiable modes of learning that scholars usually argue are the guaranteed mechanisms that facilitate job transitions and mobility pathways. We further challenge these arguments in the following chapters that trace the labor market careers of the sample throughout subsequent stages in the migratory circuit both in the United States and upon return to Mexico.

working classes and the industries in which they labored became increasingly exposed to globalization, recurrent devaluations, and financial crises. These urban sojourners joined other displaced workers from the countryside as part of Mexico's great migration of the 1990s and 2000s, when hundreds of thousands of persons crossed the border into the United States every year.

Although migration from Leon is the result of the powerful transformations and dislocations that economic restructuring produced in urban Mexico, this flow unfolded in the wake of Guanajuato's long tradition of sojourning in the United States. Leon is the economic capital and largest metropolitan area of Guanajuato, a state that has long been one of the top three migrant-sending states to *el norte*.[4] The Mexican Migration Project (MMP) registered sojourns in the United States as early as 1909, while Robert Redfield's pioneer study of Mexican immigrants in Chicago identified *guanajuatenses* working in the city's railroad yards and slaughterhouses in the 1920s. Manuel Gamio's national studies of migration and remittances during the same period placed Guanajuato as the second most important source state of U.S.-bound migrants.[5] During the Bracero Program, which lasted from 1942 to 1964, large numbers of workers enrolled and obtained visas to labor in the United States, consolidating Guanajuato's position as a major migrant-sending state. International migration persisted as a mass phenomenon in the post-Bracero era, when *guanajuatenses* of every region in the state embarked on undocumented sojourns to the United States. During the period that Jorge Durand and Douglas Massey have called "the undocumented era" (1964–86), Guanajuato trailed only Jalisco and Michoacán in numbers of emigrants, a pattern that persisted after the passage of the 1986 Immigration Reform and Control Act (IRCA).[6] IRCA's Legal-

ization Program regularized the status of previously undocumented *guanajuatenses* who were subsequently able to sponsor
legal migrants through the family reunification provisions of
U.S. immigration law. Clearly, Leon's location at the heart of a
region with a long history of U.S. sojourning and a vast reservoir
of migratory social capital provides the city's residents with a
potent social infrastructure for migration.

Most of the migration from Leon captured in our sample
took place during Mexico's great migration, a period that started
in the second half of the 1990s and continued until the mid-
2000s. During this period, between 250,000 and 400,000 Mexicans left their homeland to live and labor in the United States
every year.[7] Analyses of the U.S. Census show that between 1990
and 2000, the Mexican immigrant population more than doubled, from 4.3 million to 9.2 million people. Other sources estimate that by 2007, this population reached 11.4 million, nearly a
third of whom had arrived in the United States in 2000 or later.[8]
As the numbers of migrants grew, their geographic origins and
destinations expanded as well. In Mexico, southern states like
Oaxaca, Guerrero, and Veracruz experienced a massive exodus
of peasants and small farmers. At the same time, metropolitan
areas such as Mexico City, Guadalajara, Monterrey, and Leon
began to appear on the map of U.S.-bound flows.[9] Mexico-U.S.
migration had become national—it was no longer a phenomenon characteristic of a particular region of the country.[10] At the
dawn of the twenty-first century, one-fifth of Mexico's working
age population resided in the United States.[11]

Historically, Mexican migrants traveled to live and labor in the
Southwest, California, and the Chicago metropolitan area. But
beginning in the 1980s, the geography of Mexican migration began
to change. Mexican sojourners started to relocate to destinations

outside the historic states of concentration abutting the border. This dispersal of the Mexican population further into the United States gained momentum throughout the 1990s and early 2000s as hundreds of new immigrants crossed the border to settle in states other than California, Texas, and Illinois. By 2000, nontraditional states of settlement, such as Nevada, New York, Georgia, and North Carolina, hosted large concentrations of Mexican immigrants.[12]

While Mexico's great migration to the United States had its roots in a century-long history, the causes of this large migratory wave did not stem exclusively from the disruptive changes in the Mexican economy and the social capital provided by established social networks. The U.S. economic boom of the late 1990s produced a strong demand for foreign workers, particularly in occupations gradually abandoned by Americans, including construction, light manufacturing, and services. In Mexico, cheap imported merchandise, produced and sold at a fraction of local goods, threatened traditional manufacturing activities and displaced rural and urban workers, including those in Leon's shoe industry. The financial crises of 1982, 1986, and 1995, which punctuated the process of economic liberalization, also contributed to displacing workers, especially in industries like construction that are particularly sensitive to sudden economic contractions. In fact, many *guanajuatenses* who worked in construction and lost their jobs during the 1995 crisis ended up migrating and laboring in building sites across the United States.

As a result of these transformations, the profile of Mexican migrants changed. The cases of Rafael, Ana, Lalo, Christian, Ruy, and others described in previous chapters represent the changing face of Mexican migration to the United States. Rafael,

Christian, and Ana were born and reared in cities where they had accumulated work experience in urban industries, such as manufacturing, construction, tourism, and other services. While Lalo hailed from a rural section of Guanajuato and started working at a young age on the family farm, he found a job at the General Motors plant in the city of Silao. Ruy learned construction skills from his brothers while participating in the building of the family home in a rural hamlet but then applied those skills working as a mason in Leon. All of these migrants had relatively low levels of formal human capital but had acquired an increasingly varied set of skills at home and then in urban jobs during the early years of their occupational careers before moving to the United States. Although mostly learned informally, at home or at the family shop, these skills were often highly portable and could be mobilized across borders.

In this chapter, we draw from our survey of returnees to describe and explain the dynamics of migration from Leon to the United States. We address the causes and the social infrastructure of migration, the periods and duration of sojourning, the legal status of migrants, and their demographic characteristics at the time of first migration. We also draw from the qualitative interviews we conducted in North Carolina and in small towns and cities in Guanajuato to shed light on the role of migrant social networks, employers, and migration intermediaries in the mobilization of skills across borders. The quantitative and qualitative evidence indicates that migration from Leon to the United States is a relatively recent phenomenon; the timing of first U.S.-bound trips coincides with the momentous transformations in the Mexican economy over the past 25 years, but the destinations of sojourning suggest the strong role played by social networks in facilitating migration and assisting in the mobilization of skills. Our data also show that urban-origin migrants have diverse skill sets associated with the occupations and industries concentrated in cities and metropolitan areas.

PERIOD, DURATION, NUMBER OF TRIPS, AND AGE AT FIRST MIGRATION

Evidence from our survey of returned migrants indicates that, in contrast to the long-established tradition of outmigration from the rural areas of Guanajuato to the United States, sojourning from Leon to *el norte* is a relatively new phenomenon. As Table 3.1 shows, 85 percent of Leon migrants conducted their first trip to the United States during the mid-1980s and later when the financial crisis, austerity measures, and the restructuring of the Mexican economy unfolded. Moreover, nearly half the respondents undertook their first migration during the decade of the great migration—from approximately 1995 to 2005. In fact, the average year of the first migration was 1995 for men and 1999 for women. Altogether, a sizeable two-thirds of all respondents in the sample of returnees undertook their first migration between 1995 and 2009 (the year before we implemented the survey). In contrast, the Leon survey identified only a small proportion of migrants (11 percent) who started their sojourning abroad during the 1970s and early 1980s (1970–84), a period of Mexico-U.S. migration characterized by undocumented migration of largely rural origins. An even smaller proportion of Leon respondents migrated at the time of the Bracero Program and immediate post-Bracero years (4 percent from 1945 to 1969; see Table 3.1). Although many *braceros* have died, it is not rare to find them as residents of Mexico's urban centers. These rural-origin workers, who labored legally in U.S. agriculture between 1942 and 1964, often used

TABLE 3.1

Year of first migration to the
United States (n=198)

Year Intervals	Frequency
2005–2009	19%
2000–2004	28%
1995–1999	19%
1990–1994	8%
1985–1989	12%
1980–1984	5%
1975–1979	4%
1970–1974	2%
1945–1969	4%

NOTE: Due to rounding, percentages do
not total exactly to 100 percent.

remittances to finance a permanent migration from the countryside to urban areas in Mexico.[13]

As Table 3.2 indicates, the majority of the Leon migrants conducted their first U.S. trip between the ages of 15 and 29 (72 percent). On average, women migrated at a slightly older age than
men—25.3 and 23.7 years of age, respectively. Less than 20 percent of the respondents in the sample undertook their first
sojourn to the United States between the ages of 30 and 44 years
old (see Table 3.2). In terms of age at first migration, these urban-
origin migrants made their initial trips later than their rural
counterparts. In Mexican cities where a culture of migration has
not taken hold, moving for work to the United States takes place
at a later stage of the life cycle and is more of an economic strategy than the automatic response or expectation prevalent in
the countryside.[14] With more years in the labor market, older

TABLE 3.2

Age at first migration to the
United States (n=191)

Age Intervals	Frequency
<15	6%
15–19	24%
20–24	30%
25–29	18%
30–34	8%
35–39	6%
40–44	5%
45 and older	3%
Total	*100%*

migrants are more likely to have accumulated more skills, work-related experience, and years of education by the time they move abroad. City-origin migrants are more likely to benefit from the concentration of educational opportunities and infrastructure in the country's urban areas.[15]

The number of trips Leon migrants have taken abroad also speaks to the recent emergence of this urban flow. Fifty-seven percent of the Leon survey respondents have conducted only one migratory trip to the United States, while 43 percent of them have migrated two or more times. On average, Leon migrants conducted 2.5 migratory trips, but our subsample of women had only 1.6 sojourns to the United States. During their first sojourn, nearly 58 percent of Leon migrants remained abroad for a period of one to five years (see Table 3.3). Longer spells abroad offer potential opportunities for skill acquisition that migrants might be able to translate into occupational mobility in either the United States or Mexico. The repeated short-

TABLE 3.3

Length of stay during first migration
to the United States (n=199)

Years	Frequency
<1 year	34%
1–2 years	31%
2.5–5 years	27%
5 years	8%
Total	*100%*

term trips characteristic of rural streams are absent in Leon. However, the number and duration of trips of recent migrants also reflect the growing costs and risks of undocumented border crossings. As the scholarship on Mexico-U.S. migration has established, increasing border enforcement by federal authorities has produced a "caging" effect, deterring back-and-forth sojourns and extending the time unauthorized migrants remain in the United States.[16]

LEGAL STATUS

The overwhelming majority of the Leon respondents conducted their first trip to the United States as undocumented migrants: more than 92 percent lacked any form of documentation, while the rest used work permits or had already received permanent resident status or U.S. citizenship (see Table 3.4). In contrast to other urban-origin flows, migrants from Leon did not resort to tourist visas to enter the United States, which working-class individuals receive only if they can demonstrate formal employment, a steady source of income, and ownership of a home in Mexico.[17] The large percentage of undocumented migrants in

TABLE 3.4

U.S. immigration status by migratory trip

Legal Status	First Trip (n=197)	Most Recent Trip (n=85)
American citizen	2%	1%
Permanent resident	1%	1%
Temporary work permit	5%	8%
Undocumented	92%	88%
Other	1%	1%

NOTE: Due to rounding, percentages do not total exactly to 100 percent.

the Leon sample also attests, albeit indirectly, to the emergent character of this urban flow. In the Mexico-U.S. migratory system, legal status is associated with older flows and repeated trips, while undocumented and less numerous U.S.-bound migratory sojourns tend to be typical of newer streams.[18] For those who had migrated two or more times, the legal status on the most recent trip remained largely unchanged: 88 percent of the respondents crossed into the United States without documentation, while the proportion of migrants using temporary work permits increased slightly. In Leon, unauthorized entry was the dominant form of migration across trips. As we discuss in chapter 4, respondents were aware that undocumented status limited their occupational mobility and exposed them to abuses by employers and labor brokers. In the section on social networks in this chapter (see below), we show how our undocumented respondents used kinship, friendship, and workplace ties, and the services of smugglers and other migration industry actors to facilitate their migration to *el norte*.

As Table 3.4 also shows, the second-ranking legal status used to enter the United States was a temporary work visa. Ten of our Leon respondents reported that they had conducted their first migration under the auspices of the H2 visa program.[19] This program provides temporary work visas for jobs in agriculture (H2A) and assorted industries (H2B) where demand for low-wage immigrants is high, such as construction, landscaping, food processing, and hospitality.[20] After reaching a high of 180,000 visas in 2007, the U.S. Department of State issued approximately 106,000 H2 visas in 2011, a steep decline we attribute to the economic recession in the United States. Preliminary figures for fiscal year 2013 indicate that the recovery of the U.S. economy has once again sparked the demand for H2 workers. In 2013 the U.S. Department of State had issued more than 131,000 visas.[21]

In Guanajuato, U.S. firms formally recruit workers under the auspices of the H2 visa program. While the H2 program is administered by a number of departments of the federal government (Department of Labor, Department of Homeland Security through the U.S. Citizenship and Immigration Services, and Department of State),[22] in practice it is run by employers, formally incorporated contracting companies, and informal brokers that operate on both sides of the border.[23] We visited a company that recruits H2 workers in Guanajuato and interviewed the staff and contracted workers, one of whom was Circunspecto, a 37-year-old man with experience in heavy manufacturing and construction. In 2003, he was offered the chance to work in the United States through the H2 temporary visa program. As he explained,

> There is a company that works to get us visas. The people [from the company] in the United States recruit people for the businesses

and you go to take an exam here in Guanajuato, and [according to] what you get on the exam they recommend us [and] tell us "you're good for this job and you for this other one." When I went [for the first time] I asked to work in construction, in other words, as a machine operator, which is what I knew. But they told me there were no openings but [that there were] for this other work. And I said: well, as long as there's the opportunity to go with papers, and so I went.

After paying \$450 to the recruiter, Circunspecto obtained his ten-month H2B visa, which he renewed for four consecutive years, until the onset of the economic recession in the United States. During this period, he worked as a landscaper in Texas and then as a groundskeeper in Kentucky. Circunspecto did not face any critical economic circumstances when he enrolled in the H2 program, but given the wage differential between home and destination and the prospect of remitting hundreds of dollar to his family every week, Circunspecto decided to take advantage of the opportunity presented to him by the H2 recruiter to migrate legally. Our interview with Circunspecto revealed that, in addition to funneling workers to labor-intensive industries, brokers associated with the H2 visa program play a role in assessing the skills of Mexicans recruited to temporary jobs in the United States.

The interviews we conducted with workers like Circunspecto also showed that the top-ranking occupations of the H2 program, and its H2B category in particular, which includes nonagricultural jobs, such as landscaping and roofing, require skills that migrants develop in the context of prior undocumented sojourns. In fact, some of these migrants are rehired as H2 workers by firms in which they were previously employed without authorization. Take the case of Herculano, a construction worker from San Miguel de Allende. Herculano began his migratory career as an unauthorized worker. After numerous undocumented sojourns facilitated by his social networks, Herculano obtained an H2B visa to work with his previous employer in Texas, who had relied on his construction skills during prior undocumented stints.[24] Interestingly, Herculano transferred his colonial-style building skills acquired in the historic town of San Miguel de Allende to his construction jobs in the United States, and once recognized by his U.S. employer, was rewarded with higher wages and more workplace reponsibility. Herculano also reskilled in the U.S. labor market, learning new building techniques, which he then transferred to the Mexican labor market upon his return home to San Miguel de Allende.[25]

CAUSES AND REASONS FOR MIGRATION

Two-thirds of the Leon returnees migrated to the United States during or after 1995, reflecting the effects of economic liberalization and Mexico's 1995 financial crisis. Not surprisingly, nearly half of all respondents in the sample cited economic reasons for their most recent sojourn abroad.[26] Some of these urbanites used migration to accumulate funds to pay for debt contracted to make mortgage payments and keep small businesses afloat (see Table 3.5 later in the chapter). In late 1994, as restructuring and economic integration with the United States moved apace, a financial crisis brought the Mexican economy to a halt. Throughout the following year, capital flight, the dramatic devaluation of the peso, and skyrocketing interest rates paralyzed numerous industries and increased unemployment and poverty rates. Urban residents began sojourning to the United States to cope with the immediate impact of the crisis on the household economy.[27] A respondent from a small city explained how the economic down-turn had affected his entire family, leaving his father with no work, forcing siblings to join the labor market, and prompting him to migrate to the United States:

> When I was going to school at CONALEP [a vocational high school] and was about to start my fourth semester, I started working. But then the crisis here in Mexico happened. So, in order for me to continue studying, my sister had to quit school. My father was already a plumber and didn't have work and [with the crisis] he got even less work. I paid [for school], but since I am the oldest of the men in my family, I would see the fights between my parents, the needs they had and I said: I won't keep going to school just for me and won't pay attention to what is happening here in the family and I'll forget them or I go to the United States to help them. And I left because I needed to support them.

A municipal employee described the circumstances of his migration as the result of the 1994–95 economic crisis and the rising interest rates that followed: "I needed to go [to the United States] to earn much more money [because] due to the devaluation of '94 I was getting really behind on the house payments." This economic context intersected with the family life cycle, creating strong pressures for migration. Approximately 56 percent of respondents were already married at the time of their first U.S. trip and pressures to accumulate resources for the household in Mexico weighed heavily on their decisions to migrate. A return migrant interviewed in Guanajuato City explained that he had left for California in 2000 "because I wasn't making enough and I had to borrow money.... And I couldn't make enough because Mexico was going through a phase of deep crisis. I had young children and I wasn't making enough money." Similarly, Patricio, a construction worker and carpenter's assistant in Leon, migrated right after his first daughter was born because of the low pay and poor working conditions at home. He would have migrated with his entire family but his wife was reluctant to leave and stayed behind in Mexico.

In Guanajuato, rural dwellers whose employment opportunities were tied to the construction industry in nearby cities and other states in the country began to migrate to the United States to cope with the sudden disappearance of jobs. Workers like Ruy from San Antonio (featured in chapter 2) and many other small towns in the state often commute to cities where they find jobs in residential and commercial building projects. Ruy and other return migrants we interviewed in hamlets near cities like Guanajuato (the state capital), Irapuato, Dolores Hidalgo, and Leon had honed their skills in bricklaying and numerous other tasks specific to the region's construction styles. When local employment dwindled during the 1994–95 crisis, these men searched and found jobs with construction companies specializing in roofing, demolition, and repairs of large public and commercial buildings in Texas, Arizona, Florida, and North Carolina.

The opening of the Mexican economy also presented challenges for workers and small entrepreneurs in traditional and formerly protected industries, such as Leon's leather and shoe manufacturing cluster. As we explained in chapter 1, Chinese imports undercut local producers, forcing them to borrow money to continue operating and to resort to migration to repay debts. This is the case of Jorge, who migrated to the United States at the unusually late age of 35. After learning to work with leather in his parents' shoe business, he established a small shop manufacturing handbags in Leon until Chinese imports started to undercut his products. According to Jorge,

Total sales [of leather bags] went down because of the product that entered Mexico. The Chinese product, all synthetic, was cheap and disposable; so, customers buy cheaper products than leather [despite the fact that] it lasts less. With what customers used to buy one of my bags, they would now buy two or three Chinese bags. This economic situation caused my workshop to shut down. I went to the United States to earn money and pay off all the debts I was left with because I got into debt buying skin, making bags that I would store with the hope that sales would pick up; [the government] said they were going to stop the entry of Chinese product and since they didn't stop it, I tried to go on with my business, so as not to have to lay off my people. That was how I got into debt, more than anything, so I wouldn't have to lay off my employees, until I couldn't do it anymore.

Accumulating funds to buy a home or to invest in a business were also cited by a small percentage of respondents, although it is likely that many more ended up using remittances for these purposes. This use of migration as a strategy to accumulate savings reflects the barriers preventing access to credit markets in Mexico to pay off a debt, expand a business, or build a home.[28] Take the case of Humberto, a mechanic who owned a small auto repair shop. Having learned basic auto mechanic skills at his father's shop, Humberto established his own business. Later on, he migrated to the United States with the purpose of making more money to invest in his auto repair shop in Leon. Finally, slightly over one-quarter of the sample of returnees explained their migration as either a desire for adventure and an interest in the United States or as a way to pursue opportunities for self-improvement and learning new skills. A positive perception of the United States and the value placed on sojourning in *el norte* to work were shaped by the experiences of earlier returnees who regularly spoke of the success stories of coworkers and friends in

TABLE 3.5

Primary reason for last migration to the United States by gender

Primary Reason	Total (n=200)	Men (n=172)	Women (n=28)
Investing; buying, building, remodeling home	6%	6%	4%
Debt	4%	4%	4%
Economy/work/money	48%	49%	39%
Family/reunification	12%	9%	29%
Self-Improvement/opportunities to learn new skills	9%	9%	7%
Adventure/interest in learning about U.S.	18%	19%	14%
Other	4%	4%	4%

NOTE: Due to rounding, percentages do not total exactly to 100 percent.

their neighborhoods who had profited through skills acquisitions and saved earnings from living and working abroad (see Table 3.5).

While the literature confirms that women are more likely than men to migrate for purposes of family reunification, often joining a spouse, the women in our sample were also responding to economic factors.[29] The periodic crises and restructuring in Mexico and the expanding opportunities available in female-dominated, low-wage occupations in service and hospitality in the United States affected their decision to migrate.[30] Take the case of Carmen, a relatively prosperous entrepreneur who at the time of interview was 46 years of age and owner of a small *pica* that specializes in covering and stitching fabric to the heels of women's shoes. Before migrating, she had experienced mobility in the Leon labor market, moving from salaried employer to entrepreneur. Having developed cooking skills at home, she further enhanced them as a paid cook in a restaurant. Eventually,

Carmen saved enough of her earnings to launch a business specializing in women's shoes. Things were going fine until unforeseen events occurred. First, as a result of the peso suffering devaluation, her business was placed in jeopardy. During this time, she was also in an automobile accident that incurred debt. Unable to borrow from her ailing business to pay off her debt and keep her *pica* afloat, she migrated north. Five years later, Carmen had accumulated enough capital to pay off her bills and returned home to reopen her business.[31]

Family reunification and children's welfare were also important factors of cross-border mobility, particularly among our subsample of women. Take the case of Concepción, a 36-year-old woman who lives in a rural hamlet outside of Leon. She first migrated at the age of 16 to join her husband in Arkansas, who was unable to locate work in their economically depressed community in Mexico. She traveled to and from the United States for a number of years, caring for her parents in Mexico and U.S.-born children in Arkansas. Eventually, she decided to return to Mexico permanently to be with her parents (a decision she now regrets), leaving her children in the United States with their father, where she feels educational opportunities are better.

Our sample of Leon returnees exhibited a remittance behavior that is consistent with Mexican migrants in general. The median amount of each remittance at the time of the first job was $300 and was used primarily to pay for daily necessities, followed by investments in small businesses, construction and improvement of homes, the purchase of cars, to increase savings, and to repay debts. Interestingly, these urban-origin migrants rarely remitted funds to support community projects and, therefore, show negligible participation in collective remittance programs sponsored by the Mexican government, such as the 3x1 program for migrants (*Programa 3x1 para Migrantes*).[32] This pattern of remittance use remained largely unchanged between first and last job in the United States. One noticeable but expected difference across the employment career abroad is that at the time of the most recent job, fewer migrants used remittances to repay debt.

SOCIAL NETWORKS AND DESTINATION OF MIGRATION

Leon migrants have a wealth of social networks that connect them to the United States. Kinship, rural hometown connections, and urban neighborhood ties form a powerful social infrastructure to support international migration. In Leon, kinship ties are the cornerstone of this social infrastructure. U.S.-based family members provide information about jobs, offer shelter, and pay for the immediate cost of migration. A respondent to the survey of return migrants explained that "A brother of mine who was in the United States lent me 800 or 900 dollars to pay the *coyote* (smuggler). I found the *coyote* that brought me over [to the United States] there at the border." Another respondent stated that he migrated "by way of my brother's brother-in-law who is still in the United States now. He helped me pay the *coyote* and that's how I was able to leave." A female respondent, Julia, explained, "My sister who lived in the United States paid the *coyote*. I went by bus from Leon to Guadalajara, from there to Nogales (Sonora). A friend of my sister's picked me up in Nogales (Arizona) and she paid the *coyote*."

The return migrants interviewed in Leon confirmed the centrality of kinship networks not only to support the actual move to the United States but also as a source of employment information.

The case of Alberto illustrates this point. After he joined his uncle in Stockton, California, Alberto tapped this relative's contacts to find work at a local cable company, where Alberto learned how to install wires for telephone, television, and internet systems. These cross-border family ties were particularly important for women, whose first job in the United States often was caring for the children of relatives. Several female respondents explained how sisters and cousins sponsored their first migratory trip to babysit newborns and young children.

The migratory support networks of our Leon respondents have both rural and urban origins. Approximately one-fourth of the returnees we surveyed were born in rural localities of Guanajuato and neighboring states, such as Zacatecas, Jalisco, and San Luis Potosí. These migrants were able to tap into the highly developed migratory social networks that connect the small towns and hamlets of the central-western region of Mexico with myriad destinations and labor markets across the United States. These hometown networks often overlap with kinship ties through endogamous marriage, creating not only a powerful engine of migration but also a formidable mechanism to channel sojourners to employment and residential niches abroad.[33] A respondent with ties to a hometown in central Guanajuato described how a network of *paisanos* rapidly channeled migrants to a neighborhood in Oklahoma City: "We got there in '94, there were few *hispanos* ... [but] in one year there were about 500 of us living on one street, and all from here, from house to house, almost all from here."

While a substantial minority of informants in the sample have a history of internal migration, it is notable that more than 70 percent of them reported having been born in the city of Leon. Still, it is likely that their parents and grandparents moved from the countryside to Leon and other cities of Guanajuato and that, in consequence, our respondents have had access to the rural-origin social networks which the literature on Mexico-U.S. migration has analyzed in detail. At the same time, our data suggest that these Leon-born respondents have begun to develop urban-based migratory support networks through contacts with neighbors and coworkers. In the Leon districts where we collected our data, many returnees were aware of the sojourning experiences of fellow residents, suggesting that the urban neighborhoods we surveyed had begun to nurture their own migratory social capital. Social ties to coworkers also translate into access to migratory social networks. A respondent in Leon described how his coworkers shared information about an uncle who owned restaurants in the United States. Although this contact did not spare him the difficulties and costs of crossing the border without documentation, his colleague's relatives did provide information about a trustworthy smuggler and helped him secure a job when he arrived at his destination.

Social ties to other migrants do not cause migration but do greatly facilitate sojourning and decisively channel first-time border crossers to particular destinations and occupations. In the Leon sample, 80 percent of respondents chose the destination of their first trip based on the place of residence of family and friends in the United States. Showing the enduring effect of social networks in repeat migration, 77 percent of the migrants who engaged in two or more trips stated that the location of friends and relatives determined their choice of destination (see Table 3.6). Attesting to the power of this multilayered social infrastructure, a sizable 28 percent of our respondents (15 years of age and older) knew what their job in the United States would be before they undertook their first migratory trip.[34]

TABLE 3.6

Primary reason for choice of destination on first and last
migration to the United States

Reasons Given for Destination Choice	First Migration (n=199)	Last Migration (n=86)
Family and friends reside at destination	80%	77%
Work opportunities at destination	10%	10%
Informally hired without visa	4%	5%
Formally hired with visa	2%	2%
Other	5%	6%

NOTE: Includes last migration figures only for those who migrated multiple times. Due to rounding, percentages do not total exactly to 100 percent.

In fact, many of the respondents who knew the kind of job that awaited them abroad were also able to transfer skills learned in Mexico to the U.S. labor market. The welders, mechanics, auto body shop repairmen, and construction workers featured in chapter 2 represent some of the most common occupations in this subgroup. While the skills associated with these occupations are in fact quite portable across borders, friends and family members played an important role in finding a job at the destination that matched the skills developed in the country of origin.[35] This was the case of Saturnino, the owner of a collision and auto body repair shop in Leon. Taking advantage of the wage differential between Mexico and the United States, Saturnino migrated to Los Angeles, where his brother found him a job in an auto body shop. Javier, a blacksmith and welder, had a similar experience. He learned the trade during his childhood at his father's shop in Leon. A family member found a job for Javier in the United States building metal fences at a cattle ranch. Javier wanted to increase his earnings and seized the opportunity. He was able to transfer all the skills he had originally developed at his father's blacksmith and welding shop in Guanajuato.

The tourist industry, the expatriate economy, and the transnational corporations that establish plants and subsidiaries in the state of Guanajuato also offered opportunities for international migration and the mobilization of skills across borders. The cases of Ana, featured in chapter 1, and Karen, introduced in chapter 2, illustrate this point. Ana worked in a hotel owned by an American who taught her English. She continued to practice and develop her language skills until a tourist visiting Guanajuato offered her a job as a live-in nanny in Manhattan. Karen, a young woman who worked for the Australian company Fresh Select, was hired as an assistant secretary but, through in-house job training and an English class paid for by the company, moved up to administrative secretary at the company's branch office in Santa Maria, California.

Not surprisingly, social networks also played a role in channeling migrants from Leon to traditional places of concentration of the *guanajuatense* population in the United States. Nearly 70 percent of respondents moved to California, Texas, and Illinois on their first trip across the border. Los Angeles and neighboring southern California counties, such as San Bernardino, Orange, and San Diego, attracted a sizeable 29 percent of first-time migrants. While a large proportion of respondents migrated to traditional destinations, 30 percent of them dispersed across 21 other states, with noticeable clusters in Arizona, Colorado, Ohio, Florida, and Georgia. This pattern of concentration and dispersion persisted across trips: 63 percent of repeat migrants went to California, Texas, and Illinois on their most recent migration, while the rest (37 percent) dispersed across 17 other states (see Table 3.7). Although the flow from Leon to the United States is

TABLE 3.7

Destinations of first and last migration
to the United States

State of Destination	First Migration (n=196)	Last Migration (n=86)
California	43%	34%
Texas	20%	16%
Illinois	6%	13%
South[a]	12%	18%
West[b]	11%	10%
Midwest[c]	7%	7%
Northeast	1%	2%
Total	*100%*	*100%*

[a] Excluding Texas.

[b] Excluding California.

[c] Excluding Illinois.

TABLE 3.8

Year of first migration to the United States by state of destination
(n=194)

Year of Entry	California	Texas	Illinois	Arizona	Georgia	Other
1945–1979	7	6	1	1	–	2
1980–1984	8	2	–	–	–	–
1985–1989	15	4	1	2	–	1
1990–1994	9	4	2	–	–	1
1995–1999	15	3	2	2	4	11
2000–2004	24	7	2	2	1	18
2005–2009	6	12	3	2	1	13
Total	*84*	*38*	*11*	*9*	*6*	*46*

heavily concentrated in the traditional states of Mexican immigration, recent migrants appear to be choosing new destinations in sizeable numbers. As Table 3.8 indicates, 54 respondents (28 percent of the sample) who conducted their first migration to the United States between 1995 and 2009 sojourned to states other than California, Texas, and Illinois.

CONCLUSION

Most migrants from Leon took leave for the United States between 1995 and 2005, during Mexico's great migration. During this tumultuous period, economic restructuring, the opening of national markets to foreign competition, financial crisis, and devaluation launched between a quarter of a million and four hundred thousand Mexicans across the border every year. Kinship and friendship networks, some based in the rural communities of Guanajuato and adjacent states and some anchored in the urban neighborhoods of Leon, provided a powerful social infrastructure to facilitate migration and mobilize skills in the international labor market, while contacts with employers and recruiters offered additional but less common pathways to sojourn north. Still, the majority of Leon respondents have migrated only once to the United States, a fact that we attribute to the emergent nature of this flow and unauthorized status of the overwhelming majority of sojourners. Our respondents also migrated at an older age than their rural counterparts, having acquired more years of formal education and more skills and experience in Leon's urban labor market. Not surprisingly, our respondents migrated to traditional states and cities of the Mexican and *guanajuatense* population in the United States. In recent years, these migrants have started to select and disperse across less traditional destinations in the country.

4

Transferring Skills, Reskilling, and Laboring in the United States

Francisco learned the fundamentals of masonry as a young boy. His father was a well-established *maestro albañil* (master mason) in Leon, and from him Francisco learned the craft of adobe construction, how to mold and dry clay for bricks, and how to cut and lay brick and stone by hand. In the United States, Francisco was able to apply his masonry skills to a different type of job: a friend and established immigrant from Leon found him an entry-level position in a manufacturing company that makes airplane parts in Ohio. Though the production relies on advanced technology for molding rubber and steel parts, Francisco's experience in molding bricks from mud and manure by hand and then firing them in ovens gave him an advantage in learning the new technology for the job. He was a fast learner, and through informal interaction with coworkers on the plant floor and on-the-job observation and practice, Francisco reskilled, mastering how to operate the machinery that molded the material. When asked how he learned his machinist skills at the factory, he responded, "from other workers." As he explained, "When they noticed how

I watched them operate the machinery, they asked if I wanted to learn. When I said yes, they showed me." From his fellow workers, Francisco learned specific steps in the processing and production of rubber tires and aluminum parts. He loved his work because he was continually learning about new technology and materials and the importance of precision, a skill and approach to performing tasks that he argued was not emphasized in his work experience in Mexico. Despite being satisfied with his job at the factory, he eventually left because of the low hourly wage, a condition he credited to his undocumented status and lack of English skills, which prevented him from negotiating with his employer for higher wages. Through the recommendation of a friend in his immigrant network, he secured a job as a mason in a construction company that specializes in residential patios. Here, his work experience in the construction industry in Mexico enabled him to assist his *patrón* in many explicit ways, but one experience stood out:

> One day we were building a brick chimney for a barbecue grill. Our job was to build a circular stone chimney. I realized that the other workers [all co-ethnics] had no experience working with stone and that they didn't know a basic technique in building with stone or brick—that one had to *sacar la línea,* install a mason's line or twine, which is the line that keeps the stones straight on the wall and thereby allows for greater accuracy and faster laying. When the boss came to check up on our work he asked who installed this line. Upon finding out that I had installed it throughout the chimney foundation, front and back, the *patrón* said, "*¡Qué buena cabeza tienes, qué buen trabajo!*"—What a good head you have, what good work! As Francisco commented, "I will never forget that moment."

Francisco was far from "unskilled" when he entered the U.S. labor market. Although he never finished primary school,

Francisco had acquired substantial masonry skills from his father in Mexico, and he was able to transfer those skills to the United States in both implicit and explicit ways. His working knowledge in molding materials in Mexico remained hidden until he expressed interest in learning how to operate the machinery that molds the plastics and thereby demonstrated his talent. In addition, Francisco was able to reskill in the U.S. labor market because of the ways in which skills were embedded in the social organization of work on the plant floor; he learned the new molding techniques through interacting with and observing coworkers, not through explicit instruction by a boss. He soon acquired skills in operating state-of-the-art industrial machines. His working knowledge also included learning and appreciating what he called the importance of precision— a competence not related to technique but to the ways in which specific types of work are approached and organized—and despite his unauthorized status, relatively low levels of formal education, and lack of English, Francisco jumped across occupations and different manufacturing sectors of the economy, where he went through additional reskilling: building walls and chimneys and laying stones for residential patios exposed him to new and more efficient technologies for cutting, installing, and polishing tile and stone.

Francisco took a risk and quit his job in the airplane parts factory, even though he loved his work and had no other jobs lined up. Drawing on contacts in his immigrant network he eventually located work where he could apply his source-country skills. In essence, he relied on the skills he had brought from Mexico, his social capital, and his own agency to *brincar* (job jump). In his new job as a mason, his boss recognized and valued his masonry and problem-solving skills, and he was rewarded with an increase in responsibility and hourly wage. Like many of the migrants in our study, Francisco not only transferred work experience from Mexico but also underwent a process of reskilling in which he learned to apply new technologies to do things in a different way. In the long run, the willingness and ability both to transfer source-country skills and to develop new ones in the United States empowered Francisco to embrace job jumping, a strategy to escape exploitation and improve work conditions.

For many first-time migrants a lack of English fluency, limited knowledge about work opportunities, and exploitive work conditions in the secondary labor market represent major mobility barriers in the United States. Given low levels of formal human capital and broader structural constraints, newcomers like Francisco rely on a co-ethnic network to direct them to jobs in the unregulated sector of the economy where work authorization may not be required and demand for English is minimal.[1] And, as the case of Francisco demonstrates, sometimes migrants can apply source-country skills in these gateway jobs to advance their opportunities. The empirical evidence about what happens after they enter these first jobs paints a mixed picture, reflecting the complexity of the labor market integration and economic mobility of Mexican immigrants.

Perspectives on the long-term mobility opportunities largely fall into two camps. On the pessimistic side are those who argue that when immigrants with low levels of formal human capital initially arrive in the United States they are relegated to the secondary labor market characterized by job insecurity, low wages, and low skill requirements.[2] In many of these secondary sector jobs, newcomers are crowded into "brown collar" occupations that provide little if any opportunity for higher wages, occupational mobility, and advancement.[3] Lack of English language skills and unauthorized status place many Mexican workers at the mercy of recruiters, labor contractors, employers, subcontractors, and co-ethnic bosses in institutionalized and exploitive migration industries.[4] In this scenario, workers adjust by shifting back and forth between jobs in the informal and ethnic economies. Ironically, these movements re-create the very conditions of isolation, inequality, and blocked mobility that they are trying to escape.[5] Because they are concentrated in a largely unregulated secondary labor market, their mobility opportunities are restricted and, if embedded in ethnic networks, they experience what Nobert Wiley terms *ethnic mobility entrapment*.[6]

The optimistic side argues, as Roger Waldinger often puts it, "migration is good for immigrants." By traveling to more developed countries, migrants can realize opportunities not available at home, such as higher wages, the chance to accumulate capital, and the prospect of learning and applying new skills. As Douglas Massey, a leading scholar of Mexican migration, recently wrote after reading a first draft of this book, "Migrants are motivated, creative agents who are always looking for ways to get ahead and given half a chance they are likely to experience significant social mobility within the United States if they accumulate significant time north of the border." Rather than constraining opportunities, optimists argue, the secondary labor market provides shelter for newcomer immigrants who lack English language skills and knowledge about the United States. Working with co-ethnics can provide newcomers with access to information about their host country, opportunities for skill development, and time to adjust to new conditions. Collectively, these ethnic networks and the entry-level jobs serve as stepping-stones to better jobs and entrepreneurial ventures in the informal sectors of the economy such as landscaping and construction where disadvantaged immigrants can apply skills learned at home and innovate opportunity.[7] Through co-ethnic networks in the informal economy some Mexican immigrants find weekend projects to augment their wages, while others start small businesses in co-ethnic communities.[8] Increasingly, then, scholars recognize that working-class immigrants or those with low levels of education are not always relegated to the secondary labor market, and that even in this largely unregulated sector of the economy, mobility opportunities exist.[9]

We find some support for both scenarios, demonstrating the complexity of the work experiences of immigrants, especially undocumented Mexican immigrants who must navigate multiple institutional and structural barriers to mobility. In this chapter, we argue that the way immigrants are incorporated into the U.S. labor market also depends on the work experience, skills, abilities, and knowledge they bring with them from their home communities. We further the debate on the employment experiences of immigrants by showing how cross-border skill transfers and reskilling in the United States shed light on why some individual immigrants, including the undocumented, can escape bad jobs while others cannot. We call into question conventional wisdom that the immigrant labor force resembles an hourglass—wide at the top and bottom and narrow in the middle. Like other scholars we find considerable skill development and mobility among Mexican immigrants in the United States.[10] Rather than explain this dispersal as solely a function of formal education and training as most researchers do (in large part because of the U.S. Census and Labor Bureau metrics they rely on to measure skills), we argue that informal learning environments at home and abroad can provide migrants with skills and competences that they then mobilize to advance their opportunities in the U.S. labor market.

In this chapter, we tell the story of how the dual processes of skill transfer from Mexico and reskilling in the United States influence the work experiences and job opportunities of immigrants. To place the discussion in social context we begin the chapter with an overview of the U.S. geographic and industrial venues where migrants in our study arrived, a discussion that has an important bearing on the types of skills demanded in the U.S. economy. We then move on to identify the different types of skills these migrants brought to their U.S. jobs from Mexico with a focus on the gendered nature of those skill transfers. What then follows is a discussion of how the social context of skill transfers and reskilling shapes the occupational trajectories of migrants in the U.S. labor market.

ECONOMIC, GEOGRAPHIC, AND SOCIAL CONTEXTS OF ARRIVAL IN THE UNITED STATES

The large majority of the Leon migrants initiated their migratory careers in the mid-1990s, following the impact of the Mexican government's abandonment of its model of import- substitution industrialization in favor of market liberalization and an export-oriented growth approach. As we discussed in chapter 3, these neoliberal economic policies displaced and uprooted workers throughout the country, but especially hard hit were those laboring in once-protected industrial sectors in urban areas such as Guadalajara, Mexico City, Monterrey, Tampico, and Leon. For many urban Mexican workers, U.S.-bound migration became a new strategy to overcome deteriorating economic conditions at home and to develop new opportunities.[11]

While the economic restructuring and the crises of the 1980s and 1990s in Mexico were major macrostructural factors behind emigration, the destinations and specific first jobs of Mexican migrants were largely determined by their network ties in the United States, the total human capital they brought with them, and the demands of the U.S. labor market. The Mexican sojourners who came to the United States in the 1980s, 1990s, and even the early 2000s entered a booming construction market and an economy that was undergoing a major process of restructuring characterized by the movement of production to low-wage sites, the expansion of certain industries and the contraction of others. Facing international competition resulting from the elimination of barriers to trade between countries, including NAFTA, firms in the United States increasingly shifted to a smaller and more flexible labor force and moved production to cheaper labor sites both overseas and throughout the country, especially the Southeast. Also, while some sectors and geographic areas of the U.S. economy such as mass manufacturing in the Northeast and Midwest declined, other sectors, including manufacturing-based technology and finance, flourished in the Sun Belt. To support the increase in specialized manufacturing and professional service occupations, the U.S. economy experienced a parallel growth in low-wage manufacturing and service jobs—janitors, restaurant and other hospitality workers, construction workers, and domestics—or what Nigel Harris calls the "sweated trades in developed countries."[12] These jobs were filled primarily by unauthorized migrants fleeing the economic crisis in Mexico and political turmoil in Central America.

Table 4.1 lists the U.S. states and industries in which the Leon migrants lived and worked during their first trip to the United States. As we explained in chapter 3 and show again here, 63 percent

TABLE 4.1

Percent distribution in each industry by state of destination
for first migration (n=197)

	Arizona	California	Illinois	Georgia	Texas	Other States	Overall Industry Distribution
Agriculture	25	15	0	17	18	4	*13*
Construction	38	7	18	17	28	27	*18*
Manufacturing	25	21	9	33	13	16	*18*
Hospitality	0	20	27	17	15	27	*20*
Domestic	0	6	9	0	5	4	*5*
Other services	13	30	36	17	21	22	*25*
State distribution	*4*	*43*	*6*	*3*	*20*	*25*	*100*

NOTE: Due to rounding, percentages do not total exactly to 100 percent.

of the Leon migrants in the study migrated to the traditional gateway states of California and Texas, with smaller numbers concentrated in Arizona, Illinois, and Georgia. The "other states" category is a diverse one, including a handful of newcomer migrants who arrived in the late 1990s and early 2000s, and settled in new destination states such as North Carolina, Virginia, and Nevada. Collectively, these nontraditional destinations parallel the contemporary geography of migration tracked by other scholars of Mexican migration.[13] In all of these gateway and new destination states, the men and women in our sample were concentrated in three immigrant-heavy sectors: agriculture, manufacturing, and service. In California, the agricultural workers were all men and clustered in produce picking, including seasonal crops like grapes, mint, and strawberries, while in Arizona, Texas, Wisconsin, and Utah, they were primarily husbandry workers, laboring in the care of cattle and the grooming and training of horses.

The construction industry was also a major sector of employment for Leon male migrants in all of the states, except California. This sector experienced tremendous growth during the U.S. housing and real estate boom of the early 2000s and it became increasingly dependent on immigrant labor.[14] In this industry, our sample primarily included roofers, bricklayers, general laborers, carpenters, and framers on residential and commercial projects, earning fairly high wages in comparison to jobs in agriculture and the service sector. In some states in the South, because of the absence of unions, the construction industry is increasingly organized through subcontracting. While working for subcontractors placed our workers in precarious and sometimes exploitative conditions, it also provided opportunities for skill development.[15]

In all states, migrants also labored in food processing, transportation, and auto repair, and semiskilled positions in plastics and metal fabrication industries. In Georgia and other new gateway destination states men worked in low-wage poultry, meat, and other food processing sectors that are increasingly drawing migrants to new destinations. Both women and men found first jobs in the service industry where men labored primarily as gardeners and janitors and women as chambermaids in hotels, as food preparation workers, as cooks in restaurants, and as live-in and day domestics in private homes.

TOTAL HUMAN CAPITAL TRANSFERS
FROM MEXICO TO THE UNITED STATES

Three central questions organize the findings we present in this chapter. First, did the migrants bring human capital skills from

Mexico to their U.S. jobs and, if so, what did these skills look like? Second, for those who did bring skills, under what individual agency strategies and institutional and structural conditions were they able to mobilize them to improve their economic situation in the U.S. labor market? Finally, what are the social and institutional mechanisms through which employers and co-ethnics block or facilitate the learning and mobilization of skills in the United States? Each of these questions is addressed by industrial sector and through a gendered lens, recognizing that the social context of learning and labor market opportunity varies dramatically for men and women.

Beginning with the first question: Did the Leon migrants bring human capital skills with them? Table 4.2 shows the skills that the return migrants reported acquiring and transferring from all jobs in Mexico to the United States. The table shows most Mexican migrants bring very little traditional human capital with them to their U.S. jobs as measured through host-country language facility, formal education, vocational classes, and on-the-job training programs; among the Leon sample these composed only 3 percent. Yet, although small, these transfers were useful in some work environments and jobs in the secondary labor market of the U.S. economy. While most of the men laboring in service and construction reported that English language skills were not initially valuable because they worked alongside co-ethnics, several men reported using English and mathematics learned in secondary school in Mexico in their U.S. jobs. Two young men said that their limited knowledge of mathematics and English was valuable in their U.S. construction jobs to measure materials and read manuals and blueprints. Another respondent, who was a mechanic in Leon before he migrated, reported that he learned to read English by reading mechanics manuals published in the United States.

TABLE 4.2

Skill and knowledge transfers from Mexico to U.S. jobs by gender

Skill Type	Total (n=200)	Male (n=172)	Female (n=28)
Any transfer	48%	51%	26%
English	2%	1%	4%
Formal education	1%	1%	0%
On-the-job technical skills	44%	47%	26%
Off-the-job technical skills	11%	12%	4%
Social skills and competences	3%	2%	4%

NOTE: Total exceeds 100 percent since some respondents reported transferring more than one skill type.

The story of human capital transfers is different for women. Although they too transferred low levels of traditional human capital from Mexico to the United States, English language skills were more important to their initial occupations abroad than it was for men, reflecting the different entry jobs occupied by women and men. In their first and subsequent jobs as domestics, chambermaids, and sales clerks, occupations where face-to-face interaction with employers and customers requires a measure of language proficiency, women reported using the English they had learned in school in Mexico. Knowledge of English also made it easier for these women to apply existing or newly learned social and customer service skills. Recall Anna, the assistant to a receptionist in a San Miguel de Allende hotel, who was recruited for a live-in domestic position in Manhattan by an American guest at the hotel. Though her English was minimal, it did help her secure the job. Similarly, the tactful social and communicative competences she learned in her job as a receptionist also made Anna a good candidate.

Two-thirds of the sample—men and women alike—argued that some knowledge of the English language was important for long-term social mobility pathways in the United States, recognizing that without some English they would probably remain in low-wage, dead-end jobs. Though many workers did not need English to locate jobs or complete job tasks, most acknowledged English language proficiency as a stepping-stone to occupational mobility. Domestics saw it as a skill that would allow them to escape live-in work; construction workers saw it as a skill that would facilitate a transition to foreman, an intermediary position between workers and management, or enable them to initiate an entrepreneurial activity. Workers in hospitality saw it as a way to leave invisible labor in the kitchens where they worked as dishwashers and janitors and move to the front where they could work as waiters.

A number of migrants could not apply skills they had acquired in Mexico because they either were not needed on the job or because of fear of launching a subcontracting activity or an independent business due to legal status and the paperwork involved in licensing. For example, a migrant reported enrolling in a vocational program in electricity in Mexico but was unable to use his electrician skills in his construction job in the United States because of the specialized nature of the job and licensing issues. Several women who completed cosmetology training in Mexico were unable to apply their skills abroad because of English language and licensing barriers, but one did eventually open an informal beauty salon in her apartment in her U.S. neighborhood. We will return to these informal entrepreneurial activities below.

Thus, if we look only at formal human capital transfers, our findings appear to support the assumption in human capital empirical research and in policy arenas that Mexican migrants are unskilled. Yet, as Table 4.2 shows, the respondents in our sample arrived in the United States with substantial skills, reflecting extensive work experience prior to migration. More than half brought informal on- and off-the-job technical skills from Mexico to their U.S. jobs. Men were twice as likely as women to say that they transferred on-the-job skills to the United States and three times as likely to report having transferred off-the-job skills to their U.S. jobs, reflecting both their greater occupational diversity in Mexico and the emphasis on off-the-job learning among young boys and men. Common technical skills transferred from Mexico to the United States by men included machine and appliance repair, and electrical, carpentry, masonry, and metalworking skills, all of which were learned on and off the job through observation and interaction and practice. Because of the restricted job options for women compared to men, the on- and off-the-job skills women reported possessing centered on interpersonal competences, such as caregiving, and on food preparation skills, reflective of women's domestic roles as homemakers and their jobs in food production and preparation.[16]

TRANSFERRING SKILLS, RESKILLING, AND OCCUPATIONAL CHANGE: BARRIERS AND OPPORTUNITIES

Do these technical, English language, communication, and interpersonal skill transfers make a difference in the labor market experiences of Mexican migrants? Do they facilitate reskilling, job advancement, and higher wages? We find that they do, but with a caveat. Skills alone do not guarantee job advancement. Successful human capital transfers are filtered through migrant social networks, the social organization and conditions of work, and the institutional arrangements that support the learning of skills. With this in mind, we turn to the U.S. labor market experiences and social mobility processes of the Leon sample.

Table 4.3 captures four mobility pathways of migrants in the United States: acquisition of new skills, transitioned to a job requiring more skills, wage increases, and employer valorization. As the table shows, 81 percent of the sample acquired new skills, and reskilling in the U.S. labor market enabled transitions to jobs that demanded yet higher skills and increased wages.

We argue that although the personal networks of migrants assume a large role in directing them to their workplaces, mobility within the U.S. labor market is in part a function of the skills they bring with them from Mexico as well as the skills they learn on their newly found occupations, which they then can apply to leverage better jobs. Furthermore, knowledge transfers from home communities in Mexico can assume a central role in adapting and learning new skills. Next we examine these skilling interactions and mobility pathways at work in specific economic sectors.

TABLE 4.3

Economic mobility pathways in the U.S. labor market (n=200)

Learned new skills	81%
Transitioned to a better job requiring more skills	36%
Wage increase	33%
Skills recognized and rewarded	65%

NOTE: Total exceeds 100 percent since migrant workers could list multiple pathways.

AGRICULTURE

Because farmwork tasks are perceived as simple and repetitive and because of the constant replenishment of migrant labor in the agricultural industry, anthropologist Manuel Romero argues that the workforce in this sector has regularly been characterized as an easily replaceable labor force made up of transient and unskilled labor.[17] In contrast to this limited and limiting perception of low-skilled migrants with restricted occupational choices, we found substantial skill transfers and skill development among the migrant farmworkers in our sample. Of the 20 male migrants who entered agricultural jobs upon arrival in the United States, for example, 16 said that their agricultural experience and knowledge of planting and harvesting crops in Mexico helped them learn new ways of doing things in their agricultural jobs abroad. Being able to recognize when to harvest a cucumber according to specifications learned in Guanajuato facilitated learning how to pick fruit in North Carolina. This point was made by Manuel Romero in his ethnography of farmworkers laboring in orange and grape production in California's Central Valley, "Nothing to Learn."[18] To quote from his paper,

> There are in fact a number of abilities needed to do this job. Some of them are related to the commodity's specification, like recognizing the fruit that meets the required conditions and cutting it without damaging the trees, all at a pace fast enough for good productivity. Other abilities are related to becoming adapted to the job and doing it in a less exhausting way: knowing how to handle the sack, how to place and move the body over the ladder, and how to empty the sack in the box, all reducing the effort and helping to avoid the risks of accident or injury. According to the workers, this is "*el chiste*" (the key) to the job: learning how to do the activity in a way that "*le rinda*" (pays off).

Workers transfer knowledge and skills learned in Mexico through experience and observation. Our colleague Víctor Zúñiga relayed the following case, and even though it does not come from either the fieldwork or the survey we conducted in Guanajuato, it poignantly illustrates the kinds of knowledge transfers taking place in husbandry in agriculture. Arnulfo works at a hog-raising commercial farm in southern Utah, where he is in charge of an entire section. Each section functions independently, producing and raising its own pigs, which are then transported to slaughterhouses by rail. According to the manager, Arnulfo's division ranks number one in two key indicators among nearly three hundred sections that comprise the farm: number of pigs being born and their fattening rate. Arnulfo attributes his success to his knowledge of the social hierarchy among pigs, something he had learned from observation at a similar facility in Chihuahua in northern Mexico. According to Arnulfo, there are leaders and followers in every pigpen. Once the food is placed in the pen, the sole leader of the group feeds first, then the others feed. Arnulfo had also transferred from his job in Mexico detailed knowledge of the pigs' reproductive behavior, which he then applied to his new job to successfully increase the animals' rate of insemination. Despite Arnulfo's undocumented status, the farm's managers recognized his success and talents at raising pigs and regularly awarded him with financial incentives, something that had not happened in his native Chihuahua.

The literature on migrant agricultural workers portrays a disadvantaged worker relative to other immigrant-heavy industries. Migrant farmworkers earn lower wages and experience more unemployment than other workers. They live in substandard housing conditions and are regularly exposed to hazardous chemicals.[19] Despite the disadvantaged position of migrant farm-workers in the United States, a number of studies have documented that skills learned in the U.S. agricultural industry can facilitate job transitions and upward mobility.[20] Indeed, in our sample, almost half of all workers in agriculture reported learning new skills in their U.S. jobs, which then led to occupational changes. Reskilling in their U.S. jobs involved being exposed to new tools, technologies, and ways of doing things. Many of the migrants had worked on small family farms in Mexico where they completed tasks by hand with the use of simple tools. In the United States they learned their skills in a largely mechanized industry. Moreover, because of the decentralized nature of workforce management in the industry, agricultural workers often acquire their skills on the job watching and imitating crew leaders.[21]

Oscar, for example, reported learning new planting techniques through observation and practice. Several of the migrants transitioned from picking lemons by hand to operating "shake and catch" machines, which surround a tree and shake the fruit and nuts into a catching frame. One migrant, Jaime, mobilized old skills learned off the job at home to engage in what Hagan and her colleagues learned from migrants to call *brincar* (job jumping), first within the agricultural sector, and later across industries to construction.[22] Drawing on his personal network, Jaime landed his first job as a picker on a farm that raised cattle and harvested tomatoes. One day his supervisor inquired if anyone among the workers had the skills to build a corral. Jaime stepped forward and said that he had some woodworking skills, having helped his father build a doorframe and cabinet. Upon seeing the corral Jaime built, the owner was so impressed with his craftsmanship that he referred Jaime to neighbors and eventually to a friend and residential builder and developer who recruited Jaime from agricultural work. In his new job he reskilled, acquiring new knowledge about tools for working with wood and new approaches to work. As Jaime explained, "I learned to be more efficient and precise." Jaime is not the only migrant in our study who was able to job jump because he was approached by another employer: 8 percent of all respondents in the sample who reported changing jobs stated that this transition came about because they were directly recruited by another employer that valued their skills.

There are other mobility narratives in the U.S. work history of those who worked in agriculture. Take the case of Ruben, who traveled to a rural community in Wisconsin to work alongside his brother on a horse farm that trained show horses in dressage. Initially his tasks were confined to cleaning the stalls and feeding the horses. Eventually, he moved up to the position of groomer and his wages increased slightly. After two years, he moved up to assistant trainer, learning how to lead the horse in dressage steps. All of these skills were learned informally on the job and from his supervisor. He copied what he observed and then practiced it. Ruben would apply this skill on other horse farms in Wisconsin for several years before returning to Mexico for family reasons. In each of his U.S. jobs he was given the opportunity to demonstrate his skills and his employer valorized them. Skill recognition and valorization is a major ingredient in the satisfaction and pride and dignity that many in our sample found in their jobs abroad. The cases of Jaime and Ruben demonstrate several important factors about skill transfers, reskilling, and opportunities. First, migrants do bring skills from Mexico and sometimes they mobilize them in their sojourns in the United States. Second, contrary to the scenario of dead-end, low-wage jobs, migrants learn considerable new skills while abroad. As Table 4.3 highlights, more than three quarters of the respondents reported learning new skills abroad, and some of this reskilling took place in work that we consider offers few paths to mobility, such as agricultural jobs.

The decentralized nature of labor management in agriculture provides opportunities for skill development through intermediaries, but this same management style can lead to exploitation.[23] The skimming of wages by middlemen and contractors is especially problematic in the agricultural industry, which is largely controlled by employers and labor brokers in the private sector.[24] One migrant from Leon reported having to pay 50 percent of his salary earned picking tobacco and cucumbers in North Carolina to a co-ethnic intermediary. Frustrated because he could not communicate with his employer and unable to escape the exploitive conditions, he returned to Mexico.

MANUFACTURING AND CONSTRUCTION

The manufacturing sector, including construction, automotive repair, and plastic and steel production, also provided ample opportunities for transferring skills and reskilling through on-the-job training, sometimes in the form of workplace safety programs. Take, for example, construction, a sector in which 40 percent reporting transferring skills from Mexico, and another 16 percent reported learning new skills in the United States. Except for five cases of women working in food processing, the overwhelming majority of Leon workers in manufacturing were male. The urban construction industry experienced tremendous growth during the years of the housing and real estate boom and became increasingly dependent on immigrant labor.[25] In the virtual absence of unions in the U.S. South and portions of the Southwest, the construction industry is increasingly organized through subcontracting, a system that has helped corporations lower wages, deflect legal responsibility for workers' compensation, weaken union influence, and eventually make jobs largely unattractive to native-born workers.[26] Mexican and other Latino immigrants constitute a substantial percentage of the construction workforce in California and Texas, the main destinations of the Leon migrants, and a growing proportion in new destination states like North Carolina and Georgia. During the housing boom, the construction sector was one of the largest employers of immigrants. In this industry, Mexicans work primarily as roofers, bricklayers, general laborers, carpenters, and framers on residential and commercial projects, earning fairly high wages in comparison to jobs in agriculture and the service sector.

Table 4.4 shows that modes of learning are slightly different in the United States than in Mexico. First, learning through formal mechanisms in the manufacturing industry is more common in the United States, even for migrants that lack authorization and possess low levels of English and formal education. This difference can partially be explained by the importance of vocational classes and safety training in industrial jobs in the United States. Of the 14 migrants who reskilled through formal training paid for by the employer, all were men and the large majority attended a community college where they enrolled in technical courses that were required to further their job careers. At the request and expense of their employers, several of the *encargados* (foremen) in the construction industry enrolled in community colleges where they were certified in reading blueprints. Another Leon migrant, who was hired by a manufacturer of airplane parts because of the machinist skills he brought with him from Mexico, was sent to a

TABLE 4.4

TABLE 4.4

Social context and processes of learning skills in the United States

Learning Process	Total (n=162)	Male (n=143)	Female (n=19)
Formal (institutional)			
Vocational training and other schooling leading to credentials	7%	8%	0%
Formal (workplace)			
On-the-job training program designed by the workplace or explicit instruction from boss or coworker	56%	49%	68%
Informal (work)			
Observation, social interaction with coworkers, experimentation and practice	57%	57%	53%
Informal (home and community)			
Observation, social interaction with family, friends and neighbors	—	—	—

NOTE: Percentages exceed 100 since migrant workers could list multiple forms of learning.

vocational class in Ohio to learn how to operate more sophisticated and newer machinery. Another migrant took classes at a community college to learn how to operate a diagnostic computer for his job as an auto mechanic.

Federal and local government agencies also assume an important institutional role in safety-related skills training. A return migrant who worked in food preparation for a large restaurant chain in California underwent extensive in-house safety training to learn how to control temperatures when storing perishable foods, a technique that is regularly monitored by health inspectors. Migrants working in construction depended on Occupational

Safety and Health Administration (OSHA) training to learn industrial safety guidelines in their U.S. jobs. Construction workers regularly went through weekly or monthly safety training classes, learning how to use tools, operate harnesses to scale tall buildings, and follow regulations that stressed the importance of working in teams to minimize accidents. In one Raleigh construction firm, employees attend weekly toolbox safety workshops. To accommodate the immigrant laborers, workshops are conducted in both Spanish and English.

We found that workers laboring in large commercial projects were more likely to be provided with safety training compared to migrants who worked for small-scale residential subcontractors such as in roofing, where in the absence of institutional safety training, workers are largely required to fend for themselves. In this context, it is not surprising that immigrant work accidents are so prevalent. Indeed, our respondents told us of numerous fatal or near-fatal accidents of fellow migrants who perished or were crippled in roofing or window-washing accidents and their families were never compensated. One young return migrant told us that he watched his father fall to his death from a scaffold when his harness came loose. Another return migrant, a widow and mother of two U.S.-born children, reported that her husband also fell to his death in a roofing accident. As these cases demonstrate, there are few state-regulated institutional mechanisms to provide safety training and protection for unauthorized workers and as a result workers are at the mercy of their employers to provide these supports.

Table 4.4 also shows that unlike learning in Mexico, none of the migrants in the sample acquired skills off the job in the United States. Except for picking up a few English words or phrases through interaction with neighbors and store clerks, these opportunities simply did not exist. Table 4.4 also shows that as in Mexico, most migrants learned their U.S. jobs informally on the job through observation, interaction, and practice. Just as in Mexico, they must be fast learners to advance. Competition is fierce and migrant labor is plentiful. There are also similarities in informal learning in Mexico and the United States, and this is most notable in the construction and other craft industries where one learns by watching and doing. One of the interesting differences between informal learning at home and abroad is that migrants reported receiving far more feedback from co-ethnic workers and intermediaries in the United States than in Mexico. As one migrant explained, "In Mexico, we were often left to fend for ourselves, to watch and then imitate, but in the United States if a supervisor sees you are trying, he will provide feedback and encourage you to do more." The foreman, who is often a well-established co-ethnic intermediary, can assume an important role in skill demonstration and development, filling an institutional gap created by inaccessible training and credentialing programs.

Although the subcontracting system, which is increasingly characteristic of the U.S. construction industry, generally makes for precarious employment and working conditions, this system also offers entrepreneurial and reskilling opportunities to immigrants. Medium- and small-size construction firms maintain a small number of permanent employees, often in areas deemed essential, and subcontract all other tasks. Needless to say, employers appreciate the fact that subcontracting allows them to maintain lean operations, deflect legal responsibility for workers (including their legal status), and pay lump sums to subcontractors without having to worry about indirect costs. But even such a flexible system requires a measure of stability. Firms often subcontract small crews of sheetrock workers or framers composed of two hangers and one helper or two framers and a helper. Workers are only hired as members of a crew and not individually. These crews are hired continuously until a job is finished and, in some cases, throughout an entire season. In this context of relative stability, the less experienced helpers (probably recently arrived) learn from master hangers, framers, and finishers. Helpers can then move on to establish their own crews. Becoming a finisher may take longer since, as per the interviews conducted with employers, finishers must have a broader skill set and have their own machinery. Acquiring "good worksite English" is most likely a condition to establish a separate crew.

Josefina, a Colombian-born vice president of a medium-sized construction company whom we interviewed in North Carolina, offered several cases of former employees who had moved from helpers to leaders of their own crews and even small firms. In one instance, a helper named Manuel demonstrated "good work ethic and desire to learn" and he received a raise. Later, after more skill acquisition, he hired his own helper, moved up to framer, and continued to work for the company. He later left the firm. Four years later Josefina found out that he had moved all the way up to *patrón*—he had learned English and established his own business with insurance and a crew of eight men. Immigrants also form and run their own crews in jobs that have low barriers to entry in terms of either capital or skill, such as painting. Subcontracting offers opportunities for transferring skills, reskilling, and even increasing social mobility through entrepreneurship while remaining functional to the logic of a system in which one crew can undercut and displace another crew from a job.

Because many immigrant construction workers are excluded from apprenticeship and formal programs that could expose them to new technology and methods and thus help them develop their skills sets, they primarily depend on learning through observation, trial and error, and informal mentoring from a seasoned worker or supervisor. Take the case of Florencio, who arrived in the United States in 2006 when the construction industry was booming. Because he had not worked in construction in Mexico, he was hired as an *ayudante* (entry-level helper) and remained in that position for two years. During this time, he acquired new skills, learning how to frame and lay bricks. When asked how he picked up these skills, he responded, "From people I work with and my cousin, who is the *encargado* (person in charge), but most of all by watching how others did it."

On-the-job reskilling is also made possible by the way in which construction work is socially organized. From interviews with employers like Josefina and construction workers and our on-site observations, we found that crews usually consist of three to five members of one ethnic group. The team is typically supervised by an experienced worker with substantial skills or a coethnic who has English language skills and acts as intermediary between workers and management. If the crew leader is of one ethnicity (e.g., Mexican) and he supervises two immigrant crews of different national origin (Mexicans and Guatemalans), he is more likely to provide greater mobility opportunities to a coethnic from the same country. Every crew has at least one crewmember with "good worksite English." The rest of the crew seems to speak little or no English. Often the composition of the teams reflects the hierarchical occupational structure from Mexico, with an *ayudante*, and a *media cuchara*, the worker supervising the *ayudante* but under the supervision of the supervisor or *maestro*. Work experience and time in the United States are also important factors in the ways the hierarchy of teams is organized.

The younger and more recently arrived immigrants are often the helpers, but as time and knowledge of English increase, they are able to move up to framers and hangers, and with more skill and better language skills these workers could become *patrones*. As Josefina, the owner of the Raleigh firm, explained, the *encargados* and *patrones* had to speak English as they had to be able to interact with all of the workers above and below them including subcontractors, in addition to being able to read complex plans.

Despite the many skills that migrants may bring with them or learn in their U.S. jobs, they are often subject to exploitation, especially in the unregulated sectors of the economy, such as agriculture and construction.[27] That is, despite the talent that a migrant may possess, he or she may never benefit but remain exploited because of sociolegal and cultural barriers, such as English language, lack of knowledge about the U.S. labor market, and lack of authorized status, or the conditions and type of labor market where he or she works. Like agriculture, the decentralized labor management system in construction lends itself to worker exploitation. Even general contractors acknowledged the skimming of wages by their subcontractors, many of whom were co-ethnics. As one general contractor explained to us,

> Often immigrant crew leaders approach us at sites and simply tell me that he can do a better job than us. They will tell us that they can bring 20 men to the site and speed things up. Speed is everything in this competitive business. They might charge us $15 per man hour so he could make $15 every hour and pay $10 to the worker and pocket $5 for himself. Some days I will arrive at work and an extra 10 guys had popped up. I didn't care as long as the job was getting done.

This brings us to the question of to what extent limited English and unauthorized status placed immigrant workers in our sample at the mercy of their employers or co-ethnic bosses. Unfortunately, we did not directly ask the Leon returnees about issues related to worker violations such as wage theft, but in response to a follow-up question about job satisfaction in their last job, 15 return migrants volunteered information about past exploitation on their last job in the United States. Violations ranged from not being paid for overtime work to receiving no benefits. We suspect that this figure underestimates the prevalence of work violations experienced for several reasons. First, because the survey only asked about conditions in the last job, it did not capture violations or discrimination experiences in previous jobs. Second, because the return migrants were asked retrospectively about job satisfaction years after returning to Mexico, it is probable that they idealized some of their experiences abroad, highlighting the satisfactory dimensions of work in the United States, which is exactly what we found. More return migrants spoke about job satisfaction than dissatisfaction and couched the former in terms of learning new skills and earning sufficient wages to remit some money home.

In contrast, in the exploratory stage of our research project we did ask the North Carolina construction workers, who are not part of the Leon sample, directly about workplace conditions and violations at their *current* jobs, which is clearly a more reliable measure of prevalence. Although workers reported high average hourly earnings in their construction jobs (from $9–$25 in 2005), they reported systematic violation of labor laws and practices in the construction industry. Workers laboring in small residential firms and working for contractors appeared especially prone to violations.[28] One quarter of the North Carolina sample of construction workers reported violations of labor laws and practices, clustered into several categories, including:

(1) not being paid for work done; (2) denied meal or other breaks during the workday; (3) paid late; (4) verbal abuse by employers; (5) retaliation by employer for complaints; (6) not paid for overtime; and (7) being paid under the table and in cash (*al contado*).

All migrants who reported experiencing violations chalked it up to their unauthorized work status and poor English skills. One return migrant, who worked for a construction firm for two years in Morrisville, North Carolina, reported that the only way to keep a job if one is undocumented is to either withstand these violations or to jump jobs. As he explained, "Asking for time off or benefits will just get me fired." Several established workers, who wanted a paper trail of their work history just in case the U.S. government implemented a legalization program, left their construction jobs because they were being paid under the table. Another migrant, Juan, who worked as a framer had not been paid for several months. When he asked his boss about it, he was told that he would not be paid until there was more work. Marco, a pipe layer for a highway construction firm in North Carolina, reported not ever being paid for his overtime weekend hours. Still another migrant, Jorge, who was recruited to work as a gardener for a landscaping company in the heat of the summer in Wilmington, North Carolina, was forced to live and work in horrible conditions. He was required to pay rent at a steep price for a dilapidated trailer that had no air conditioning and was at the mercy of his contractor for rides to work and the grocery store. As David Griffith found in his research on guest workers in the United States, migrants who depend on contractors are regularly forced to live in deplorable conditions.[29]

Despite the circumstances migrants often face in the construction and building trades, we found that the opportunities for skill transfers, reskilling, and social mobility in those areas were substantial and exist in other manufacturing sectors of the U.S. economy as well. Industries such as construction and auto repair offer desirable jobs not only because they offer higher wages and greater mobility relative to other sectors of the economy where migrants are concentrated, such as agriculture, food, and hospitality services, but also because workers learn largely by doing rather than through formal education and they can apply skills learned at home as well as learn new ones in these U.S. jobs.

For these reasons, there was little movement out of manufacturing, auto repair, and construction, especially among the migrants who labored as semiskilled or skilled carpenters, masons, auto mechanics, and machine operators. Skilled manufacturing workers were most successful in changing jobs to improve wages or working conditions. Take Rodolfo, who first migrated to the United States fairly late in the career of a migrant, at the age of 35. Before leaving Leon, he worked as an *ayudante* (helper / apprentice) in his father's auto repair business. In this capacity he learned the basics—how to change tires, do tune-ups. Off the job, he read trade books ("how to" manuals). He eventually opened up his own repair shop, and to expand the business, he decided to move to the United States, where a friend had secured him a job as an auto mechanic working for a Japanese company. There, Rodolfo had the opportunity to apply all the skills he had learned at home plus learn new skills and approaches to the work. Like many others who labor in the auto repair industry in the United States, Rodolfo underwent a reskilling process in which he learned to work with new technology and tools that enabled him to approach both familiar and new job tasks in a different and often more efficient way.

Some migrants who arrived in the United States with a set of integrated skills were only able to transfer some of their skills, indicating a simultaneous deskilling process. Deskilling was most evident in the construction industry, where workers reported that their craft is far more fragmented and specialized in the United States. Twenty-six percent of the sample working in construction reported deskilling on the job. Take the case of Manuel, who in Mexico was a master mason or *albañil,* one who knows how to make bricks from scratch and is knowledgeable about working with all materials except steel and glass. In the U.S. construction industry, as a result of advanced technology in brick production and the very specialized nature of construction tasks, his skill is restricted to the single task of laying bricks. Or take the case of Cesar, a construction supervisor, who told us about his brother who in Mexico was a master stonemason specializing in interior residential stone work in the tourist resort city of Cancun. There he was a master craftsman who could cut and install floors, countertops, patios, and fountains. He also learned how to take damaged or chipped stone and sand and buff it so that it looks new. In the United States, as his brother explained, a chipped or scarred piece of stone would be discarded, so it is rare that he can use this skill. In his current job, because of the specialized nature of stone production and installation, his task is limited to installing marble countertops.

Not all migrants were able to transfer skills and knowledge acquired in Mexico to their U.S. manufacturing jobs. In some cases, place of arrival, local and regional opportunity structures, and social networks drew migrants to particular sectors of the economy where their skills were not applicable. Other times, their skill sets did not correspond to the skills demanded in the U.S. labor market. For example, 63 percent of those that worked as machinists in Leon's shoe and leather industry were unable to transfer any technical skills to their jobs abroad, especially within the same occupation or industrial sector. But there were exceptions. Take the case of Javier. Before migrating to the United States he worked as an industrial stitcher in a shoe-manufacturing firm in *El Coecillo,* the Leon neighborhood where the vast majority of manufacturers of shoes and other leather goods in the city are located. Javier identifies as a skilled stitcher. At a very young age and under the direction of his father and uncle, he learned tasks associated with all stages of shoe production, from cutting to stitching to molding to finishing. In Mexico, he not only operated the industrial stitching machine, but learned how to disassemble it, clean it, and reassemble it. When he migrated to San Francisco in 1992 at the age of 28, he located a job as a stitcher through a friend at a firm that manufactures ice skates. Because of his experience in Mexico he was able to adapt quickly to the new and more sophisticated machinery. His skill and aptitude were valued by his employer, who gave him a raise and more responsibility within several months on the job. In addition to learning to operate and clean the machinery, Javier also learned the importance of punctuality, organization, and efficiency, skills he stressed were not as important in the shoe industry in Mexico.

RETAIL, HOSPITALITY, AND PERSONAL SERVICES

Opportunities for transferring skills, reskilling, and improving social mobility also exist in the service sectors of the U.S. economy, where almost 40 percent of the men and women in the sample labored as janitors, dishwashers, gardeners, parking lot attendants, chambermaids, and live-in domestics when they first arrived in the United States. Yet, many did reskill while abroad (48 percent) and some, but not many, were able to mobilize these skills to improve their economic situation, transitioning out of their low-wage jobs as dishwashers and janitors and other service positions (60 percent) to more desirable and better paying jobs as waiters, assistant chefs, line cooks, and hostesses. Some of the men acquired skills in landscaping that they were able to convert into better jobs in construction. Similarly, some men entered as laborers in janitorial and maintenance work and moved into management positions within the industry. These were the exceptions, as many of the men in service remained in low-paying positions like dishwashers until they could find work in more lucrative industries such as manufacturing, construction, and auto repair.

All but five of the women were concentrated in hospitality, restaurants, retail, and personal services, and their labor market experiences paint a mixed picture. As countless other studies have found, immigrant women with low levels of education are concentrated in niches in the service and hospitality industries where they work in low-wage, undervalued jobs as domestics, janitors, and entry-level food service workers, occupations that offer few avenues for mobility.[30] The women in our sample followed this pattern. In the United States they were clustered in hospitality and other personal and support service categories. In these industries, they located jobs as private household domestic workers, chambermaids, janitors, or food-preparation workers. Despite the low wages and prestige associated with these positions, all the women reported transferring on- or off-the-job skills in cleaning, cooking, and caregiving from Mexico to their U.S. jobs. That is, though restricted in the choice of occupations, their labor market experience at home proved to be relevant and adaptable to jobs abroad. Unfortunately, these skill sets provided limited opportunities for transitioning to better jobs. Opportunity structures for the women in the U.S. labor market were largely influenced by the way in which their work is socially organized. Concentrated in the service and hospitality industries, women often labor in isolated conditions in low-wage and undervalued jobs as domestics and chambermaids, where management enjoys the upper hand and work conditions offer limited opportunities for skill development and economic mobility.[31]

For example, of the ten women who worked as domestics, none were able to move out of this type of occupation and seven remained in their first job (as a live-in domestic) during their entire migratory sojourn. However, two women did transition from live-in to day domestic work, thus potentially broadening their social networks and acquiring additional information and resources toward eventual movement out of this line of work. Overall, as other research has documented, live-in domestic labor is isolating and the social relations at work are limited to unequal personal interactions and exchanges with employers, rendering it almost impossible to transition to other or better types of jobs.[32]

Women working in food processing or hospitality-related occupations also said they were able to transfer cooking skills learned on and off the job in Mexico to their jobs in the United States. These women also acquired new skills abroad, learning English and management and customer service skills. Unlike the women who labored in domestic work, however, workers in the hospitality industry reported being able to transition to better occupations within the industry, from chambermaids, food-preparation workers, or janitors to jobs as waiters, assistant cooks in restaurants, or supervisory cleaning positions in hotels. In these jobs they reported wage increases and increased autonomy, and also spoke of learning new and improved skills, such as preparing different types of food and developing teamwork and leadership skills.

Take the case of Carmen. In Leon, Carmen was a cook in a restaurant and then owner of a small shoe factory that specialized in covering and stitching fabric to the heels of women's shoes. She incurred a debt and migrated to the United States with the goal of paying off the debt. When she arrived in Washington, DC, in 1995, she found work as a busgirl in an Anglo-owned Mexican restaurant, earning $5.50 an hour. Though she spoke no English when she arrived in the United States, she was eager to learn. She watched television in English and practiced with the staff at work. After about eight months on the job, Carmen was promoted to food-preparation assistant where she fixed salads, placed condiments on plates, and arranged them for delivery to customers. Carmen was quick to remark to the lead cook that they were using the wrong peppers for the *chiles rellenos* (stuffed peppers) dish. Both the chef and manager were quite taken by her initiative and so asked her to teach them how to prepare the dish "the Mexican way." By the time she left the restaurant, having paid off her debt and returned to Mexico to be with her daughter and rekindle her business, she had been promoted to one of two lead cooks, was earning $12 per hour, and had acquired enough English to communicate with her manager and coworkers.

SKILL DEVELOPMENT AND
ENTREPRENEURIAL OPPORTUNITIES

Entrepreneurial skills also proved difficult to transfer from Mexico to the U.S. labor market. Like many poor and working-class persons in Mexico, a number of the migrants in our sample had worked as minor entrepreneurs in the informal sector before migrating. None of these men and women was able to transfer these activities to the United States, including a handful who had had some vocational training (cosmetology and hairdressing, electrician) in Mexico. Lack of documentation, English language skills, and knowledge about the U.S. labor market acted as major barriers to transferring individual ventures. However, with time in the United States and the acquisition of new skills and the English language, a few in the sample did moonlight and launch informal entrepreneurial ventures on the side. One woman opened up a beauty salon in her home; another woman prepared Mexican specialty food items and sold them from her apartment and the back of her husband's truck. Several of the men who labored in the construction industry in North Carolina also participated in the informal economy, moonlighting in painting and home renovation projects on weekends or evenings. On their side jobs, these men applied skills they could not use in their formal occupations. Clients for side projects are usually found through social networks. As we found in North Carolina, sometimes an immigrant foreman or *patrón* will recruit members of the work crews he manages through their day jobs to labor on a side project. Other times, immigrants locate these additional projects through unofficial day laborer sites.[33]

Side projects also facilitate entrepreneurship activities as they offer skilled workers opportunities to build client networks and augment management skills.[34] This is especially the case in the construction industry where it is relatively easy for more established immigrants, who have work experience, knowledge of the U.S. labor market, contacts, and some English, to open up their own operations. One subcontracting operation in which Latinos are concentrated is residential painting, an irony given that this is not a skill transferred from Mexico but one learned in the U.S. labor market and acquired rather rapidly for a fast learner.

Take the case of Ricardo and Miguel, who migrated from Guanajuato to the Research Triangle Park of North Carolina in the mid-1980s. Among the pioneer migrants from a medium-sized town in Guanajuato, the two brothers arrived at a time when the construction industry was booming. Although neither brother had any experience in construction, they were fast learners and found regular work in the painting sector of the industry. In their last jobs as salaried employees, they were the only two Mexicans in the crew, which pushed the brothers to learn some English. Several years later, the crew was almost all Mexican, and most were immigrant friends and relatives from Guanajuato. Recruiting and training newly arrived immigrants, the brothers became helpful intermediaries between the owner of the painting company and newcomer Mexicans, a position that was facilitated because of their English language capital. On weekends, the brothers regularly marketed their painting skills in the informal sector, attracting clients by word of mouth. Over time, they acquired their own clients while the workload from their regular job also increased, though they were not being rewarded with a higher salary for the increased responsibility. They had enough. As Ricardo figured, "We got tired of working for my employer. We worked for him for 15 years and in that time made him into a millionaire. So we decided to start our own businesses." Ricardo and Miguel had acquired enough confidence and clients and learned enough painting and interpersonal skills to launch their own business. Some knowledge of English sealed the move. Today, Ricardo and Miguel each owns his own painting business. As the brothers' narrative reveals, economic success abroad is more than the result of the credentials and work experience that immigrants bring from their home communities. Additionally, advancement in the U.S. labor market cannot be explained only by access to social capital provided by co-ethnics. Equally important are the years of work experience and reskilling that immigrants acquire and the not-so-measurable competences of self-confidence in taking risks.[35]

THE RECOGNITION AND VALORIZATION OF SKILLS

As the case of Carmen, the cook at the American-owned restaurant, demonstrates, when employers recognize skills migrants are sometimes rewarded for their talents. As Table 4.5 shows, 65 percent of the total sample reported that their talents were rewarded through either higher wages, more autonomy, a promotion, or opportunities to teach their skills to others. Over half of those rewarded for skills received higher wages. This means that one-third of the entire sample received higher wages because of their talent, be it transferred from Mexico or learned on their U.S. jobs (also see Table 4.3). These remarkably high figures are most likely an underestimation of actual wage increases since they only reflect wage augmentation as a result of recognized skills by employers. Higher wages, increased responsibility, and opportunities to teach skills to coworkers translated into increased job satisfaction among the sample; 84 percent of our sample reported that they found their last U.S. job satisfying, compared to only 16 percent who stated they were indifferent or dissatisfied.[36] Job satisfaction came not only from earning wages and acquiring new skills, but also from being

TABLE 4.5

Types of rewards for recognized skills in U.S. labor market (n=197)

Boss did not notice or reward respondent's skills	34%
Boss recognized and rewarded respondent's skills	65%
Received raise	52%
Boss asked worker to teach others	12%
Received more freedom at work	19%
Given more responsibility at work	17%

NOTE: Due to rounding, percentages do not total exactly to 100 percent.

rewarded for their talent and problem-solving skills—know-how that came with years of work experience.

The skills that employers valued include both technical and hard skills, along with what some scholars call soft or people skills. Both types of skills can be tacit or hidden but hard skills are easier to identify, conceptualize, and quantify or measure once recognized. Not so with soft skills. Why? Because unlike hard skills, which are about a worker's technical ability to perform a certain type of task or activity, soft skills are interpersonal and often invisible except through interaction. Soft skills are about *behavioral* competences and are broadly applicable. Often referred to as interpersonal or *people* skills, they include a heterogeneous group of proficiencies such as communication, problem solving, and negotiation competences, personal effectiveness, creativity on the job, strategic thinking, and team building. These skills can be applied to multiple work environments but are often grouped together under the limited and rather ambiguous term of "soft skills." In our analysis we refer to these interpersonal skills and abilities as competences because the term more clearly reflects the social skills and abilities of the individual worker and person.

Competences mean different things to employers and workers. In general, the migration literature associates soft skills with what an employer desires from his or her workers, and scholars see them largely as demonstrating the exploitive nature of immigrant work conditions (follows orders, shows up on time, works hard). We too found that while employers recognize these skills, they do not always valorize them with higher wages or more responsibility. One subcontractor in the North Carolina construction industry implicitly revealed this exploitive attitude when speaking of soft skills like flexibility, dependability, and long hours that make immigrants more attractive than native workers. As he described, "Most native-born workers only want to work four or five days and from nine to five. Immigrants will work around the clock ... that's their marketing core. They are always on the job, from dusk until dawn. They have the old work ethic." In other studies employers identify motivation and customer and coworker interaction as skills, but because they refer to attributes associated with relationships with bosses, they take on, as Roger Waldinger and Michael Lichter argue, a political connotation of unequal power between workers and bosses, which is exactly what the term is designed to hide.[37]

With few exceptions, sociologists only look at soft skills from the perspective of the employer, too frequently dismissing them and treating the concept solely as an ideological category that is constructed on the basis of a political or power relation and therefore one of exploitation and condescension. But the value of interpersonal skills is much more complex. Migrants know that employers appreciate some soft skills but do not valorize them through higher wages. However, migrants also recognize that soft skills are specific to the social and cultural context of work and important for their own careers in the U.S. labor market. Take the case of Jose, who worked alongside his father in a nursery in Phoenix. Early on in the job, Jose's father noticed that the owner arrived early to the jobsite, before the workers, and stayed on the jobsite all day. He told Jose, "For us to get noticed and move ahead, we have to be like our boss and show up early and be punctual." And so they did. After several days, the owner approached the father and son and told them that he appreciated their punctuality and motivation and rewarded them with more responsibility. He also asked the men about their work experience in Mexico. Upon learning that Jose had worked as an apprentice to an auto mechanic, the owner of the nursery shifted Jose's work to vehicle maintenance, where he earned a higher hourly wage and was able to apply the skills he had acquired in Leon. Jose went on to explain that punctuality is an American skill, one that is rarely valued in the social organization of work in Mexico. As he told us, in construction work "*encargados* in Mexico never show up until later in the day, sometimes after lunch, so there is little incentive for us [workers] to arrive early."

Immigrants also recognize, as do employers, that it can be difficult to separate technical skills from social and interpersonal competences as scholars often do. Recall the case of Francisco, whose narrative opened up this chapter. Francisco's boss recognized and valorized not only Francisco's ability to install a mason's line or twine, but also his problem-solving techniques. Both sets of skills remained tacit until his boss recognized them. Immigrants also distinguish among the values of different types of competences. For example, many employers spoke of an immigrant work ethic, a cluster of abilities that usually encompasses dependability, punctuality, and willingness to work long hours. But from the perspective of the worker, it is one thing to be on time and another to work long hours willingly. While immigrants can agree with their employers on the value of punctuality, they consider efforts to compel them to work unnecessarily long hours as exploitive.

SOCIAL MOBILITY THROUGH *BRINCANDO* (JOB JUMPING)

Returning to Table 4.3, we can see that 36 percent of the sample transitioned to better jobs requiring additional skills. Migrants regularly used their own agency and mobilized skills to transition to jobs that required more skills and thus provided higher wages. Workers regularly initiate these transitions through a strategy they refer to as *brincando* or job jumping. *Brincar,* which literally means "to jump" in Spanish, occurs when workers acquire new on-the-job skills that are not being remunerated by their employer, either because these new skills have not been recognized or because obstacles, such as legal status and language, inhibit the migrant from negotiating for wage increases. After leaving a former employer, the worker must market his new or improved skills and negotiate with a potential employer for higher wages.[38] When we asked how immigrant workers locate new employers, several respondents told us that they primarily connect with potential employers through personal and work networks. Other times, workers seek new employment through the informal economy. As one worker explained, "Let's say I have learned how to work with sheetrock. Well, when a *gringo* comes by the site and asks for a *chirroquero* [a term created by immigrant workers to describe anyone who works with and installs sheetrock or drywall material] I can sell my new skill and earn $12 [an hour] as opposed to the $8 I earned as an *ayudante.*"

To connect with prospective employers, workers often engage in a signaling strategy,[39] intentionally donning clothing that markets their skills, such as wearing grass-stained overalls to suggest landscaping experience. From another example, we learned of one immigrant worker in North Carolina who, after acquiring painting and plastering skills, dressed himself in used painting slacks, a painter's cap, and a Sherwin Williams T-shirt, and advertised himself as a painter at a day labor site.

The concept of job jumping has long been recognized as an effective strategy used by both native-born and immigrant professionals to escape exploitation and market new and improved skills to secure higher wages.[40] With the exception of earlier research conducted by the authors, the concept of job jumping has not really been investigated in studies of the labor market incorporation of less educated and unauthorized immigrants. We found in both the North Carolina and Leon samples that migrants regularly took the risk and jumped across employers, from crew leaders to subcontractors, and across ethnic job niches and economies. The *brincar* strategy crosses formal and informal labor markets and intersects with various industries. One migrant from a small ranch in Guanajuato moved up within the roofing industry from *ayudante* to *maestro* roofer and then proceeded to join what Elizabeth Fussell calls the immigrant "Hurricane Chasers," roving construction crews traveling throughout the country building and repairing roofs in the wake of large storms.[41] Indeed, he told us with a wink that he had fixed the roof of the local immigration office in New Orleans in the wake of Hurricane Katrina. Among the entire Leon sample, of those who reported changing jobs, 20 percent reported going out on their own and approaching another employer; among these, 59 percent reported changing their jobs to improve wages. The practice of *brincar* relies not on the possession of formal credentials but fundamentally on the acquisition of skills in places of origin and destination, on the availability of social networks, and on an individual's self-confidence to take chances.

CONCLUSION

Because of their low levels of formal human capital, many Mexican migrants depend on a co-ethnic network to direct them to jobs in the secondary labor market where work authorization may not be required and the demand for English is minimal. Some migrants remain trapped in low-wage jobs in this unregulated sector of the labor market, while others experience substantial mobility within it. In this chapter we have demonstrated that the different mobility pathways of Mexican migrants are not only a function of where migrants are located in the U.S. labor market but also of the dual processes of skill transfer from Mexico and reskilling in the United States. Francisco, who was featured in the opening narrative to this chapter, was able to apply the brick and adobe molding skills he learned from his father, who was a *maestro albañil,* to his job in an Ohio plant that manufactures rubber and plastic airplane parts. His molding skills, acquired informally, on and off the job in Mexico, became explicit in his U.S. job as Francisco encountered new technologies, interacted with other workers, and needed to solve problems in the workplace. In contrast, Ricardo and Miguel's economic success was largely a function of reskilling that took place abroad, and after years spent acquiring skills in painting and drywall installation, venturing out on their own. Developing knowledge of some English, management know-how, and the confidence to take risks, the two brothers eventually launched a successful painting business.

Francisco, Ricardo, and Miguel are not exceptional cases. Far from being unskilled and trapped in low-wage, dead-end jobs, significant numbers of men and women in the study who were able to apply skills acquired on and off the job in Mexico and learn new ones while sojourning abroad experienced job transitions in the U.S. labor market. When recognized and valued, skill mobilization resulted in more autonomy on the job, higher wages, increased job satisfaction, and an easier transition to better jobs. The practice of job jumping, a labor market strategy that migrants employed to improve their employment situation and demonstrate new or improved skills, also enhanced mobility. Sixty-five percent of the sample reported that their skills were recognized and rewarded by their U.S. employers; 33 percent experienced wage increases; and 36 percent transitioned to better jobs that required more skills. Some of these transitions were facilitated through *brincar.*

We also find that the learning and transfer of knowledge and skills is gendered, reflecting the different social contexts and industrial sectors in which men and women acquire their skills at home and abroad. In communities of origin, men have more opportunities to acquire and expand their technological skills in construction, manufacturing, and auto repair, and these skills were often rewarded in the U.S. labor market that valued construction and auto repair skills. In contrast, women are more likely to acquire and transfer skills associated with their gender such as cooking, caretaking, and hospitality, skills that landed them domestic and low-wage service jobs that are undervalued in the U.S. labor market. These gendered occupational findings on skill transfers demonstrate the importance of treating learning and skill development as a lifelong process and recognizing the different social contexts in which men and women learn their skills throughout their life and migration cycles.

The ability of migrants to transfer skills acquired in Mexico and to transfer and develop skills across occupations and industries within the United States represents an important but relatively unexplored mobility pathway. Accounting for the role of skill transfers offers an alternative explanation as to why some "unskilled" migrants are unable to escape low-wage "gateway jobs," while others achieve significant labor mobility and successfully increase wages by improving existing skills and developing new ones.

Returning Home and Reintegrating into the Local Labor Market

Enrique emigrated with an uncle as a teenager, making the overland journey from Mexico to San Francisco where they joined another uncle and his family. Before leaving Leon, Enrique was attending a local primary school and working evenings and weekends in his father's *piquita,* the family-owned and -operated shoe-manufacturing firm located on the second floor of his family's home. After graduating from high school in the United States at the age of 19, he found work in an Anglo-owned and -run Mexican restaurant. Because of his Spanish and English language skills, he quickly moved up the ladder from busboy to waiter to assistant manager. Enrique married a Mexican American woman and had two children, but eventually they divorced and Enrique lost custody of his young children. He then wrestled with the decision to return to Mexico. After careful consideration, he withdrew his savings and returned to his hometown of Leon; here he could be close to his parents and siblings. Because Enrique returned with English skills and savings, he was able to bypass shoemaking and become a self-employed taxi driver, catering to the international English-speaking business clientele who travel to Leon to purchase leather goods. His services are unique, providing airport transfers, tours of the city, and chauffer service for the day. When asked about the skills he learned in the United States, he referred to a set of integrated personal, self-improvement, and social skills that he had learned from his boss in the restaurant: confidence, responsibility, initiative, and customer service. As he exclaimed, "the stuff of American entrepreneurship."

Victor was only eight when he traveled by bus and foot with his two older brothers and parents to Los Angeles. In 1986, his parents applied for and were granted permanent resident status under the Legalization Program of the Immigration Reform and Control Act (IRCA). Through the family reunification policy, Victor and his brothers also became permanent residents. At the age of 15, Victor dropped out of school and joined a gang. He held a number of service jobs here and there but nothing steady. In 1990, he left the formal labor market, went underground, and started dealing marijuana. Within several years, he had moved from dealing marijuana to growing and selling hydroponic marijuana to local dealers. In 1995, he was arrested and received a five-year sentence, which he started to serve in a Los Angeles prison. In 1998, under the federal Criminal Alien Program, Victor was removed directly from jail, deported to Mexico, and barred for life from reentry. His return to Leon and reintegration into Mexican society has been problematic. Shunned by many in his neighborhood because of his deportee status and tattooed body, Victor spends much of his time alone in the family home of his childhood.[1] He has applied for and been turned down for several jobs because of his less than perfect Spanish and the visible tattoos that crown his shaved head and cover his exposed arms and legs. He survives from day to day by selling from his porch used clothing sent monthly by his parents from the United States.

Maricely migrated in 1987 at the age of 19 to join her husband, brother-in-law, and a community of friends and family who lived in a Dallas suburb. They had two children, both born in Texas. Her husband, Juan, worked for a roofing company traveling throughout the state removing and installing new shingle roofs. He made good money: $25 an hour. Maricely found occasional work as a day domestic where she pulled in about $50 a house. Juan became a permanent resident through IRCA and through his new status his wife applied for permanent residency. They hired a lawyer to assist them with the process and deposited a $500 retainer with the lawyer, in addition to paying a hefty fee for the application. But before Maricely could receive her green card, her husband had a fatal fall while working on a roof. She lost her opportunity for permanent residence status and received no compensation from her husband's boss. With no recourse, she returned to her hometown in rural Guanajuato. There she lives with her mother and father, and the two children are struggling in a local school because they do not speak Spanish.

The cases of Enrique, Victor, and Maricely demonstrate the complexity of the return migration process and how closely it intersects life-cycle events.[2] Enrique and Victor left Leon at a young age and spent their youth in the United States, where they attended school, learned English, and became permanent residents. Maricely joined her husband and was planning to

into general economic, social, political, and family-related categories. A further distinction can be made between push and pull factors.[4] An economic downturn, for example, in the country to which migrants have emigrated may push them back home.[5] Alternatively, target earners may be pulled back by increased job opportunities at home or to realize a specific objective, such as investment of their savings in a business.[6] Social motives for return also include push and pull mechanisms—discrimination or anti-immigrant hostility and exclusionary policies in the host country may push migrants home. On the other hand, nostalgia for home or the opportunity to experience an elevated social status through launching a new business or building a new home may draw migrants home.[7] Family and life-cycle events weigh heavily in the decision to return, with some migrants returning home to marry, to be with their children, to care for elderly parents, or to retire. Some members of the family might favor return, while others adamantly oppose it.[8] Political factors may drive return migration, such as forced removal or curtailment of migrant rights by the government of the country to which people emigrated, or migrants may be drawn home by opportunities to diffuse political ideas or engage in political activities there.[9]

Just as there are multiple and shifting causes behind return migration, so are there varied and overlapping social, cultural, political, and economic effects of returning home. Historical and comparative evidence suggests that migration abroad facilitates some upward mobility for returning migrants and a transformation of the local social structure, sometimes widening the middle class,[10] other times exacerbating class, gender, and regional inequalities.[11] On the other hand, social reintegration presents many adjustment problems that are strongly differentiated by life cycle and gender. Women, for example, who experienced a more independent lifestyle and paid employment abroad, often face traditional employment discrimination barriers upon return.[12] The literature on the economic effects of return migration focuses primarily on wages, employment opportunities, and economic development. A useful distinction, and one that we will employ in this chapter, is between the economic welfare of the individual returning migrant and the aggregate contributions return migration makes to the local economy, region, or community of origin. In this chapter, then, our main concern is with how living abroad and being exposed to new approaches to work and acquiring new skills influences the labor market experiences of individual return migrants in Leon. Within this analysis we are especially interested in how this process is differentiated by gender.

As we stated in earlier chapters, we believe that most respondents are unlikely to remigrate abroad. The mean age at the time of the interview (39 years) suggests that, for them, return migration is a permanent event. Overall, repeat sojourning is uncommon among urban-origin migrants. In contrast to their rural counterparts who tend to journey recurrently to the United States, Mexican urbanites conduct one or two trips abroad during their migratory careers. As we discussed before, 57 percent of the Leon sample undertook only one trip to *el norte*. The fact that men have been home for nearly eight years on average suggests a low probability of remigration. As we show below, most returned not because they were unable to locate work in the United States, but because they were drawn home to be with family or had completed their migratory aims.

We begin the chapter by examining return patterns among the Leon sample, situating the discussion of why and when the Leon migrants returned within the larger economic and political context of changing patterns of migration between Mexico and the United States. In the next section, we complement the departure discussion with a brief overview of the economic context of arrival in Leon and then move on to the heart of the chapter, examining the labor market experiences of return migrants. Within this discussion we are concerned with how skill transfers shape the job trajectories and economic opportunities of return migrants.

CONTEXT OF DEPARTURE
AND REASONS FOR RETURN

As we discussed in chapter 3, Mexico-U.S. migration grew steadily after the passage of IRCA in 1986, with the total Mexican immigrant population in the United States increasing from 2.8 million in 1979 to 11.5 million in 2009.[13] This increase is largely attributable to undocumented migrants who comprised roughly 60 percent of the growth.[14] In 2006, migration patterns between Mexico and the United States began to change, suggesting a major reversal of flows in the history of the U.S.-Mexico migratory system. Recent data from the Pew Hispanic Center and the Mexican government show a net rate of unauthorized migration fluctuating near zero, with some evidence that more Mexicans are leaving the United States than arriving, particularly unauthorized Mexicans.[15] Scholars explain this change in migration patterns as a consequence of multiple factors, including the U.S. recession, stepped-up border and interior enforcement, increasing abuse of migrants by smugglers and transnational criminal organizations, and growing job opportunities in Mexico.[16] As jobs in the United States became scarce after 2006, especially in the construction and restaurant industries where they were concentrated, fewer Mexicans felt compelled to migrate while others returned home. The Pew Hispanic Center estimates that the number of Mexicans and their children who moved from the United States to Mexico between 2005 and 2010 rose to 1.4 million, roughly double the number who had done so in the five-year period a decade before.[17]

State-imposed deportations of Mexicans have also increased return migration. Since 1996, and especially in the wake of 9/11, the U.S. government, with the assistance of local and state officials, has implemented a series of laws and policies that make it easier to arrest, detain, and deport undocumented migrants. Between 1995 and 2011, yearly deportations (with orders of removal) skyrocketed from 50,924 to almost 400,000, representing over a 600 percent increase in just thirteen years.[18] Of the 1.4 million people who have migrated from the United States to Mexico since 2005, a significant minority has been deported and remains in Mexico. Precise data on this phenomenon are unavailable, but the Pew Hispanic Center estimates based on government data from both countries that 5–35 percent of these returnees may not have moved voluntarily.

Can patterns of return migration among our sample shed light on changing Mexico-U.S. migration patterns or tease out the multiple factors of causation? Table 5.1 lists the periods and primary reasons for the most recent return among the Leon sample, and Figure 5.1 displays them by gender. As the table shows, the majority of returns are recent, and family, economic, and political concerns played prominent roles in the decision to return. (With the exception of deportation, which was dominated by men, the reasons did not significantly vary by gender.) As Table 5.1 shows, more than half the sample returned to Leon since 2006, the year in which both Mexican and U.S. census data

TABLE 5.1

Primary reason for last return by period of return (n=204)

Date of Return	Family	Health	Nostalgia	Economic	Completed objectives	Deported	Visa/Legal problems	Discrimination	Other	Total	
2006–2010	54%	3%	6%	10%	5%	11%	5%	0%	7%	*58%*	(119)
2001–2005	46%	3%	8%	8%	14%	11%	3%	0%	8%	*18%*	(37)
1996–2000	47%	0%	0%	12%	24%	12%	6%	0%	0%	*8%*	(17)
1991–1995	44%	0%	22%	11%	0%	0%	0%	0%	22%	*4%*	(9)
1986–1990	43%	0%	14%	14%	0%	14%	0%	14%	0%	*3%*	(7)
1961–1985	60%	7%	7%	0%	7%	7%	7%	7%	0%	*6%*	(15)
Total	*51%*	*2%*	*7%*	*9%*	*8%*	*10%*	*4%*	*1%*	*6%*		
	(105)	(5)	(14)	(19)	(16)	(21)	(9)	(2)	(13)		

NOTE: n=204 because we have missing data for 13 migrants and some migrants listed several primary reasons.

began to document a reversal in migration. Another 18 percent of the sample left after 2000, bringing the total number of migrants who returned home to Leon since 2000 upward of 76 percent. Many may have intended to return even sooner (the average stay in the United States was four years) but postponed the move because they recognized that remigration would be costly and dangerous due to the militarized border. On the other hand, the rather lengthy stay abroad could also indicate that some planned to settle permanently but were pushed out because of economic and political conditions in the United States, a discussion to which we now turn.

Fifty-eight percent of the sample returned to Mexico in the wake of the U.S. economic recession. Among these, 10 percent reported that economic concerns in the United States drove

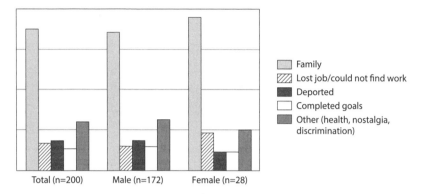

Figure 5.1. Primary reason for return to Mexico by gender.

their return to Mexico. While substantial, the numbers are lower than one would expect in light of the prominent role that scholars and pundits have given to the recession in explaining the increase in return migration flows. Only one migrant who returned because of economic conditions cited "economic crisis in the United States." Others cited "unable to find work," "not making what I expected," or "company where I worked closed." It is probable that some of these were recession related, but some of these economic failures—not finding work or earning too little—could have occurred for other reasons. Limited knowledge about the U.S. labor market, worker exploitation, and weak social networks could also weigh heavily on economic considerations in the decision to return.[19]

While the effect of economic factors on return migration can be debated, there is little doubt that political factors played a prominent role in the intended return. Overall, 21 reported being deported by the U.S. government, but 8 were deported twice, bringing to 29 (11 percent) the total number of deportations in the sample.[20] This figure falls in the middle range of recent estimates of involuntary returns to Mexico.[21] Interestingly, although the laws making it easier to detain and deport people were enacted to remove criminal aliens, only one of the migrants—Victor—was removed for committing an aggravated felony. Six were removed by Immigration and Customs Enforcement (ICE) agents at their work sites; another five were apprehended by local officials for public intoxication (which in some states is considered an aggravated felony) and then detained and deported for not having *papeles,* or authorization to work or live in the United States; one was arrested in a barroom brawl and then detained for not having papers; three were stopped at traffic checkpoints and detained after not producing a valid driver's license; and in the remaining deportations, the migrants were stopped in various public places by local police and then detained and deported. Another political factor behind return was "visa or legal problems," which meant in most cases that a migrant's temporary visa had expired or they were unable to renew work authorization and decided to return home.

While the anti-immigrant climate and economic recession in the United States pushed some migrants to return to Leon, the pull factors associated with the positive attraction of going home had more influence in return decisions.[22] As Table 5.1 shows, just over half the sample cited "family" as the primary motive behind their return. Given that more than half the sample were married at the time of their first migration, reunifying with a spouse and children would naturally be a primary motive. Recall, for example, Carmen, the young woman from Leon who achieved mobility within the restaurant industry in the United States, a process that was triggered when she corrected the cook on the way he prepared *chiles rellenos* and then demonstrated the Mexican way. While Carmen migrated to earn money to pay off a debt, it was the pull of being with her son that brought her back. Others, however, like Enrique and Maricely, wanted to be close to their parents, siblings, and friends. Still others cited returning to care for ill or aging parents. Another 7 percent reported that they returned home because they missed their life in Mexico, citing the greater freedom there compared to U.S. society. A final category that reflects the desire to return home permanently and supports the target income theory is "completed objectives." Some in this category migrated with the intention of earning enough money abroad to start a business upon return, but others, like Enrique, first acquired skills and ideas in the United States and only then returned home to launch a business, retire, invest in better technologies, or buy more land.[23]

While the pull of family dominates motivations for return, it is important to recognize that in the contemporary era of migration between the United States and Mexico, political and economic forces interact with family reasons for return.[24] The human costs of family separation have intensified as a consequence of stepped-up border enforcement. Migrants, who would have otherwise sojourned home to visit family, have no recourse but to stay longer than desired in the United States, thus lengthening the time away from family and intensifying the suffering of separation from loved ones. Expanded border enforcement operations have also pushed up *coyote* costs, which are typically shouldered by migrants living and working in the United States. Yet, in the context of declining economic opportunities for migrants in the U.S. labor market, some migrants lack the economic resources to finance *coyotes* to bring up family members. Consequently, we can suspect that some migrants return to Mexico to be with their families because of the political and economic barriers to reunifying abroad.[25]

ECONOMIC CONTEXT OF ARRIVAL IN LEON

As we pointed out above, the majority of respondents (58 percent) in the Leon survey returned to Mexico between 2006 and 2010, during a period characterized by economic growth followed by abrupt decline and a promising recovery. Driven by a strong demand for its manufactured products in the United States, the Mexican economy grew at a rate of 5.1 percent in 2006 and 3.3 percent in 2007. Mexico's exports continued to increase steadily until 2008, before declining sharply in 2009 as a consequence of the U.S. economic recession and the global financial crisis. In fact, Mexico's integration with and dependence on the economy of its northern neighbor produced a dramatic reduction in the country's gross domestic product (−6.6 percent) in 2009, the largest of any Latin American nation that year. As a result, the unemployment rate rose, while industrial production, real wages, and private consumption declined. The peso lost 15 percent of its value in 2009, and remittances, which had reached $26 billion in 2007, declined to $21.3 billion in 2009.[26] The proportion of Mexicans living in poverty increased from 44.5 percent in 2008 to 46.2 percent in 2010. In Guanajuato, the poverty rate increased from 44.2 percent in 2008 to 48.5 percent in 2010. The rise in the number of impoverished *guanajuatenses* resulted in part from the decline in remittances sent to the state, which dropped from a high of nearly $2.38 billion in 2007 to approximately $1.94 billion in 2009.[27]

The economic recession had an uneven impact on the state of Guanajuato but some of its effects were readily visible. On the highway that leads to the Bajío International Airport, near the small city of Silao, the yards of the General Motors plant, once packed with SUVs and pickup trucks ready to be shipped to the

United States, were empty in 2009. Auto assembly and auto parts production had represented nearly 69 percent of all state exports in 2007.[28] Responding to decline in demand for its cars across the border, General Motors–Silao eliminated shifts, laid off workers, and stopped production for several weeks that year. GM's local network of suppliers experienced similar production stoppages.[29]

Traditional industries did not experience the sharp downturn that export-driven sectors suffered. Largely oriented toward the internal market, the shoe industry benefited from the slight devaluation of the peso, which made imports more expensive and Mexican footwear more competitive in the international market. Still, the Mexican shoe industry only exported a small percentage of its overall production—5 percent in 2008. Instead of opening new markets abroad, national shoe manufacturers were concerned about keeping their share of the domestic market. Clustered in Guanajuato and in the city of Leon in particular, the Mexican shoe industry had suffered a long period of decline as a result of the unilateral opening of the national market to imports. A falloff in output had begun in the late 1980s, when production dropped from a high of 245 million pairs in 1988 to 200 million pairs in 1989. After a brief period of growth in the late 1990s, the industry lost ground again, dropping to a new low of 170 million pairs produced in 2002. As production declined sharply, imports rose to 23.5 million pairs and shoes introduced illegally into the country as contraband totaled 40 million in 2003. Despite these challenges, the Mexican shoe industry began to recover in 2003 and, by the period in which most of our respondents returned to Leon (2006–10), had finally returned to its 1988 production levels of about 245 million pairs per year.[30] Furthermore, an ever greater share of the national production of footwear was becoming concentrated in the cluster of shoe manufacturers located in Leon and adjacent municipalities.

Simultaneously, however, Leon footwear manufacturers also faced the looming threat of a wave of Chinese imports. Tariffs imposed on shoes and other leather products made in China started to phase out at the end of 2007; these tariffs had been negotiated by Mexican authorities as part of China's entry into the World Trade Organization in 2001. The Mexican government had introduced tariffs as early as 1993 to protect its flailing industry battered by cheap imports and contraband from Asian countries. Other traditional industries, such as garment manufacturing, were also bracing for a flood of inexpensive Chinese imports, which threatened to displace goods produced by manufacturers clustered in the twin cities of Moroleon and Uriangato in the state of Guanajuato.

Despite the effects of the great recession and the uncertainties local producers faced, by the time we completed data collection Guanajuato's economy was experiencing a strong recovery. In 2010, Guanajuato resumed growing at rates above the national average, becoming the sixth most important state in terms of its contribution to Mexico's gross domestic product (4.1 percent of the national GDP).[31] Manufacturing played a key role in the state's economic recovery; by 2011 contributing 30.2 percent to the state's gross domestic product, the largest sector of the local economy in both absolute and percentage terms.[32] Guanajuato has attracted new flows of direct foreign investment, which has expanded the existing cluster of car and auto parts factories in Silao (where General Motors is located) and opened new hubs in Salamanca and Celaya, in the southern and southeastern parts of the state, respectively. Most of this production is destined for export. Between 2010 and 2013, Volkswagen, Mazda, Honda, and Pirelli had started construction of new plants to assemble cars, produce car engines, transmissions, auto parts, and tires for export to North, Central, and South America. Dozens of companies that are part of the supply chain of the large auto manufacturers were also setting up shop in the state's industrial parks. By 2013, Mexico had become the fourth largest exporter and eighth biggest producer of cars in the world. Leon's manufacturing base was also part of these trends. Taking advantage of this city's specialization in leather products, international and local firms were establishing new partnerships and opening plants in Leon to supply the auto industry with leather seats.[33] In an informal conversation with one of the authors, the owner of a medium-sized dairy plant in Celaya remarked how the development of the automotive industry in the state was creating upward pressure on local wages. His workers now had other options. In order to attract and retain workers, he has had to raise his employees' salaries.

Clearly, our survey respondents returned to a dynamic and evolving economic context. As Enrique, the return migrant and self-employed taxi driver who opened up this chapter, told us in 2012, "The economy has never been stronger. It is the best since I returned ten years ago. My schedule is so busy that if I wanted I could work every day, interpreting for and chauffeuring Japanese, German, and American businessmen to and from the airport to work sites." Several owners of shoe factories repeated Enrique's optimism, mentioning an upturn in foreign investment not only in leather manufacturing, but also in aerospace and automobile manufacturing, agribusiness, and food processing.

HUMAN CAPITAL TRANSFERS FROM THE UNITED STATES AND LABOR MARKET EXPERIENCES IN MEXICO

It is within this strong economic climate in Mexico that we investigated skill transfers from the United States. Several questions dominate the analysis in this chapter. First, what kind of skills did migrants bring back from the United States? Second, are they different from those learned in Mexico and, if so, why? Finally, how do skill transfers shape the labor market experiences of return migrants and prospects for local development? Guiding this analysis is our underlying argument that skill acquisition and development is a dynamic process influenced by social relations, economic conditions, and the culture of learning environments and knowledge sharing at both ends of the migratory stream.

As Table 5.2 shows, skill transfers from the United States are substantial among the sample; more than half (51 percent) reported transferring skills learned in the United States to at least one job upon return to Mexico. Indeed, transfers back to Mexico are slightly higher than those to the United States, and the gains are greater for women than men, a reversal of gender patterns compared to Mexico-U.S. transfers. As Table 5.2 and Figure 5.2 show, the skill sets that migrants take back to their jobs in Mexico are different in a number of ways from those they bring with them. The skills are more diverse than those transferred to the United States, including English and technical skills learned formally in institutional environments, along with technical and social skills learned informally on the job. While only 2 percent reported transferring English skills acquired in Mexico to their U.S. jobs, 11 percent reported bringing these back from the United States and applying them to the jobs they held at the time of our interview.

TABLE 5.2

Skill and knowledge transfers across the migratory circuit

	Mexico to United States			United States to Mexico		
	Total *(n=200)*	*Men* *(n=172)*	*Women* *(n=28)*	*Total* *(n=200)*	*Men* *(n=172)*	*Women* *(n=28)*
Any transfer	48%	51%	26%	51%	50%	56%
English	2%	1%	4%	11%	10%	18%
Formal education	1%	1%	0%	2%	2%	0%
On-the-job technical skills	44%	47%	26%	39%	40%	32%
Off-the-job technical skills	11%	12%	4%	0%	0%	0%
Social skills	3%	2%	4%	19%	17%	32%

NOTE: Percentages exceed 100 because some respondents transferred multiple skill types.

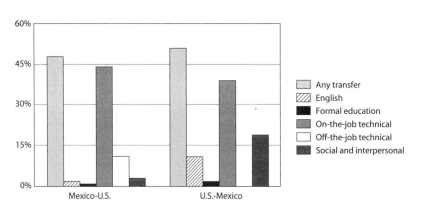

Figure 5.2. Skill and knowledge transfers across the migratory circuit (n=200).

As we shall discuss below in a subsequent section on skills and job transitions in Mexico, such language transfers are concentrated primarily in the business and tourist sectors of the local economy.

Women were almost twice as likely as men to report transferring English skills, reflecting the types of jobs they held in the United States (domestic workers, chambermaids, assistant cooks and cooks, waitresses, sales assistant clerks), which required regular interaction with English-speaking employers and their children, managers, and customers in service jobs. In contrast, men who were largely concentrated in the secondary labor market working alongside co-ethnics in construction and service jobs had needed little or no English, an observation documented in other studies of migrant labor market incorporation.[34]

The acquisition of skills through formal institutions is also more prominent among migrants in the United States compared to Mexico, where informal learning is the norm in industries such as construction. However, many of the skills learned through these formal mechanisms are not easily transferrable to the Mexican labor market. As we discussed in chapter 4, government agencies assume an important institutional role in safety-related skills training in the United States. Some of the skills migrants learned through safety programs provided by federal and state government agencies were transferred to Mexico, but by and large, most were not, reflecting the weaker regulatory environment and the different levels of industrial technology between the two countries. This technology differential accounted as well for the fact that most of the skills acquired through vocational classes at community colleges in the United States were also not transferrable, excepting training in diagnostic computer systems for auto repair and blueprint reading in the building and trades sector.

Table 5.2 and Figure 5.2 also show that neither men nor women learned skills off the job in the United States, which was a common social environment for learning across the life cycle in Mexico. This absence of off-the-job learning in the United States is possibly a function of the age of the migrants; that is, most off-the-job learning took place at a young age in home communities, before respondents entered paid employment. As the table highlights, the large majority of the migrants—men and women alike—learned skills in the United States informally, on the job, through social interaction with coworkers, close observation, practice, informal mentoring, and trial and error—interpersonal not institutional experience. While men reported the transfer of construction, carpentry, and automotive repair skills learned in their U.S. jobs, women reported food and beverage preparation skills and some support and managerial skills, such as computer and data entry knowledge.

The most notable feature of Table 5.2 is the substantial number of nontechnical skills that were transferred, especially by women. These social or interpersonal skills are numerous and diverse. They include hard-to-measure competences that may invoke new ways of doing things or new work habits such as punctuality, teamwork, supervisory and leadership skills, entre-preneurial skills (initiative), self-confidence, and follow-through—personal attributes that can enhance and, as we show, do improve an individual's job performance and career prospects. As noted in chapter 4, in the migration literature social or "people" skills are exclusively associated with what an employer desires from his or her worker, and in general are seen as having a demeaning connotation (follows orders, shows up on time, works hard) in that they can demonstrate the unequal and often exploitive nature of immigrant work conditions. In this chapter, we tell the employment story from the perspective of the worker, identifying the social skills that migrants themselves reported learning in the United States and applying to their Mexico-based jobs. Many of these personal skills and competences, we find, are particular to the culture of work in the United States, and as we shall highlight below, some migrants were able to mobilize them to further their labor market careers upon return and, in particular, assist in the launching of entrepreneurial activities.

Table 5.2 and Figure 5.2 also show a gendered dimension to skill transfers associated with the different types of work that immigrant women and men perform in both the United States and upon return to Mexico. While technical or "hard" skills dominated men's transfers to their jobs in Mexico, women were twice as likely to report transferring interpersonal skills, reflecting both the greater propensity among women to hold service jobs in the United States and upon return, jobs in which communication, management, and customer service skills are required.

BARRIERS TO AND OPPORTUNITIES FOR TRANSFERRING SKILLS, RESKILLING, AND OCCUPATIONAL CHANGE UPON RETURN

Do these English, technical, and personal skill transfers make a difference in the labor market experiences of migrants when they return home? Do the skills acquired in the United States influence the types of jobs and industries that migrants enter and advance to in the Mexican labor market? Our findings are mixed. Like much of the literature on return migration, we find that there are a number of factors that influence whether or not return migrants can mobilize skills learned abroad to advance their economic circumstances upon return. As the literature documents and we further found, reintegration into local labor markets upon return home is a complicated process. Beyond the obvious resource of savings remitted home, which plays a paramount role in entrepreneurship ventures, we find that the ability to transfer skills from the United States to the Mexican labor market depends on multiple interacting variables, including the compatibility of occupations and industries in both labor markets; time abroad as well as time away from social contacts at home; whether the return was forced or voluntary and thus planned; and institutional and discriminatory labor practices.

Some studies show that industries and occupations in which migrants work while abroad do have a bearing on their ability to repatriate with improved and higher wages, although the wage returns vary by gender because men and women are often clustered in different occupations abroad.[35] Taking it one step further by accounting for labor market context upon return, other scholars have found that occupation-specific experience abroad does have a positive impact on wages upon return if migrants can channel this experience into comparable industries and occupations.[36] That is, return migrants achieve the most economic gains when their Mexican jobs match their U.S. occupations. Collectively, the scholarship on return migration and labor market reintegration suggests that migration improves the labor market experience of return migrants by improving occupation-specific skills, and if men and women are clustered in different occupations abroad, the returns may also be gendered, sometimes benefiting women, other times men. In a similar but expanded vein, as we will discuss below, we too found that migrants experience the most occupational mobility when they can apply skills learned in the United States to their Mexican jobs upon return; however, as we also show, skills are not synonymous with occupation and wage gains are not the only benefits from skill transfers. Knowledge acquired abroad includes technical know-how along with interpersonal competences that may facilitate different mobility pathways upon return. Sometimes skills are mobilized from a U.S. job experience in a similar occupation and industry in Mexico, but other times skills are mobilized across occupations and industries or create new labor market experiences altogether as in the case of an entrepreneurial activity.

At times, however, industries at home and abroad are not compatible. Some skills in landscaping and construction, for example, are not transferable because of the different building styles of the two countries. For example, none of the respondents who worked with specialty gardening techniques, such as pruning, yard design, or curbing, transferred these techniques because of the lack of local demand for these services in Mexico. One young man had worked his way up in a landscaping firm in Arizona, beginning as a *chalán* and advancing to a paver, learning to operate the machinery used to install the decorative paved trimmings that surround garden beds and line driveways. Although he did install them in his yard and the product was admired by numerous neighbors, almost none of the homes in the small Guanajuáto city of Dolores Hidalgo had the yardage to develop flower beds, let alone trim them. Only a handful of return migrants who worked as roofers, sheetrockers (*chirroqueros*), or painters in the United States were able to transfer any technical skills to their Mexican jobs because of different residential building techniques in the two countries. In contrast to the United States, where roofing consists primarily of asphalt shingles, most residential homes in Mexico are roofed with tile or plaster. Similarly, while sheetrocking is common in both residential and commercial construction north of the border, in Mexico the technique is restricted to commercial buildings. Moreover, most working-class Mexicans plaster and paint their own homes.

Other scholars point to the importance of duration abroad in the ability to repatriate skills and achieve wage gains. Theoretically, optimization of time abroad (a proxy for work experience in human capital parlance) allows migrants to acquire and diversify their skills in the likelihood that they can transfer them upon return. If the duration abroad is a year or two, for example, the opportunity for skill acquisition and diversification may be limited. If the period abroad is very long, then the returnee may be too old or too disconnected from the community of origin or local labor market.[37] Empirical studies examining the relationship between duration abroad and labor market performance of return migrants offer mixed results. While some studies show that additional time abroad increases the earnings of return migrants, other studies do not find any wage premium associated with duration abroad.[38]

Along with Christian Dustmann, we find that time abroad, which is a proxy for U.S. labor market experience, is an incomplete predictor of labor market gains upon return because migrants extend or shorten their tenure abroad to achieve their goals. For example, over their migration careers, the Leon sample had worked an average of four years in the United States, a period during which substantial skills could potentially develop, yet we did not find that those who spent more time abroad were any more likely than those who spent less time in *el norte* to transfer skills. The findings could have been affected by the repeat migration among our sample. That is, some migrants, with a history of repeat migration, were unable to acquire or transfer any skills because they were not at one job long enough or held multiple jobs of different types. What we did find is that some migrants reported being gone too long from home and unable to access the familiar social networks of the past to find work. That is, emigration for some resulted in a loss of social capital at home, which diminished access to information and job referrals upon return.[39] Of the 160 migrants who entered wage work upon return (excluding entrepreneurs), for example, only 42 percent found these jobs through social networks, whereas before migration 57 percent had relied on family, extended kin, and friends to obtain their jobs, and 75 percent relied on social networks to gain access to their first jobs in the United States. In the absence of job referrals through networks, many return migrants relied on classified advertisements and their own agency, canvassing employers and marketing their new skills and talents. Some were successful using these strategies, while others were not.

Some particular formal skill sets are not country specific and have universal transferability. English language capital and Information Technology (IT) skills are among those that have been identified as especially important in explaining wage increases and occupational change among return migrants.[40] English language skills open up employment prospects in industries such as international business, trade, and tourism, in which English is the primary language of communication. According to the literature, highly skilled migrants appear best able to mobilize the formal human capital skills they acquired abroad for economic gain upon return. In their study of five different types of skilled return migrants in Slovakia, Alan Williams and Vladimir Baláž found that upon return from the United Kingdom, most Slovak migrants benefited economically from the formal human capital they had acquired.[41] Professional and managerial workers who possessed IT and English language skills exhibited the biggest gains. But as we found, the gains to formal skills acquired abroad are not limited to professional workers. As we shall discuss below, migrants in our sample also benefited economically through the English language skills they had learned in the United States and that this learning experience was gendered. Because women worked in retail, food processing, and caregiving, they learned more English than their male counterparts who had worked primarily alongside co-ethnics in unregulated construction and other manufacturing sectors of the U.S. economy.

We found that employer preferences and discriminatory labor practices also influence reintegration. Some employers value migrants workers for their "disciplined work ethic," while others were put off by insistence on fair pay and time off, labor rights they had learned about in their U.S. jobs.[42] While English skills and local labor market demands certainly benefited some of the women returning to Leon, the older female return migrants reported being unable to apply skills learned abroad because of age discrimination against women in the Mexican labor market. Take the case of Erika, who eked out a living selling shoe soles to local shoe manufacturers. In the United States, she worked at a McDonald's, where she learned how to prepare and grill hamburgers and make pastries. When she returned to Leon in her mid-thirties, it was only natural that she would try to locate a job at a local McDonald's. She was denied the position, however, possibly because of her age and employer preferences. Unable to market her skills, she found a low-wage job as a janitor in a mall. Returning home with technical and customer service skills and English language acquired through migration did not help Erika or other older women; they were bypassed when employers in the retail and service industries seemed to favor younger women.

SKILL TRANSFERS AND LABOR MARKET
TRANSITIONS UPON RETURN

Despite barriers to labor market reintegration, we identify three important labor market transitions resulting from skill transfers from the United States to Mexico: (1) a transition from manual jobs in agriculture and the shoe, leather, and textile industries to service-based jobs in retail and hospitality; (2) occupational mobility within an industry; and (3) a transition from salaried worker to entrepreneur, which sometimes involves upward mobility from working to middle class. To illustrate these transitions we draw on three comparisons. First, we look at the industries in which the return migrants worked before and after migration. We then compare the industries in which the Leon sample worked at the time they were interviewed with the labor market profile of a 2010 census sample of all workers of the same age and gender in the city of Leon. Finally, we compare the job status of our sample with a census sample of the Leon population of the same age and gender, with an eye toward illustrating and explaining the rate of entrepreneurship among the sample.

Table 5.3 lists the last industry in which the migrants worked before emigration and the industry in which they labored in summer 2010, when we conducted our interviews. Several notable industrial transitions stand out in the table. When our sample arrived home in Mexico, less than 1 percent turned to agriculture and only 17 percent turned to the shoe industry, the biggest manufacturing employer of migrants before emigration.

TABLE 5.3

Distribution of Leon sample before and after migration
by economic sector (n=200)

Last Industry before Migrating	Last Industry after Return (% of total in the last industry before migrating)[a]						
	Agriculture	*Construction*	*Leather*	*Other manufacturing*	*Service*	*Not in labor force*	*Total*
Agriculture	0	13	13	0	75	0	*4*
Construction	0	61	11	4	25	0	*14*
Leather	0	0	40	9	40	11	*24*
Other manufacturing	3	6	3	42	26	19	*16*
Service	0	4	11	4	74	8	*38*
Not in labor force	0	0	20	0	60	20	*5*[b]
After return distribution	*1*	*12*	*17*	*10*	*51*	*10*[c]	*100*

NOTE: Due to rounding, percentages do not total exactly to 100 percent.

[a] Table interpretation: 75% of return migrants who worked in the agricultural sector just before migrating were working in the service industry when they were interviewed for the study.

[b] Among those not in the labor force before migration were 7 unemployed and looking for work, 2 university students, and 1 homemaker.

[c] Among those not in the labor force at the time of the interview were 10 unemployed and looking for work, 3 migrants who had just returned from the United States (within a month) and were not yet looking for work, 2 retired persons, 1 university student, 1 disabled person, and 2 homemakers.

In contrast, the number of those working in service, especially retail and hospitality, increased substantially. We found that the transition from traditional industries, including construction, shoemaking, and manufacturing, to retail and hospitality after migration was in part determined by the industrial characteristics of the local economy to which they returned, along with the interpersonal and English skills and the new self-confidence they brought back with them. For some migrants, social skills and competences acquired abroad opened up service positions in hotels and restaurants and retail shops, while English language skills opened up employment prospects in Mexican industries in international business, trade, and tourism.

The women in our study were especially competitive for these positions because of the English language and social skills they had acquired in their U.S. jobs as domestics, nannies, chambermaids, and food preparation workers. For example, before migration Lara worked on a family farm picking cucumbers. In the United States, she worked as a nanny where she acquired considerable social skills and improved her English. When she returned to Leon she moved into retail—selling women's clothing—a position, she told us, that allowed her to use her U.S.-honed skills. When we interviewed her, she was in the process of opening up her own retail store that would sell used clothes sent from the United States. Or take the case of Marcelina. In the United States she had worked in a steak house where she learned not only how to store, prepare, and serve beef, but also developed customer service and teamwork skills through interaction with coworkers. She returned to Mexico for family reasons and was hired as an assistant clerk in an OXXO, a chain of convenience stores in Mexico. When we interviewed her, she had moved up the ladder to manager, a transition she believes was facilitated by what she termed "*relaciones públicas*" she learned in the United States. Others who worked in the retail and hospitality industries before emigration found themselves in an improved position with greater social status upon return. Rovina, who worked in a stationery store before leaving Leon, improved her English through interaction with coworkers and management at the restaurant where she worked in the United States. When she returned to Mexico, she located a job at a cyber café and now uses her English frequently with customers and translating for coworkers and even her boss, whom she says "relies" on Rovina's English skills.

Like Enrique, the taxi driver who was featured in the introduction of this chapter, a number of the men who returned to Leon turned to driving a taxi or chauffeuring, using the English and customer service skills they had acquired in the United States. One return migrant, Miguel, found work as a taxi driver catering to English-speaking tourists and businesspersons. Other taxi drivers accuse him of "brown-nosing," but he argues that he is just providing good customer service, something he observed in the culture of work in the United States. As he concluded at the end of his interview, "*El que tiene más saliva, come más pinole.*"[43] When asked what this *dicho* (saying) meant, he explained the literal and symbolic meaning: "Well, *pinole* is a dry corn-based powder that you mix with sugar. It is very dry so having more saliva means you can eat more of it. In Mexican society it means that the person with the most skills has the greatest advantage over others. In my case, because I have more English and customer service skills, I get more clients than other *taxistas.*"

Large cities with a diverse industrial base such as Leon, or expatriate and tourist communities such as San Miguel de Allende and Guanajuato City, provide return migrants like Miguel with multiple labor market opportunities in which to apply English language and customer service skills. In these cities, return migrants often labor as waiters, clerks in retail stores, taxi drivers, and guides. English language capability has enabled some female return migrants, like Anna, to bypass traditional domestic service and gain work as English teachers or move to tourist towns where they can demand a higher salary because of their language skills. In San Miguel de Allende and several other tourist towns in the state of Guanajuato, we interviewed a number of return migrants who had left their home communities to seek better labor market opportunities. Except for teaching, we found very little opportunity for migrants to apply their English language skills in rural hamlets and small towns as there is simply no demand in these local economies.

Even those who returned to the same industry in which they had worked before they emigrated often experienced occupational mobility. For example, among the 19 return migrants who returned to work in the shoe industry, 10 advanced from their positions as salaried employees to being self-employed manufacturers. This transition to entrepreneurship was facilitated largely by remitted savings from U.S. jobs and Leon's rebounding manufacturing sector. Several entrepreneurs, including Rafael, the tailor featured in the introduction of this book, also returned with technical and social skills that enabled their entrepreneurial activities.

Although we only came across a handful of cases where technical cobbling and tailoring and upholstering skills acquired in the United States facilitated occupational mobility among salaried workers, they are memorable cases. Francisco, for example, learned the craft of upholstering furniture at a young age in his father's home-based factory—how to measure and stretch fabric and then fasten it to furniture with industrial staple guns. In the United States, he located a job in a factory that manufactured upholstery for hotel furniture. According to Francisco, "I learned to work with more sophisticated designs in the United States, such as Louis XV, rococo, and baroque designs." Rather than working with his father upon return to Mexico, he mobilized his new skills and located a well-paying job in a factory that manufactures upholstery for residential and commercial furniture. Like several others in the study, Francisco's move from the role of unpaid family worker before migration to a salaried position after migration represents a trajectory of personal freedom and emancipation.

Javier also acquired manufacturing skills in his U.S. job that he was then able to mobilize to advance in Leon's shoe industry. Before migrating, Javier worked as a stitcher in a medium-sized shoe factory that manufactures men's shoes. In the United States, a friend referred him to a company that manufactured ice skates, and because he was able to communicate and demonstrate his skills to the factory supervisor he was also hired as a stitcher. He caught on fast, learning how to operate the sophisticated machinery developed to produce ice skates. Javier was very contented in his U.S. job because he was exposed to new technology and materials and because his skills from Mexico were recognized and valued by his employer. Unfortunately, for health reasons he was forced to return to Mexico. In Leon he was able to demonstrate his machinist skills to several prospective employers and was hired at a competitive salary to fill a position in one of Leon's biggest and oldest shoe factories. Though his job title position remained a stitcher, he was also responsible for teaching other workers how to use the industrial machinery in the factory, a job he embraced with his newfound self-confidence.

Technical know-how in construction and automotive repair ranked high among technical skill sets successfully transferred to the Leon labor market, and often their transfers facilitated occupational advancement. Most working in these two industries at the time of the survey had had premigration experience, but smaller numbers were first-time workers. Several factors explain the successful transfer of these skills: the extensive informal training workers had at home and abroad in these industries; the prestige associated with positions at the top for persons with low levels of formal education; and the strong demand for construction and automotive skills in both Mexico and the United States.

As we illustrated in chapter 2 on learning, many young men acquired their construction and automotive skills at a very young age and often in the social context of home and community long before they entered paid employment in Mexico. Once in the formal labor market, if they elected to pursue a career in automotive repair or the construction trades, they would pick up additional on-the-job skills and then through migration further reskill in the United States, learning how to work with new technology and materials. Thus, learning and skill development over the migratory circuit enabled some migrants to move up the occupational ladder from *ayudante* or helper before migration to master mason or mechanic upon return.

Take the case of Fernando, an auto body repair worker who transferred skills in both directions of the migratory circuit. Fernando worked repairing crashed cars and eventually became the owner of an auto body repair shop in Leon. In Mexico, he used electro-mechanic tools and equipment to straighten cars and reshape them to their original dimensions. Fernando also repainted vehicles and, as the owner of a small business, he knew how to estimate the cost of repairs and was familiar with other administrative tasks. Fernando's brother found him a job as an auto body repair mechanic in the United States, a job to which he transferred all the skills he developed in Mexico. While abroad, he became acquainted with computerized machines, lasers and spotters and other technology that provided the exact measurements of the cars according to the year and model. Fernando transferred his newly acquired skills back to Mexico where he is in charge of an auto body repair shop. Even though he does not work with exactly the same advanced technology available in the United States, Fernando managed to buy and import some of the new tools and equipment. During the interview, he reported that his employer appreciates his ability to work with more sophisticated technology. Fernando is now in charge of purchasing new tools for the shop and training the other employees in the use of the recently acquired equipment. He also reported substantially higher earnings at the present job than at the position he held before migration.

As noted in an earlier section in this chapter, Guanajuato has attracted new flows of foreign investment that have expanded the existing cluster of car and auto parts manufacturers in Silao, the town adjacent to Salamanca and Celaya, in southern Guanajuato. Most of this production is for export and out of reach of many working-class Leon residents. Like most Mexicans who cannot afford to purchase a new car, they rely on maintaining used cars. Thus, the automotive repair industry is big business in Leon, and a number of the migrants in our sample worked in this industry before migration, while abroad, and upon return, all the while improving their technical skills and advancing their positions in the labor market. For example, take the case of Jorge. Before migrating to the United States, Jorge worked as an *ayudante* to a mechanic, repairing tires, motors, and transmissions of large diesel trucks. He migrated to the United States with the desire to learn more automotive skills, but unable to find work in automotive repair or manufacturing, he settled for a job as a laborer in a natural gas plant where he installed gas piping. Learning of his mechanical skills, his supervisor regularly called on Jorge to repair equipment and work on firm vehicles. Eventually, Jorge found work in a company that designed and manufactured trailers. In this job he developed new skills in electricity and learned how to operate sophisticated tools and equipment so that when he returned to Mexico he was able to transfer his new skills to a construction firm that hired him to operate and repair heavy machinery.

The low levels of formal human capital required for entry into the *albañilería* (construction) trade draw some young men into the construction industry in Mexico. The skills they learn at home and then in the Mexican labor market come in handy when they migrate to the United States where the demand for immigrant labor in the construction and building trades is high. Like the mechanics in our sample, many of the construction workers developed skills throughout the migratory circuit and benefited from this knowledge upon return home to Leon. Take the case of Guillermo, who learned basic masonry skills from his father. Once in the formal labor market, he developed new and improved skills: how to mold and lay brick, install concrete flooring, plaster walls, and read blueprints. By the time he migrated to the United States he had moved up the occupational ladder from *ayudante* to *media cuchara* to *albañil*. In the United States he located work with a construction firm where he was able to apply skills learned in Mexico. In his U.S. job he reskilled, learning framing, roofing, plumbing, and electrical skills. According to Guillermo, he has been able to apply everything he learned to his current Leon job, where he is a subcontractor for a large construction firm that builds commercial buildings. His status in the trade of *albañilería* is *maestro albañil* or master mason. In his closing narrative, he told us that his plans were to launch his own construction company with his two sons.

In the tourist town of San Miguel de Allende return migrants who had worked in construction in the United States, especially with skills involving wood and stone, framing, and landscape design, reported that these skills gave them an edge in the occupational niche of local construction and building trades that cater to expatriate building styles. Herculano worked in construction in the United States for five years, advancing from *ayudante* to skilled worker in carpentry, framing, adobe, and electrical and plumbing skills. In his last job abroad, he built adobe and Spanish-colonial homes in New Mexico, using a style he called "rustic colonial." He returned to San Miguel de Allende and markets this style to many expatriates who purchase and renovate homes there but must meet local housing and building specification. As Herculano explained, "Americans want a frame house with large windows but the *municipio* has rules against just any building style. We have a restricted use of wood in building because we want to retain the stone facades of homes. Americans have had to adapt their building desires to the architecture of San Miguel de Allende. I can help them to do this through marketing my rustic colonial building style." What makes the case of Herculano and other return migrants working in San Miguel de Allende so interesting is their ability to mobilize the skills they had acquired in the United States to carve niches in a local economy that is driven by the building desires of the expatriate community.

Table 5.4 compares the industrial distribution of the sample with a 10 percent sample of the economically active population of Leon in 2010. As this table shows, the return migrants and the Leon populations are equally represented in shoe and leather production. The return migrants are as likely to be in agriculture relative to the total Leon working population, but more likely to

TABLE 5.4

Economic sector of return migrants and
Leon city working population (2010)

Industry	Leon sample	Leon (city)
Agriculture	0.5%	0.4%
Construction	12.4%	6.2%
Shoe, leather, and textile manufacturing	20.0%	20.1%
Other manufacturing	9.7%	9.1%
Automotive and bicycle repair	7.6%	1.3%
Retail and hospitality	36.8%	29.3%
Other services	12.9%	32.4%
Other industries (mining, utilities, and unspecified)	–	1.1%

SOURCE: Leon city population, INEGI, *Censo de Población y Vivienda* 2010, Micro-datos de la Muestra. www.inegi.org.mx/sistemas/microdatos2/default2010.aspx.

be concentrated in construction, auto repair, and retail, transitions we have argued and demonstrated are facilitated by skills transferred from work experience in the United States. Men who entered their U.S. jobs as laborers in construction or auto mechanics and reskilled in these jobs were able to apply new skills to their Mexican jobs to improve their economic opportunities. Those who had worked in service and retail and hospitality in the United States were able to move to these industries upon return, a transition especially facilitated by English language skills.

SKILL TRANSFERS AND ENTREPRENEURSHIP

Does migration facilitate entrepreneurship, and if so what are the factors driving this mobility pathway? Numerous studies docu-

In Table 5.5 we document the high percentage of self-employed among the return migrant sample relative to the Leon population. We distinguish between two groups of return migrants who own their businesses: those who are self-employed and those who are self-employed and have employees, the latter of whom are identified in the table as *patrones*. In the former category are return migrants who reported opening up small businesses, primarily ambulatory food and beverage stands in the informal sector, as a survival strategy to overcome institutional and social barriers to labor market reintegration, as some scholars would predict. The costs of entry into these small business ventures is minimal and some return migrants saw self-employment as a short-term career strategy, expecting to eventually transition to salaried employment.[48] Deportees, like Victor, whose narrative opened up this chapter, were largely concentrated in this category, reflecting the problems of labor market reintegration for migrants who are forcibly repatriated. These migrants return with few resources and are often stigmatized upon arrival home. Women also were concentrated in this category and reported turning to self-employment as a response to social barriers to reintegration, including absence of established contacts in the Leon labor market and the gender and age discrimination they experienced in the mainstream labor market. Some were able to transition out of self-employment and apply skills acquired abroad to enter salaried work, but others were not. The business activities of this group of self-employed migrants were concentrated primarily in small sundry shops, ambulatory food and beverage vending stands, and secondhand clothing stores, enterprises that did not necessarily depend on skill transfers or substantial remittances from the United States.

On the other hand, as the table shows, 15 percent of the migrants did become *patrones,* a figure five times the *patrón* per-

TABLE 5.5

Labor market status of return migrant sample and
Leon population over 20 years old, by gender

Work Status	Total		Male		Female	
	Sample (n=200)	*Leon (n=22,229)*	*Sample (n=172)*	*Leon (n=10,587)*	*Sample (n=28)*	*Leon (n=11,642)*
Salaried worker	48%	47%	51%	61%	30%	33%
Self-employed[a]	27%	15%	26%	19%	30%	12%
Patrones	15%	3%	16%	4%	11%	1%
Unemployed[b]	5%	2%	4%	4%	15%	1%
Homemakers	1%	24%	0%	1%	4%	45%
Others[c]	5%	9%	3%	11%	11%	7%

SOURCE: Leon city population, INEGI, *Censo de Población y Vivienda* 2010, Microdatos de la Muestra. www.inegi.org.mx/sistemas/microdatos2/default2010.aspx.

NOTE: We selected the Leon population 20 and older because 20 is the age of youngest return migrant in sample. Due to rounding, percentages do not add up to 100%.

[a] Without employees.

[b] Looking for a job.

[c] E.g., retired, disabled.

centage for the city of Leon (see Table 5.5). In a separate analysis in which we include the nonmigrant Leon sample, we found that migrants who transfer skills have significantly greater odds of becoming *patrones* than nonmigrants.[49] The large majority of return migrants who became *patrones* were target migrants, that is, they moved to the United States with the chief objective of accumulating enough capital to open up a viable business upon return. These target migrants identified three factors that facilitated their entrepreneurial activities: skill development in the United States, remittances, and skill transfers. Eighty percent of all *patrones* used their savings to start their businesses. Moreover, those who reported improving their skills in the United States were over twice as likely as those migrants who reported no skill improvement while abroad and more than twice as likely as nonmigrants to launch an entrepreneurial activity that employed workers. Furthermore, 68 percent of all return migrants who became *patrones* applied skills learned in the United States to their current businesses. Skill transfers rank as the most important factor in explaining entrepreneurship among the study's target migrants.[50]

Among the return migrants who became *patrones,* 64 percent reported transferring technical skills acquired in U.S. jobs from auto repair, carpentry, construction, and restaurant work. Several used their new skill sets and savings from migration to start their own businesses and hire employees. For example, Rosalío, who at 61 years of age was one of the older men in the Leon sample, had worked before migrating as an *ayudante* in his father's wood and carpentry *taller* (a small to medium-size factory). From his father, he learned to build the huge wooden drums that tanneries use to soak, lime, and dye hides. Out of curiosity and seeking adventure, he immigrated to the United States. There he worked for a high-end wood-manufacturing firm that produces theater seats, cabinets, window frames, and specialty floors. In this job he was able to apply everything he knew about woodmaking from his days in his father's *taller,* and then he reskilled. Recognizing Rosalío's skills and admiring his initiative, his boss taught him how to use, assemble, and disassemble sophisticated machinery that he had not been exposed to in Mexico. When he returned home because of the pull of family, Rosalío brought with him sophisticated woodworking tools and machinery, which, along with remitted savings and newfound technical know-how, enabled him to open up his own woodworking factory and hire three employees.

But technical skills are not the only skills that facilitate entrepreneurial activities and diversify local economies. Equally important are the nontechnical skills successful return migrants bring back with them. Thirty-five percent of the sample reported transferring English skills to their entrepreneurial ventures; these entrepreneurs were concentrated in industries that involve face-to-face interaction with customers, including retail and hospitality, taxi and chauffeuring services, and a smaller number of manufacturers in the shoe and leather industry that worked with foreign businesspersons. Fifty-four percent of the *patrones* and 76 percent of the self-employed return migrants cited specific nontechnical on-the-job skills that they acquired in the United States and were able to apply to their business ventures. These personal skills and competences involve new approaches to the way work practices are technically and socially organized.

Some like Juan, who opened up an auto repair shop in Leon, emphasized social skills such as customer service: "It wasn't just working with new tools that I learned there. I also learned how to treat people. Maybe this is even more important if you are going to have your own business; you have to be able to trust your clients and treat people well. Let me tell you something. There are a lot of really good mechanic shops in Leon, but they don't know how to listen to clients, attend clients. This I learned in the United States." Manuel, who opened up a café upon return to Leon, also cited the customer service skills he had learned in the States: "Public relations, how to interact with customers, that's what I learned and that is key to the success of my café." Others, like Jorge who opened up a carpentry shop, told us that the organizational skills he had observed in his U.S. jobs and applied to his own business made work operate more smoothly and efficiently. As Jorge stated: "It is not just the machines that make the work faster, it is how workers approach work there. Everything is more organized and I was able to work faster, something I try to do here as well." Themes of efficiency and organization emerged in a number of interviews. Josefina, a return migrant who opened a small sundry shop, told us, "Working as a domestic I learned more English and how to be more efficient in my own work. I am more organized now." Another attribute that entrepreneurs reported as influencing work practices is discipline. As one owner of a *pica* told us, "I am more disciplined in my work now, return migrants work harder, they are more disciplined and more focused. I see it all the time. I think it has to do with knowing that you can advance faster in the United States, it makes you more disciplined. It makes you want to work harder."

Many of the self-employed migrants opened up businesses in industries where they had worked before migration, such as leather manufacturing firms, indicating economic mobility—from salaried worker to factory owner—within the city's dominant industry. Others opened businesses directly related to skills that improved in the United States (see table 5.6). For example, of the 11 return migrants who opened auto repair and bicycle repair shops back in Leon, 10 said they applied technical skills learned on the job while abroad. Another 9 (out of 11) applied technical cooking skills they had learned in restaurants in the United States to restaurants or food carts they operated upon return. One young man worked as a short-order cook in a small town in Wisconsin, where he learned to make hamburgers "the American way." When he returned to Guanajuato City, he opened up a small café where he serves Mexican specialty plates, along with hamburgers with onion rings, a combination that is especially popular with locals.

Dolores Hidalgo, the cradle of Mexican independence, is also known today as home to one of the largest *tianguis* (flea markets)

TABLE 5.6

Business types of self-employed return migrants

Business Types	Patrón (n=30)	No employees (n=53)
Manufacturing (shoe/leather, textile, furniture, ceramic/tile/glass)	27%	23%
Auto/bicycle repair service	17%	17%
Small convenience stores	13%	15%
Retail (produce, shoes and clothing, hardware, flea market)	10%	34%
Formal restaurant/coffee shop	10%	4%
Informal food/juice vendors	7%	6%
Residential/commercial construction	17%	2%

NOTE: Due to rounding, percentages do not total 100 percent.

in the state. Each week, thousands of *guanajuatenses* flock to the open-air market to purchase everything from *chicharrones* (pork rinds) to used clothing to secondhand equipment and vehicles. At the *tianguis* we met several dozen return migrants, some who were selling used clothing they arranged to have shipped to Mexico on a regular basis; others who learned or improved their auto repair skills in the United States were selling cars they had purchased, repaired, and driven home to sell at the *tianguis*.

Overall, 88 percent of all self-employed return migrants transferred skills acquired abroad to their self-employment ventures upon return. The types of skills transferred varied by gender. Women benefited less than men from the return of technical skills acquired abroad. Only 25 percent of women transferred technical skills, compared to 39 percent of male respondents. Of the seven women who did transfer technical skills, three opened their own businesses. Another woman became the manager of a cyber café. Similar to male return migrants, women benefited from the return of cooking techniques. Both women who opened their own restaurants in Leon reported transferring technical skills acquired in the United States to these entrepreneurial ventures. The limited transfer of technical skills among women likely results from the occupations women held abroad. While a few women worked as cooks and food preparation assistants, some were servers and bartenders, and others worked as secretaries and in other service capacities. Unlike men, who predominantly worked in technically intensive jobs such as construction and auto repair, these women did not always have an opportunity to acquire technical skills.

CONCLUSION

The findings presented in this chapter reveal the complex and contingent dynamics of skill transfer when migrants return to the home country. The majority of our Leon respondents returned to Mexico during the 2006–10 period. Although the great recession and the U.S. policy of deportation played a role in fostering return for many Mexicans, most of our respondents invoked family reasons to explain the end of their migratory sojourns. We conclude that while economic and political factors are important to understand the context of departure, family reunification creates a positive pull for return, which persists across periods of migration. Migrants returned to an evolving economic landscape in Guanajuato. Modest but consistent growth in 2006 and 2007 was followed by the steep decline of the 2008–09 global recession. As the gross domestic product and remittances declined, unemployment and poverty rates increased. By 2010, the national and state economies were in full recovery with modest but sustained positive GDP rates. In this context, slightly more than half of our respondents managed to transfer skills upon return.

For return migrants, the transfer of skills is part of a broader process of local labor market reintegration. Time abroad, the individual's local social networks, employer preferences, and the development of and transportability of skills across occupations and industries—all played a role in this process of reintegration. Technical knowledge in construction, carpentry, and mechanics was often cited by men as the most successfully transferred skills, but our respondents also cited employers who did not recognize these skills or discriminated against older workers, especially women. Our findings demonstrate that the transfer of skills is contingent on multiple factors, including gender, occupation, and industrial sector. Migrants transfer English language and technical knowledge as well as interpersonal skills acquired through institutional mechanisms and on-the-job experience. Women and men undergo this process differently; employed in service jobs in the United States, women were more likely to transfer English language skills to Mexico than men, who, in turn, had developed technical skills working among Spanish-speaking workers. English, social skills, and new work habits facilitated women's transition to higher-paid jobs in tourism, a booming economic sector in Guanajuato.

Our findings highlight three important transitions associated with the transfer of skills upon return. First, there is a transition from lower-paid, less-skilled, and less-esteemed occupations to higher-paid, multiskilled, and more-prestigious jobs within an industry, such as construction. In Guanajuato, skills acquired in the United States also allowed returnees to cater to a growing expatriate population and other return migrants seeking to build homes in the American style. The shoe industry illustrates the second of these transitions, namely, the passage from salaried worker to entrepreneur and from employee to employer. Although several of our respondents returned to the shoe industry, they did so equipped with capital and new skills acquired abroad. Finally, for some of our respondents, the skills acquired in the United States and transferred upon return to Mexico also facilitated the mobility from manual jobs in agriculture and manufacturing to service-based occupations in the hospitality and retail industries.

of his U.S. *patrón* who taught him everything he knows about cooking and how to run a kitchen. Despite the land inherited from his father, Ricardo most values and identifies himself with the skills that he acquired in the United States. As he exclaimed, "All that I have basically is from working in the United States."

At the age of 16, Laura traveled with her aunt to Chicago where they joined her parents. She quickly adapted to life in the United States, enrolling in high school and learning the local culture, including English. After graduating from high school, she first found work as a cashier in a *panadería* (bakery) and then as a waitress in her second and third jobs. In these, she acquired customer service skills and learned to bake Mexican pastries and other food specialties. In 2009, several of her relatives pooled their resources and opened up a small Mexican restaurant. It was only natural that they would hire Laura as manager of the family business. In charge of day-to-day operations, Laura supervised the preparation of specialty foods, learned how to keep the books, and interacted with customers on a daily basis. The business folded in 2010 as a result of the continued U.S. recession, and Laura decided to return to her hometown of Morelia, Mexico. Unable to locate a job where she could use her skills, she moved with a girlfriend to San Miguel de Allende because of the tourism industry of the city and thus the opportunities it would provide to apply her English language, customer service, and management skills. When we interviewed Laura, she was working as a cashier and clerk in the carryout section of a restaurant that caters to expatriate Americans. Earning 700 pesos a week and unable to apply her cooking skills, she expressed dissatisfaction with her job. Though she had repeatedly requested work in the kitchen or management, the U.S. supervisor of the restaurant with low levels of education. First, as we demonstrate in our analyses of learning at home and abroad, many so-called unskilled and low-skilled migrants possess technical and interpersonal skills learned in informal contexts through observation, interaction, and cooperation. For low-income Mexicans, skill acquisition begins at a young age before paid employment through participation in household and community projects and work related to family-owned businesses. Cooking, cleaning, fixing a car, and building a house or an addition to an existing home are common tasks in which working-class men and women are involved regularly early on in their lives. These experiences, together with basic literacy and numeracy skills learned in elementary and secondary schools, provide a baseline for these individuals to further develop and transfer skills. In the shoe and leather industry of Leon, Guanajuato, young men start to work in the small, family-owned, and almost always informal *picas* (shoe and leather manufacturing enterprises). The location of these enterprises on one of the floors of the family's home allows young men to join the shop after school and observe and learn from their fathers and other workers. These family-owned businesses—not the vocational and technical schools of the Mexican education system—are the training grounds of many of the workers who later go on to labor in the large and medium-sized factories of the city.

Once in the United States, many newcomer Mexicans with few credentials and little knowledge of the labor market depend on a co-ethnic network to direct them to jobs in the secondary labor market, where work authorization may not be required and the demand for English is minimal. As we have demonstrated in this book, while some migrants remain trapped in low-wage jobs in this unregulated sector of the economy, others achieve substantial mobility within it. Ironically, we find that mobility opportunities may be greatest in unregulated or informal sectors of the economy. In industries such as agriculture, construction, and landscaping, disadvantaged immigrant workers can apply source-country skills and learn new ones, all the while furthering their economic opportunities abroad. These are also sectors that provide substantial on-the-job training, another factor in the mobility equation.

The different mobility pathways of Mexican migrants are not only a function of where migrants are located in the U.S. labor market, but also of the dual processes of skill transfer from Mexico and reskilling in the United States. More than half of the migrants in our study were able to transfer skills learned on and off the job at home to further their careers abroad. The success of others, like Ricardo and Laura, was largely a result of reskilling in the U.S. labor market. Ricardo became a seasoned cook in Chinese cuisine after learning the craft through observation and informal training by his employer. Developing knowledge of English, management know-how, and the confidence to take risks, Laura quickly moved from cashier to waitress to management within the hospitality industry. Ricardo and Laura are not exceptional cases. Significant numbers of men and women in the study who were able to apply skills acquired on and off the job in Mexico and learn new ones in their U.S. jobs, experienced occupational transitions in the labor market market. When recognized and valued, immigrants expressed more satisfaction and experienced increased autonomy at work, higher wages, and a smoother move up to yet better jobs. Sixty-five percent of the sample reported that their skills were recognized and rewarded by their U.S. employers; 33 percent cited wage increases; and 36 percent were able to progress to better jobs that required more skills. Some of these transitions were facilitated through job jumping, a labor market strategy that migrants employ to improve their job situations, demonstrate new or improved skills, and circumvent exploitive conditions. Moreover, we found that migrants who transferred skills from Mexico to the United States were significantly more likely to experience occupational mobility and skill development while abroad than were migrants who did not transfer such skills. This finding resonates with Duleep and Regets' observation that "people who have learned one set of skills, even if those skills are not valued in the destination country's labor market, have advantages in learning a new set: in learning a previous skill, one learns how to learn."[3]

We also find that the acquisition and transfer of knowledge and skills from Mexico to the United States is gendered, reflecting the different social contexts in which women and men acquire their skills at home and abroad. In communities of origin, men have more opportunities to expand their technological skills in construction, manufacturing, and auto repair, and these talents are often rewarded in the U.S. labor market where the demand for them is high. In contrast, women are more likely to acquire and transfer skills associated with their limited domestic and labor market activities, such as cooking, caretaking, and hospitality, abilities that landed them domestic and low-wage service jobs that are undervalued in the United States and offer few opportunities for economic mobility. These gendered occupational findings on skill transfers reaffirm the importance of treating learning and skill development as a lifelong process and understanding the different social contexts in which men and women learn their skills throughout their lives and migration cycles.

For return migrants, the transfer of skills is part of a broader process of local labor market reintegration, and as the narratives of Ricardo and Laura demonstrate, successful transfer is not a guaranteed outcome of migration. The ability to improve one's labor market position upon return is a complex process that depends on numerous social and economic factors, including time abroad, access to local social networks, employer preferences, and the transportability of skills across occupations and industries. Men often cited technical knowledge in construction, carpentry, and mechanics as the most successful skills brought home, while women cited English language and social competences as ranking high among skills transferred. Respondents who transferred skills back home were more likely to benefit in the local labor market through additional reskilling and occupational mobility than those who did not.

But as the narratives of Ricardo and Laura also demonstrate, it is impossible to account for all the factors that go into successfully transferring skills. Both Laura and Ricardo returned to work in industries in which they had labored in the United States, reflecting their ability to acquire and transfer skills across the migratory circuit. Yet, while Ricardo expressed satisfaction with his business decision, Laura was clearly dissatisfied with her job and was not optimistic about her future in San Miguel de Allende. The divergent paths of Ricardo and Laura also suggest that motivation, luck, happenstance, and risk are involved in the acquisition and transfer of skills, elements that are impossible to capture through social science approaches to migration. It is probable that Mac, the owner of the Chinese restaurant in Chicago, recognized a desire to learn and a work ethic that persuaded him to invest in teaching his assistant how to cook, followed by a satisfaction with his mentorship that propelled him to give Ricardo used equipment. Without the equipment it is unclear whether Ricardo would have launched his enterprise. It is also possible that Laura's inability to locate the job she wanted was due to factors other than gender discrimination, given that other women in the sample reported successful English and customer service skill transfers in the expatriate community of San Miguel de Allende. Nonetheless, it is clear that the job searching and entrepreneurial moves Ricardo and Laura made in Guanajuato relied on the courage to take risks and the experiences and skills obtained through migration.

ASSESSING SOCIAL MOBILITY ACROSS THE MIGRATORY CIRCUIT

Thus far, we have investigated how modes of learning and knowledge transfers shape labor market experiences at each stage of the migratory circuit, before, while abroad, and upon return. In this remaining chapter we broaden the analysis and assess migrants' cumulative and relative welfare gains, relying on both subjective and objective measures of well-being and labor mobility. The first dimension of social mobility listed in Table 6.1 is a subjective measure and strong predictor of well-being—job satisfaction.[4] Two findings are worth noting: the overall high levels of job satisfaction before, during, and after migration, and the percentages in the sample reporting that job satisfaction was highest in the U.S. labor market. Our qualitative interviews in Guanajuato reveal that high levels of job satisfaction in the United States are associated with different dimensions of working abroad: earning higher wages, learning new skills, receiving rewards and recognition for existing skills, and more job autonomy, the latter a factor especially mentioned by women. As we reported in chapter 4, 70 percent of the sample held only one or two jobs in the United States, a statistic of sig-

TABLE 6.1

Indicators of social mobility across the migratory circuit

Social Mobility Indicators	Before Migrating		In the United States		On Return	
	Men (n=168)	*Women (n=22)*	*Men (n=171)*	*Women (n=28)*	*Men (n=161)*	*Women (n=20)*
Satisfied with job	69%	78%	84%	89%	73%	76%
Transitioned to a higher-skilled job[a]	32%	27%	39%	27%	29%	44%
Mean skill level[b]	1.8	1.5	1.8	1.4	2.1	1.6

[a] Among those who had more than one job at any given stage.

[b] 1=work that requires little training and involves one repetitive task; 2=work that requires experience and formal or informal training. Involves multitasking or mastery of one specific skill; 3=work is based on extensive occupational mobility over time and mastering of all skills within an occupation through extensive formal or informal training. (See Table 1.1 for more discussion of skill codes and definitions.)

nificant job stability that we, in turn, associate with high levels of satisfaction.[5] The cases of Ricardo and Laura, featured in this chapter's opening vignette, illustrate many of these facets. Both Laura and Ricardo derived much satisfaction and enhanced dignity and self-esteem from the new cooking skills they acquired in the United States, so much so that they sought a similar creative opportunity upon return. Needless to say, high levels of job satisfaction do not exclude the exploitive work conditions many migrants encounter because of limited English, unauthorized legal status, and lax (and at times nonexistent) enforcement of labor laws.[6]

The second indicator of social mobility in Table 6.1, "Transitioned to a higher skilled job," reflects occupational mobility associated with skill transfers and in our opinion is the most direct evidence of migrant agency and job jumping. According to the literature, immigrant workers may try to escape exploitation, discrimination, and blocked mobility in the secondary labor market by shifting back and forth between jobs in the informal and ethnic economies, but rarely do they experience real economic mobility.[7] In contrast, we find that roughly one-third of our sample transitioned to higher-skilled and more-prestigious prestigious jobs across the migratory circuit, and these transitions were found to be significantly associated with job skill transfers. Men's moves to better paid, more skilled, and more prestigious occupations were greatest in the United States. This reflects the craft skills that men brought with them from Mexico, along with their greater occupational choices and skill opportunities relative to women, who entered the U.S. labor market as domestics, chambermaids, and food-preparation workers. But men also gained from reskilling in the United States, especially in automotive and construction work. In these industries, men were introduced to new building and manufacturing techniques and learned to work with more sophisticated and efficient tools, which enabled occupational mobility while abroad.

While some women moved on to higher-skilled and more prestigious jobs in the United States, many remained trapped in low-wage domestic and hospitality work. As Table 6.1 shows, their occupational mobility levels remained flat while abroad. On the other hand, upon return women trumped men, reflecting their ability to mobilize their English language capital and social skills learned abroad to land better jobs at home. Reintegration into the Mexican labor market was more difficult for women than men, but most women appeared to benefit economically and socially from migration. Women were well aware of the difficulties of labor market reintegration, which is why they were less enthusiastic about their return compared to men.[8]

Some faced institutional discrimination because of age; for others, it took time to market their English language capital and interpersonal and customer service skills acquired in the United States. As a result, many of the women, upon return, first entered traditional jobs requiring few skills, such as domestic service, but some managed to transition to higher-skilled jobs requiring multitasking, such as management and customer service or English. In some of our rural research sites, several of the women job jumped from relatively low-wage service jobs to higher-paying and more prestigious positions as English language teachers in local primary schools. English language capital also enhanced their social status in the community and increased self-esteem and confidence among the women who could apply it to their jobs in Mexico.

Finally, as Table 6.1 also shows, both men and women experienced a modest growth in their skill levels across the migratory circuit, moving from less skilled jobs characterized by repetitive tasks, such as dishwasher and leather cutter, to more skilled jobs defined as those that involve multitasking or the mastery of a specific skill (see table 1.1 for skill-level definitions).

THEORETICAL AND METHODOLOGICAL IMPLICATIONS

Our findings have wide implications not only for how we conceptualize and measure skills among many migrants but also how we think about inequality, economic mobility, and social change in migration and labor studies. Although scholars have studied migration as the outcome of structural transformations and deep-rooted economic dislocations, this book shows that migration also functions as a fundamental driver of social change. The transitions we identified in chapter 5 attest to the power of migration to foster social and occupational mobility upon return to the home country. While the connection between U.S.-bound sojourning and social mobility is not new, it is a dimension of international migration that has not been sufficiently analyzed. During the Bracero Program era, many return migrants used their savings to finance their move from rural areas to medium and large cities in Mexico.[9] Instead of investing their earnings in farms, former *braceros* purchased plots of land and homes in urban areas. International migration fostered, at least in part, the urbanization of Mexican society by providing the means to sustain internal mobility.[10] For these return migrants, rural to urban migration also signified an industrial and occupational shift from agriculture to urban jobs in construction and manufacturing. Our findings echo similar and highly consequential transformations for present-day Mexico. With new skills and, at times, capital in hand, return migrants are transitioning from manual occupations to service jobs, to higher skilled occupations within a given industry, and from salaried occupations to self-employment as entrepreneurs.

By engaging the international migration, labor studies, and human capital scholarship with the literature on knowledge and learning, we have been able to explain how Mexican migrants with low levels of education and other forms of human capital acquire and mobilize skills across the migratory circuit. Unlike professional or skilled migrants whose human capital is largely acquired in formal learning environments leading to credentialed and codified knowledge, migrants with low levels of education acquire most of their skills informally through interaction and observation both on and off the job. This is not to say that migrants with formal credentials do not acquire some skills informally prior to migration, but the point we are emphasizing here is that for migrants with low levels of formal education, job skills are socially constructed and learned primarily in informal settings, such as household-based businesses and community projects, rather than classrooms and officially recognized programs, and thus are often hidden skills. It is therefore especially important that the assessment of migrant economic and social gains based on models of human capital must account for the acquisition of lifelong human capital. Engaging the literature on learning and knowledge transactions also sheds light on social, methodological, and practical competences that migrants acquire in their workplaces. As we have shown in this book, the acquisition of competences is not limited to the skilled, but is dispersed across educational levels, jobs, and labor markets. The migrants in our study also returned home with enhanced social and personal skills developed in new work environments in the U.S. labor market.

The results of this study demonstrate that so-called unskilled and low-skilled migrants possess and deploy skills, learn new ones while abroad, and transfer those skills to the home country economy upon return. Why then do scholars, policy makers, and the public insist on referring to these workers as unskilled or low skilled? As we argued at the beginning of this book, migrants with low levels of formal education and performing jobs shunned by natives are ascribed lack of skill as a social category.[11] In that sense, the terms unskilled and even low skilled are part of a lexicon of inequality that justifies lower wages, bad working conditions, and marginal labor rights. Categorizing migrant workers as unskilled and ignoring the qualifications they acquire and mobilize through the process of migration reinforces inequality. A broad theoretical discussion about the unequal treatment of workers in the labor market requires understanding how and why the skills of the so-called unskilled remain invisible and how this invisibility is compounded by variables such as legal status, nationality, gender, and age. The recognition of these skills is part and parcel of the revalorization of the work done by migrants with low levels of formal education.

Our findings also have implications not only for how migration scholars define human capital but also for how social scientists more generally measure skill levels, relying primarily on observable and easy-to-measure skills included in census data and large secondary datasets. Our methodological approach, including surveys, in-depth interviews, and worksite observations on both sides of the border, has allowed us to examine the cumulative process of skill development and skill transfers across occupations and all stages of the migratory circuit: before migration, while abroad, and upon return. At the same time, our concept of *lifelong human capital* enables us to capture a range of indicators for hard-to-measure skills. Moreover, although most migration research categorizes migrants as skilled or unskilled, we found that many migrants are able to advance from low or apprentice-level skills to semiskilled and increasingly highly skilled jobs as a result of the skills they acquire across the migratory circuit. In a similar vein, traditional scholarship identifies migrants with only primary levels of education as "unskilled," yet formal education, even if limited to a few years, can be important in the acquisition and application of certain technical and language skills. Thus, classifying individuals into a "less than primary school category," as is usually done in empirical research, may miss the diversity within that group. Since most surveys do contain information on the years of schooling, scholars may be better served by using a continuous measure or more refined categories.

Finally, our research also suggests that the occupational and industrial contexts of learning and skill transfers matter for the long-term mobility opportunities of return migrants. On-and off-the-job work experience in construction, metalworking, automotive repair, and English language skills are easily transferrable to the United States and back to Mexico, where demand for these services and skills is high. This is especially the case in large cities with a diverse industrial base and a thriving service economy, including tourism. Other skills are country specific and cannot be transferred (e.g., the techniques used in roofing and some aspects of agriculture and husbandry in the United States not applicable to work in Mexico) or are place specific in that largely urban-based skills are not applicable in *ranchos* and small agricultural towns with a limited industrial base. This could explain in part why returnees to Mexico are increasingly attracted to destinations such as border cities, tourist towns, and large metropolitan areas[12] where their skills may put them at an advantage over non-migrants. If this is the case, then skill transfers are an important but unexplored linkage between internal and international flows.[13]

A lingering question remains, however, one that has enormous policy and theoretical implications: Will those who have successfully transferred skills remain in Mexico? Will those who acquired new skills in the United States but were not able to successfully transfer them back home be compelled to emigrate again? To tease out this complex research question, we plan to return to Guanajuato in 2015, five years after we implemented our study, and re-interview our sample, with an eye toward understanding how family, life-cycle processes, labor markets, and state and local institutions have shaped the lives of the return migrants and how they in turn have shaped their local economies.

POLICY IMPLICATIONS AND SUGGESTIONS

International migration is very much a social process through which migrants learn valuable but hard-to-recognize or measure skills and transfer them across international labor markets to broaden their opportunity structures and facilitate local development. The development of skills takes place in a migratory circuit that is shaped, on the one hand, by individual life course events and, on the other, by the ebb and flow of local, national, and regional labor market demands. As we have shown, many Mexicans migrate to the United States on a temporary and repeated basis with the goal of maximizing earnings to contribute to the household economy. In the United States they are drawn to sectors where demand for low-wage labor remains high—agriculture, manufacturing, construction, hospitality, and other services. Once the work careers of these migrants were complete, kin and cultural familiarity drew many of them back home.

The progressive hardening of the border, however, has interrupted the mobility rhythm of Mexico-U.S. migration, which was long characterized by its circularity. The linking of national security and migration after the September 11 attacks has contributed to the further criminalization of undocumented migration between the two countries. While comprehensive immigration reform should include the collaboration of Mexico and the United States to regularize the long-term undocumented population and decriminalize migration, each country can also develop strong institutions to recognize and valorize the skills of migrant workers with low levels of formal education, prevent labor and human rights abuses, and maximize the social mobility and developmental impact of the skills acquired and transferred through migration.

Debates in and out of Congress ignore the competences migrants bring to the United States and neglect to weigh the value of skills they import from the home country and deploy in U.S. labor markets. Proposals for immigration reform still hinge on the policy goal of attracting immigrants with high levels of formal education and credentials. For example, the two-tiered, merit-based point immigration system introduced in the Border Security, Economic Opportunity, and Immigration Modernization Act, or S. 744, in 2012, heavily weighs on formal education and university degrees, a bias that as we have shown ignores the high level of informal skills that most Mexicans bring to the U.S. labor market, especially to industries like construction that the native born have partially vacated but that has traditionally been fertile ground for the transfer of skills and the acquisition of new ones.

As we have demonstrated in this book, the skills that migrants with low levels of formal human capital possess are varied and hard to measure, ranging from English language and social skills to job-specific tasks. Moreover, these skill sets increase over the course of a migrant's life and migration cycles. The same classification scheme of hard-to-measure skills that we introduced in chapter 1 (see Table 1.1) could also be considered as a tool for screening and classifying migrant skills. Currently, employers who recruit through day labor centers or informal day labor sites request a skill and a migrant is assigned to a job. In most cases, the employer has no knowledge of the migrant's work experience and the migrant is unable to communicate or demonstrate his or her skills because of language barriers. Developing and relying on a prescreening and classification method along the lines that we have created would enable the worker to demonstrate and market her or his lifelong human capital to a potential employer, and thus increase a migrant's bargaining power in negotiating a higher wage and better working conditions. English skill categories, for example, could be expanded to reflect different levels of English language for a specific job task. Similarly, rather than measure work experience through the usual way—time in labor force—migrants could report the specific on-the-job skills and years and positions in a particular occupation, drawing on the classification scheme in Table 1.1.

Needless to say, much of this is contingent on the involvement of institutions, such as day labor centers and workforce development programs, which can adapt and implement this classification. In this regard, in the Los Angeles metropolitan area, the single most important destination for the respondents in our sample, the latest news is not encouraging. As we were completing the final draft of this book, the City of Los Angeles cut funding and ended its contracts with several community organizations administering day labor centers. Two of these labor centers had stopped providing services and several others were facing imminent closure.

Our findings have policy implications for Mexico as well. While we have demonstrated that a majority of migrants transfer skills acquired in the United States when they go home to Mexico, we have also shown that a substantial minority face obstacles to gainfully deploying these skills upon return. The story of Laura at the start of this chapter reflects how despite notable experiences of new skill acquisition and reskilling, return migrants may struggle to find jobs that match their qualifications and even experience gender and age discrimination at the hands of local employers.[14] Unable to make use of these skills, some migrants have to settle for less desirable jobs. The difficulties some return migrants encounter in applying their newly acquired qualifications might be a factor in their decisions to remigrate.[15]

While our study has treated the return as a fairly permanent event, the survey instrument included a remigration question. When asked whether they plan to return to the United States, a few of the younger men answered yes, more of the younger women and seasoned migrants said maybe, but over 60 percent, including the aged, the married, and those with successful transfers, reported a definitive no. In a follow-up open-ended question, respondents revealed the rationale behind their decision, citing family primarily, a successful business or anti-immigrant sentiment secondarily, followed by preference for Mexico as the primary attractions of staying put. Yet, as we have demonstrated in our previous discussion of why people migrate and why people return, decision making as it relates to migration is a complex and ever changing process influenced by social relations, life cycle, and economic opportunities and events at home and abroad. The historical evidence suggests that while some returning migrants experience long-term social mobility, others are unable to overcome the adjustment problems of reintegration.

Also notable in Laura's account at the beginning of this chapter and in the stories of many other migrants featured in this book is the absence of any institutional actor facilitating their reintegration into the Mexican labor market after a long stint abroad. This is not an accident. Mexican governmental institutions play a negligible role in the labor market reintegration of returning migrants. Despite a few symbolic efforts to reintegrate returnees, historically the Mexican government has left reintegration in the hands of the family, local communities, and market forces. Even though return migration is a long-standing characteristic of the Mexico-U.S. migratory system, neither the Mexican government nor the large employers in the private sector have developed policies to assist migrants and to take advantage of the qualifications they have acquired as a result of migration.[16] During the spring of 2014, the federal government launched the Migrant Support Fund (*Fondo de Apoyo a Migrantes*), a program that awards small and short-term grants to facilitate the labor market reintegration of return migrants. The fund seeks to foster collaboration between state and municipal-level agencies and several federal vocational and technical institutions to train migrants and help them launch entrepreneurial ventures, among other specific goals. The program provides a total of 200 million pesos (nearly $15.4 million) to 24 different states in Mexico. Since the program was announced in March of 2014, it was too early (at the time we were completing this book) to determine the impact of this fund.[17]

Interestingly, the notion that Mexico could benefit from the skills temporary migrants acquire in the United States was an integral part of the government's emigration policy during the first half of the twentieth century.[18] Faced with the refusal of the U.S. government to reestablish a temporary worker program after the Bracero Program ended in 1964, Mexican federal authorities largely abandoned their efforts to manage emigration and to actively link return migration and development. By the late 1980s and early 1990s, new economic and political realities, including the signing of NAFTA with the United States and the advent of competitive elections, forced the Mexican government to reconsider its "policy of no policy" toward migration. At the federal level, both PRI and PAN administrations have developed different programs to keep the diaspora population and its organizations engaged with the homeland. In doing so, Mexico has pursued two goals, namely, to keep collective and family remittances flowing back home, and to enlist Mexican and Mexican American organizations in support of its policy objectives in the United States.[19] In recent years, the Mexican government has used its large network of consulates and the Instituto de los Mexicanos en el Exterior (Institute for Mexicans Abroad or IME) to establish programs and partnerships with U.S. institutions to improve the well-being and facilitate the integration of its expatriate population into American society.

These programs and agreements vary significantly in nature and reach, however, and depend on the activism of consuls, the cooperation between different ministries of the Mexican government, and the availability of resources and effective local partners. Questions also linger as to whether these programs actually involve the sustained participation of significant numbers of migrants. As we reported in chapter 3, very few of our Leon respondents had benefited from government programs for migrants. Seven percent had participated in *Bienvenido Paisano,* a largely testimonial program designed to inform departing and return migrants and settled immigrants visiting Mexico about their rights and to protect them against the abuses of corrupt police. Three percent had participated in *Directo a México,* a program created to lower the cost of sending family remittances, and only 1 percent had been involved in the 3x1 program to foster and channel collective remittances mostly to rural areas. Not surprisingly, 82 percent of our respondents said that the Mexican government does not help migrants.

The experience of Mexico's Consul General in Raleigh, North Carolina, Javier Díaz de León, illustrates the difficulties of creating projects that recognize the skills migrants transfer upon return. During his tenure as executive director of IME, Díaz de León attempted to develop a program to certify the skills migrants learn in the U.S. labor market so that employers would readily recognize those competences when the worker returns home. According to Díaz de León, he quickly ran into institutional barriers in Mexico as CONOCER,[20] the department of the Ministry of Public Education (Secretaría de Educación Pública or SEP) in charge of certifying skills, was unwilling to verify abilities and competences learned informally. Instead, CONOCER proposed that returning Mexican workers participate in formal training programs, clearly a mismatch with the way most labor migrants learn and transfer skills.[21]

In 2005, IME launched a pilot program to identify and certify the skills of Mexican migrants in localities in the United States. This program sought to mobilize institutional resources in both countries,[22] to certify the skills of migrant workers in the U.S. labor market, provide the corresponding documentation to the individual, and facilitate the "integration and/or occupational mobility of Mexicans abroad."[23] The pilot program certified dairy operators in Wisconsin and Minnesota, restaurant and construction workers in Texas and Illinois, and hospitality employees in New York. According to figures reported by IME, between 2007 and 2012 only 406 workers had participated in the certification process. This certification program faced several challenges. Identifying and certifying competences are not IME-directed activities. Consequently, IME has not been able to institutionalize the program and has remained a facilitator and coordinator of willing partners. Even though the Mexican government has developed a network of more than 400 adult education centers in the United States called *Plazas Comunitarias* (Community Plazas),[24] these centers operate in widely different settings, ranging from churches to community colleges, and are coordinated by unpaid volunteers. While the *Plazas Comunitarias* could be used to implement a variety of skills certification programs, not all of these centers have the capacity to do so. Needless to say, a *Plaza Comunitaria* established at a community college, a union local, or a trade association facility is more likely to have the necessary know-how to coordinate a certification program compared to a Plaza located at a church or library. Finally, although officials like Díaz de León believe that U.S. certification would benefit workers once they go back to Mexico, the pilot program in question is largely preoccupied with the integration of Mexican migrants in the United States and does not specify mechanisms for skill recognition upon return.[25]

While the Mexican government has a limited capacity to launch and coordinate skill certification programs abroad, it can do much more to develop policies that reintegrate returning migrants to local and regional labor markets and harness the skills acquired in the United States and transferred back home. We argue that individuals, businesses, and local economies can benefit from programs that screen return migrants, identify their skills, and match them with potential employers. Mexico's federal government does not need to undertake this program alone. Over the past two decades, many Mexican states have created centers, institutes, and even local-level secretaries to deal with migrants' issues. Mirroring federal-level policies, some of the newly created institutions have sought to harness the developmental and productivity impact of migrants' collective remittances. Others have tried to intervene in the management of emigration by monitoring and marginally regulating the recruitment of Mexican workers through the H2 temporary visa program.

For example, the state of Nuevo Leon created an office of migrant affairs in 2005 to manage the flow of H2 workers passing through the city of Monterrey, regulate the growing migration industry organizing this flow, and deal with the abuses of recruiters and other intermediaries.[26] In 2010, this office approached the government of Utah to establish an agreement to channel local unemployed workers to jobs in that state. Interestingly, the agreement included a skill certification program through which the state of Nuevo Leon would identify and guarantee the qualifications of prospective workers. It is not far-fetched to think that a similar program could be established to identify the skills acquired after working abroad. More recently, the government of San Luis Potosí has organized events to attract employers and brokers using the H2 visa program to recruit workers in the state. Once again, state and municipal governments in Mexico can also develop programs to connect return migrants with local employers.[27] By using this growing institutional capacity, Mexico's federal and state governments could establish employment information centers run locally by the migrants' affairs institutes to recognize skills and maximize the developmental impact of the qualifications of return migrants.[28]

The Mexican government can also enlist the participation of the private and academic sectors in the effort to reintegrate and utilize the skills of returning migrants, particularly in many of the mid-size cities around the country enjoying rapid economic growth.[29] As the report of the *Binational Dialogue on Mexican Migrants in the U.S. and in Mexico* states, "in these growth centers, there have been marked improvements in the status of returned migrants, with more having formal sector jobs."[30] In these urban centers, the Mexican government can establish partnerships with the private sector to identify and formally certify the skills of return migrants and create jobs that will anchor them to the local economy. As the report continues, "Some [migrants] … return to Mexico in a position of strength, having acquired and reinforced their assets, skills, and institutional know how."[31] It is time for Mexico to acknowledge the hidden skills and the total human capital of its migrant population.

METHODOLOGICAL APPENDIX

Skills of the "Unskilled" is a five-year study based primarily on two stages of exploratory fieldwork, a survey of a representative sample of return migrants in Leon, Guanajuato, and two community case studies. Based on findings from the migrant interviews, we selected 15 work sites in Mexico and the United States to observe informal learning and training, and at these work sites we interviewed employers, supervisors, and workers. In communities in Mexico, we also interviewed officials serving the labor and family needs of return migrants, and in the United States we interviewed members of trade associations along with a selected number of Mexican officials working with Mexicans abroad.

Stage One (2007–09) involved a study of roughly 50 immigrant construction workers in North Carolina, a relatively new immigrant gateway.[1] Between 1990 and 2000, the Latino population of North Carolina grew by 394 percent, numbering 378,963 by the end of the decade. From 2000 to 2008, the Latino population almost doubled, reaching 694,185 and comprising 7.4 percent of the state's population.[2] We selected the construction industry for several reasons. First, at the time of the exploratory stage of our study, 2007–09, the construction and building trade was the fastest growing employer of Mexican immigrants in the state and had become increasingly dependent on immigrant labor in the urban areas of the industry.[3] In the absence of union influence in the South, corporations, management companies, and subcontractors have lowered wages to such a point that construction has become increasingly unattractive to native-born workers. Currently 30 percent of the state's construction workforce is Latino, with estimates reaching as high as 70 percent in some urban areas.[4] Laboring primarily as roofers, bricklayers, general laborers, carpenters, and framers, at the time of our study Latinos earned fairly high wages by North Carolina standards, ranging from $9 to $22 per hour.[5] The potentially high wages, along with the opportunity to apply old skills and learn new ones, makes construction jobs attractive to immigrants who otherwise might have to labor in less rewarding jobs in other immigrant-heavy industries such as hospitality (e.g., restaurant work and housekeeping) and agriculture.

We also selected the construction industry because most jobs in construction depend heavily on learning by observation and interaction rather than formal education and involve multiple levels of skill. For example, in Mexico an *albañil,* or skilled mason, holds a respected job requiring skills in masonry, tile setting, and woodworking, yet the requisite skills are acquired through work experience (observation and on-the-job training) rather than institutional learning. As this industry provides a prime setting in which to study on-the-job skills acquisition and the social context in which it takes place, we conducted a half-dozen worksite observations. From this North Carolina research, we learned that on-the-job skills learning in places of both origin and destination is fundamental to understanding the mobility pathways of immigrants with low levels of traditional human capital. The ability to transfer construction-related skills from their jobs in Mexico and to acquire new ones on the job in North Carolina empowered more than half of the immigrants we interviewed to take the risk and job jump (*brincar*) to apply newly acquired skills and successfully augment wages.

We accessed the construction workers through a variety of venues, connecting with some in public places such as food stands, work sites, parks, flea markets, day labor sites, laundromats, and restaurants. From several of these initial contacts we relied on snowball sampling, a strat-

egy commonly employed for locating hard-to-find or sensitive populations, and a technique two of the authors have long used successfully in
their research on undocumented migrants.[6] The interviews lasted
about one hour each and all were conducted in Spanish by students
and faculty on the research team. Most interviews were recorded;
however, in some instances immigrants requested that we only take
notes. The interviews included 20 open-ended questions covering the
following themes: labor market history in Mexico and the United
States; learning and knowledge sharing in the U.S. labor market; and
psychological, social, and economic dimensions of labor mobility in
the United States. To understand skilled immigrant labor market
experiences in the construction industry, we also relied on interviews
conducted with supervisors and employers, institutional and community actors, including representatives from construction industry associations, training centers, and immigrant advocacy organizations. To
examine skill formation and knowledge sharing at the work site, we
also conducted observations at several residential and commercial
construction projects.

The large majority of the immigrants in the construction sample
arrived after 2005 and came from the Mexican states of Guerrero, Distrito Federal, Veracruz, Guanajuato, and Chiapas.[7] A few came from
small ranchos, but like more recent Mexican immigrants to the United
States, many came from urban areas including Mexico City, Leon,
Guanajuato City, Celaya, and Veracruz. Coming from both urban
and rural labor markets, many of these men possessed varied skill
sets and workplace experiences. In Mexico, the respondents worked
primarily in the construction and agricultural industries (90 percent),
though small numbers also worked in manufacturing and personal
service jobs. Not surprisingly, their U.S. construction jobs were varied
and multiple, making it difficult to group the workers into fixed
occupational categories. Some workers identified themselves as
ayudantes (helpers); others as *albañiles* (skilled masons); others as roofers, bricklayers, painters, electricians, *chirroqueros* (sheetrock workers),
and framers. A few of the men were entrepreneurs, but also worked for
pay for another employer. A number of the men worked for one
employer, but performed side jobs in the informal economy on the

weekend. Many of the workers we interviewed had relatively stable employment, staying with a housing or commercial project for several months. Some managed to follow their employers to various projects in the region, sometimes taking them to other U.S. states in the Southeast. A few shifted between the informal and formal sectors of the industry, working temporarily for one employer for several weeks or months on a project and then returning to a day labor site and working as *jornaleros* (day laborers) until they found another more permanent job with some stability.

Despite their considerable work experience at home and abroad the Mexican component of the construction worker sample possessed relatively low levels of traditional human capital. Close to half (44 percent) of those who responded to the question on education had completed nine or fewer years of education, and an additional 56 percent had some secondary education but had not earned degrees. Overall, the sample's English language skills were minimal. With the exception of 11 workers who attended some high school or technical training at a community college in the United States, the workers reported speaking no or little English. Although we did not directly ask about their legal status in the United States, most volunteered that they entered the country without authorization.

Based on our initial findings, that many migrants in the construction industry bring some skills with them and return home with additional ones, it was only natural to extend the exploratory stage of the study to examine skill transfers back to Mexico. Thus Stage Two (2009) involved exploratory field research in Guanajuato, Mexico. We selected Guanajuato, first, because we had network connections in the state; second, because it includes both rural and urban areas that are well-established migrant-sending areas; and third, because of its dynamic yet uneven development and diverse economic structures, features we sought for the variety of skill transfers we might find. In contrast to other states in Mexico, Guanajuato has a system of cities of varied size and economic specialization, with some urban areas structured around services and others organized around manufacturing for the international or the internal market. Guanajuato is home to traditional industries such as shoe and garment manufacturing, and is part of the Bajío region, the historic granary of Mexico. In 2009, a team of researchers traveled to Guanajuato and conducted lengthy interviews with 79 return female and male migrants, working in different occupations, industries, and communities, ranging from cities to small rural villages. As in Stage One, we recruited respondents at public places, work sites, and through snowball sampling. Realizing that industrial context was likely to influence the types of skills that could be transferred from the United States, we interviewed return migrants in 12 communities selected for diverse demographics: in the state's largest city, Leon; in small ranchos of less than two thousand in the *municipios* of Irapuato, Ocampo, Apaceo el Grande, Valle de Santiago, and San Luis de la Paz; and in small to medium-size cities in the *municipios* of Guanajuato, Santa Cruz de Juventino Rosas, and Dolores Hidalgo.

The interviews included 20 open-ended questions covering the following themes: labor market history in Mexico and the United States; learning and knowledge sharing in the U.S. labor market; and skill transfers from the U.S. to the Mexican labor market. As in Stage One, we also relied on interviews conducted with supervisors and conducted observations at several residential and commercial construction projects. Coming from both urban and rural labor markets and working in multiple jobs across the migratory circuit, many of these men possessed varied skill sets and workplace experiences. In Mexico, the respondents worked primarily in construction as welders and masons; in manufacturing (shoe and auto) where they labored as machinists; in service where they worked in restaurants and individual homes as cleaners; and in agriculture. In the United States, they worked primarily in construction, manufacturing, and service jobs.

Despite their considerable work experience at home and abroad, the return migrants possessed relatively low levels of traditional human capital. More than half of the sample had completed nine or fewer years of education. Overall, the sample's English language skills varied, reflecting the types of jobs they held in the United States. Many of the men who worked in construction in the U.S. labor market learned very little English, while some of the women who worked in homes as caregivers or in hospitality as chambermaids learned considerable English and were able to transfer their language capital to better jobs upon return.

From this second stage of exploratory research we discovered the importance of off-the-job learning to working-class Mexicans with low levels of traditional human capital. Indeed, it was in the context of family and community that many of the skills transferred to the United States were learned. We further found that many migrants reskilled in the United States, learning to work with new technology and approaching work tasks in new ways. We also found that some skills are place specific and cannot be transferred to Mexico (e.g., certain techniques used in roofing, sheetrocking, and some aspects of agriculture and husbandry), while others are easily transferable (e.g., skills in metalworking and automotive repair, and English language skills that often create economic opportunities upon return). We also identified a number of nontechnical skills that migrants are exposed to in their U.S. jobs and bring back with them from the United States, such productive intangibles as customer service, punctuality, and organizational and leadership skills. As expected, we found that the industrial context of return matters. For example, some migrants who returned to their small rural communities were unable to apply their customer service and language skills in these limited arenas and so opted to migrate to tourist towns and international business centers where their new skills could be applied to promote economic opportunity. Recognizing the importance of industrial context for skill transfers, in 2012 we conducted two case studies of transferability, one in a rural village in Guanajuato and the other in the Guanajuato tourist town of San Miguel de Allende. These case studies, which involved lengthy interviews with 20 return migrants at each site, enabled us to examine further the relevance of local institutions and industrial contexts of return for encouraging and supporting skill transfers.

Stages One and Two revealed the acquisition of skills in Guanajuato and in North Carolina's construction industry, but neither captured the learning careers of migrants nor the entire process of transnational human capital acquisition and its implications for economic mobility. The only way to truly understand these processes was to interview the migrants across the migratory circuit, and identify the skills learned and mobilized at each stage. Thus, in Stage Three we drew on our qualitative findings and developed a survey instrument that would retrospectively capture the skill acquisitions of women and men across the migratory circuit, detailing work experiences, learning techniques, and skill transfers before migration, while abroad, and upon return. Recognizing the importance of industrial context, we selected Leon, Guanajuato, as our strategic research site to interview a random sample of 200 return migrants.

Obtaining a random sample of return migrants in the city of Leon was problematic. Due to the low proportion of return migrants in the city (roughly estimated at around 1 percent of the total Leon population), we would have had to survey a prohibitive number of households in order to reach the targeted sample size. So, to obtain a representative sample of return migrants we first identified neighborhoods in the city where we had a higher probability of finding them. The Mexican Population Census provided us with a good proxy for the presence of return migrants at the block level (*manzana* in Spanish). Indeed, it includes a question on whether any current household members were living abroad five years ago. We then drew a random sample of the blocks where return migrants were identified in the census. In the end, a total of 77 *manzanas* were visited in order to obtain a sample of 200 return migrants. We had to exclude a handful of selected *manzanas* that were considered unsafe to survey in order not to expose our students. Those *manzanas* were identified thanks to a city map recently edited by a local newspaper, which identified neighborhoods where dangerous street gangs were active.

A team of six students from the University of Guanajuato, along with the authors, administered the survey from June to October 2010. We went door-to-door and screened the selected *manzanas* in Leon for return migrants. In order to perform the screening, the students would first ask whether a member of the household was a return migrant, and in cases where there were none, whether they knew one in the *manzana*. The survey's 150 closed-ended answers, which capture detailed job and migration histories and skill acquisition and transfers, were coded into STATA. The responses to an additional 30 open-ended questions were transcribed into a word processing file and organized by theme. Finally, to conclude the interview, each respondent relayed, via a voice recorder, a personal narrative of lifelong work experience and skill development and transfers. These narratives were also transcribed and then organized by gender, occupation, industry, and by additional themes as they emerged from a review of the data.

QUESTIONNAIRE: SURVEY ON RETURN MIGRATION TO GUANAJUATO

A: Information to be completed by the interviewer, just before or after the interview.

1. Interview Number:
2. Interviewer:
3. Date and time of the interview:
   a. Day:
   b. Month:
   c. Year:
   d. Hour and Minute:
4. Municipality where interview took place:
   a. Excel sample codes:
   b. Location:
   c. Agep (geographic unit of the statistics office):
   d. Block:
5. Where did the interview take place?
   a. Home of the interviewee
   b. Workplace of the interviewee
   c. Church
   d. Store
   e. Street or park
   f. Other
6. How was the interviewee contacted?
   a. Recommended by friend or family
   b. Recommended by a manager or coworker at work
   c. Recommended by another former migrant

    d. Recommended by another interviewee (non-ex-migrant)

    e. Recommended by a former migrant living in United States

    f. Recommended by a community leader (e.g., a priest)

    g. Interviewer met him on the street or another place

    h. He / she was part of the 2003 IPLANEG survey

    i. Found and screened on the selected block

    j. Other

7. Name of the interviewee:

    a. Age of the interviewee:

    b. Sex: Male / Female

8. Neighborhood and municipality of the interviewee:

    a. Neighborhood:

    b. Municipality:

B: Work History in Mexico Before Migrating

I am going to begin the interview by asking you about the work you did in Mexico before migrating to the United States.

9. What jobs did you have before migrating to the U.S.? Include the name of the workplace if possible (company, institution, etc.).

    a. No Jobs

    b. Job 1:

    c. Job 2:

    d. Job 3:

    e. Job 4:

    f. Job 5:

Note to interviewer: You must proceed as follows:

If he / she didn't have any jobs, go directly to #46 in the "Migration History" section.

If he / she had 3 or more jobs, read this aloud to the interviewee:

Now we will ask you in detail about your first and last paid jobs in Mexico that lasted more than 6 months before migrating to the United States. If the first and last did not last 6 months, then we will ask about the jobs that lasted the longest.

FIRST JOB

10. We will start with the first job. What was your first job? (Interviewer: write the job number from previous question. Include occupation and if possible the name of the workplace / company / institution)

11. What were your tasks, activities, and work responsibilities in this job?

12. Was the place where you worked owned by a foreigner or an ex-migrant?

    a. Yes

    b. No

13. How long did it take you to find this job?

    a. Years:

    b. Months:

    c. Days:

14. Where was the job located?

    a. State:

    b. Municipality:

15. How did you get this first job?

    a. Friends or relatives recommended you to the employer.

    b. Friends or relatives told you about the job.

    c. You were hired by a friend or relative.

    d. You approached the employer.

    e. The employer approached you.

    f. Classified advertisements

    g. Other

16. How much did you earn in Mexican pesos? (Frequency code: 1=Day, 2=Week, 3=Month, 4=Year)

    a. Salary when you started:

    b. Specify if this salary was per day, week, month, or year:

    c. Salary when you ended:

    d. Specify if this salary was per day, week, month, or year:

17. What were the starting and finishing dates of this job?

    a. From: _____ Month _____ Year

    b. Until: _____ Month _____ Year

Interviewer: If he / she had only one job before migrating, go to #27.

LAST JOB BEFORE MIGRATING

FOR THE FIRST TIME

18. What was your last job in Mexico? Please give a detailed description.

19. What were your tasks, activities, and work responsibilities in this job?

20. Was the place where you worked owned by a foreigner or an ex-migrant?

    a. Yes

    b. No

21. If yes, who was the owner?

    a. A former Mexican migrant

    b. A foreigner. Nationality: _____

22. How did you get this last job?

    a. Friends or relatives recommended you to the employer.

    b. Friends or relatives told you about the job.

    c. You were hired by a friend or relative.

    d. You approached the employer.

    e. The employer approached you.

    f. Classified advertisements

    g. Other

23. How long did it take you to find this job

    a. Years

    b. Months

    c. Days:

24. Where was the job located?

    a. State:

    b. Municipality:

25. How much did you earn in Mexican pesos? (Frequency code: 1=Day, 2=Week, 3=Month, 4=Year)

    a. Salary when you started:

    b. Specify if this salary was per day, week, month, or year:

    c. Salary when you ended:

    d. Specify if this salary was per day, week, month, or year:

26. What were the starting and finishing dates of this job?

    a. From: _____ Month _____ Year

    b. Until: _____ Month _____ Year

27. Did you learn new tasks and activities in this job?

   a. Yes

   b. No

If no, go to #30.

29. How did you learn these new tasks and activities? Please choose all that apply.

   a. Observing at work.

   b. My boss / manager or coworker taught me.

   c. My boss / manager paid for me go to a school to learn.

   d. I learned at school (primary school, secondary school, technical school / high school).

   e. Other

30. Did you manage or supervise other workers at this job?

   a. Yes

   b. No

31. Did you ever receive a promotion or move up in this job?

   a. Yes

   b. No

If no, go to #33.

32. What was your new position? Why did you get moved up to this new position? Was there an increase in salary with this move? If yes, how much?

33. Of the following, please tell which of the following were important in this job. Choose all that apply.

   a. Punctuality

   b. Quality of service

   c. Teamwork

   d. Taking initiative

   e. Commitment to finish the job (even if you had to work extra hours without pay)

   f. Management of assignments and responsibilities assigned by the boss

   g. Safety of workers (knowing how to operate machinery, knowing what to do in case of emergency)

   h. Importance of competition

i. If other, please specify.

34. How much do you think your skills increased or improved in this job?

   a. They did not improve.

   b. They improved some.

   c. They improved a lot.

35. Do you think the skills and experience you gained in this job transferred to your current job?

   a. Yes

   b. No

   c. If yes, how much did the skills transfer? (1=No transfer. 2=Some transfer. 3=High transfer.)

36. Which of the following best describes your level of satisfaction with this job in Mexico?

   a. Satisfied

   b. Indifferent

   c. Unsatisfied

37. *(Interviewer: Fill in the blank with the answer to the above.)* Why do you say that you felt _____ in this job?

38. Do you think that you learned to do other things, tasks, activities, or new skills outside of work while you were in Mexico? (For example, fixing broken things at home, building a home for your family, etc.)

   a. Yes

   b. No

If no, go to #40.

39. What skills did you learn and how?

40. Did you happen to own a business before migrating? Did you start your own business?

   a. Yes

   b. No

If no, go to #46.

41. What type of business was it? In what year did you start your business?

42. Where did you get the money you used to start your business?

   a. With my own money, belongings, or savings.

   b. My family in Mexico helped me. If so, who:

   c. My family in the U.S. helped me. If so, who:

   d. I got a loan from someone outside of my family. If so, from where? (bank, loan company, friend, etc.)

   e. Other

43. How much money did you use to start your business?

44. In this business, how many people did you employ?

If "0" go to #46.

45. How many of these employees were ex-migrants?

C. Migration History

Now we are going to talk about your migration history.

46. How many times have you gone to the U.S. to work in total?

47. In which year did you go to the U.S. for the first time?

48. Where did you go?

   a. State:

   b. City:

49. Why did you go there?

   a. I had family or friends there.

   b. I knew other Mexicans who lived there.

   c. I knew there were work opportunities.

   d. Someone informally contracted me, and I didn't have a visa.

   e. Someone formally contracted me, and I had a visa.

   f. Other

50. How long did you stay the first time?

   a. Months:

   b. Years:

51. In what year did you go to the U.S. for the last time?

52. Where did you go?

   a. State:

   b. City:

53. Why did you go there?

   a. I had family or friends there.

    b. I knew other Mexicans who lived there.

    c. I knew there were work opportunities.

    d. Someone informally contracted me, and I didn't have a visa.

    e. Someone formally contracted me, and I had a visa.

    f. Other

54. How long do you normally stay in the U.S. each time you go? Please specify in months.

55. How long did you work in the U.S. in total?

    a. Years:

    b. Months:

56. Can you give me three reasons you left Mexico the last time you left?

    a. Reason 1:

    b. Reason 2:

    c. Reason 3:

57. Have you ever been deported from the U.S.?

    a. Yes

    b. No

If no, go to #61.

58. How many times have you been deported?

59. When were you most recently deported?

    a. Year:

    b. State:

60. Why do you think you were deported? Explain in detail.

61. Do you have plans to return to the U.S.?

    a. Yes

    b. No

If no, go to #63.

62. Which of the following reasons explains your decision to return to the U.S.? Choose all that apply.

    a. I haven't found work in Mexico.

    b. I would like to learn more things and skills in the U.S.

    c. I want to rejoin my family in the U.S.

    d. I want to make and save more money.

    e. Other

Continue to #64.

63. Which of the following reasons explains your decision not to return to the U.S.? Choose all that apply.

    a. The recession in the U.S.

    b. The current anti-immigrant environment in the U.S.

    c. I don't have enough money for the trip.

    d. I reached my goal last time I returned from the U.S., and I don't need to go back.

    e. Family reasons

    f. Other

64. The first time you went to the U.S., did you know what job you would do?

    a. Yes

    b. No

65. Did they contract you in your first job because of your skills or work experience that you acquired in Mexico (knowledge, way of doing things, techniques, etc.)? If yes, explain why, what you knew how to do, how your boss knew of your skills, etc.

D. Work Experience in the U.S.

Now, let's talk about your work experience in the U.S.

66. What were all of the jobs you had in the U.S.? Include the name of the place you worked if possible (company / institution).

    a. No Jobs

    b. Job 1:

    c. Job 2:

    d. Job 3:

    e. Job 4:

    f. Job 5:

Interviewer: Decide which is appropriate.

If he / she had no job, ask why and go to #109.

If he/she had 3 or more jobs, read the following to the interviewee:

Now I will ask you in detail about your first and last paid jobs in the U.S. that lasted more than 6 months. If they did not last more than 6 months, I will ask about those that lasted the longest.

FIRST JOB

67. We will start with the first job. What was your first job in the United States? (Interviewer: Include occupation and, if available, the name of the job, company, institution, etc.)

68. In this first job, please tell me what you did. What were your jobs and responsibilities?

69. From which date to which date did you work in this first job?

    a. From: (month and year)

    b. To: (month and year)

70. How did you get your first job?

    a. A friend or relative recommended you to the employer.

    b. A friend or relative talked to you about the job.

    c. I was hired by a friend or relative.

    d. You approached the employer (at the work site, at a day labor site where immigrants gather and employers come searching for them).

    e. Classified advertisement

    f. Other

71. How long did it take you to find this job?

    a. Years:

    b. Months:

    c. Days:

72. Where was the job located?

    a. State:

    b. City:

73. How much did you make in dollars in this job? Please specify how frequently you were paid. (Frequency Code: 1=Day 2=Weeks 3=Month 4=Year).

    a. Starting salary:

    b. Ending salary:

Now, I am going to ask you a few questions about the money you sent to your family during the time you were working your first job.

74. How much money did you send to Mexico? (Interviewer: Make sure to specify if the quantity is in pesos or dollars.)

75. How often did you send money to Mexico?

    a. Each week

b. Every 2 weeks

c. Every month

d. Irregularly

e. Other

76. Who did you send the money to in Mexico? Specify relationship.

77. Can you tell me, more or less, how much the person you sent money to spent on the following:

a. Household consumption (services, food, school, health):

b. Personal investment (personal business, home, cars, etc.):

c. Savings:

d. Community (for community works where you live):

e. Debt:

f. Other: (Specify, and include amount)

Interviewer: If interviewee did not have another job, go to #90.

LAST JOB IN THE U.S.

78. What was your last job in the U.S.? Include the name of the place you worked if possible (company / institution).

79. In this last job, please tell me what you did. What were your jobs and responsibilities?

80. From which date to which date did you work in this first job?

a. From: (month and year)

b. To: (month and year)

81. Why did you change jobs? Choose all that apply.

a. More money

b. I moved to another city for personal reasons.

c. I moved to another city or state to look for job opportunities.

d. I wanted to learn new skills.

e. I was fired.

f. Other

82. How did you get this job?

a. A friend or relative recommended you to the employer.

b. A friend or relative talked to you about the job.

c. I was hired by a friend or relative.

d. You approached the employer (at the work site, at a day labor site where immigrants gather and employers come searching for them).

e. Classified advertisement

f. Other

83. How long did it take you to find this job?

a. Years:

b. Months:

c. Days:

84. Where was the job located?

a. State:

b. City:

85. How much did you make in dollars in this job? Please specify how frequently you were paid. (Frequency Code: 1=Day 2=Weeks 3=Month 4=Year).

a. Starting salary:

b. Ending salary:

Now, I am going to ask you a few questions about the money you sent to your family during the time you were working in this job.

86. How much money did you send to Mexico? (Interviewer: Make sure to specify if the quantity is in pesos or dollars.)

87. How often did you send money to Mexico?

a. Each week

b. Every 2 weeks

c. Every month

d. Irregularly

e. Other

88. Who did you send the money to in Mexico? Specify relationship.

89. Can you tell me, more or less, how much the person you sent money to spent on the following:

a. Household consumption (services, food, school, health):

b. Personal investment (personal business, home, cars, etc.):

c. Savings:

d. Community (for community works where you live):

e. Debt:

f. Other: (Specify, and include amount)

90. Which of the following best describes your level of satisfaction with this job?
    a. Satisfied
    b. Indifferent
    c. Unsatisfied
91. (*Interviewer: Fill in the blank with the answer to the above.*) Why do you say that you felt _____ in this job?

ABOUT INTERVIEWEE'S TOTAL
EXPERIENCE IN THE U.S.

92. Thinking of all the jobs you had in the U.S., do you think your work experience in Mexico before migrating helped you?
    a. Yes
    b. No
94. Do you feel that your manager / boss noticed and rewarded you in some way for your abilities, knowledge, techniques, way of working, etc.?
    a. Yes
    b. No

If no, go to #96.

95. What happened when he / she noticed? Choose all that apply.
    a. You got a raise.
    b. You got a promotion or more responsibilities at work.
    c. Your boss / manager asked you to teach other workers.
    d. Your boss / manager gave you more liberty in your work (he / she didn't supervise you as frequently anymore).
    e. Your boss / manager adopted or copied your way of completing tasks. If yes, could you give an example?
    f. Other
96. Did you learn new tasks and activities in the U.S.?
    a. Yes
    b. No
97. How did you learn to do these tasks and activities? Choose all that apply.
    a. Observing at work

  b. A boss/manager or coworker taught me.

  c. My boss/manager paid for me go to a school to learn.

  d. I learned at school (primary school, secondary school, technical school, professional school, or university).

  e. Other

98. Of the following, which were the most important in the U.S. in general? Choose all that apply.

  a. Punctuality

  b. Quality of service

  c. Teamwork

  d. Taking initiative

  e. Commitment to finish the job (even if you had to work extra hours without pay)

  f. Management of assignments and responsibilities assigned by the boss/manager

  g. Safety of workers (knowing how to operate machinery, knowing what to do in case of emergency)

  h. Importance of competition

  i. Other. Please Specify:

99. How much do you think your skills increased or improved in the U.S.? (1=They did not improve. 2=They improved some. 3=They improved a lot.)

100. Do you think your skills and work experience gained in the U.S. transferred to your current job?

  a. Yes.

  b. No.

  c. If yes, how much did the skills transfer? (1=No transfer. 2=Some transfer. 3=High transfer.)

101. Did you learn other skills or tasks outside of work in the U.S.?

  a. Yes

  b. No

103. Did you happen to own a business in the U.S.? Did you start your own business?

  a. Yes

  b. No

If no, go to #109.

104. What type of business was it?
105. Where did you get the money you used to start your business?
106. How much money did you use to start your business?
107. In this business, how many people did you employ?

If "0" go to #46.

108. How many of these employees were migrants?

E. Work History in Mexico after Returning from the U.S.

Now, we are going to talk about your work in Mexico since your return.

109. Why did you return to Mexico this last time? Choose all that apply.
    a. Family reasons
    b. I lost my job and I couldn't find another one.
    c. I was deported.
    d. I reached my original goal for migrating (I made the money I planned to make).
    e. Other

110. When did you return to Mexico?
    a. Month:
    b. Year:

111. What are all the jobs you have had since returning to Mexico from the U.S.? Include the name of the workplace if possible (company, institution, etc.).
    a. No Jobs
    b. Job 1:
    c. Job 2:
    d. Job 3:
    e. Job 4:
    f. Job 5:

Interviewer: Decide which is appropriate.
  If he / she had no job, ask why and go to #139.
  If he / she had 3 or more jobs, read the following to the interviewee:

Now, I will ask you in detail about your first job since returning that has lasted more than 6 months (or the job that has lasted longest) and your current job.

112. Let's start with the first job. What was your first job upon returning to Mexico? (Interviewer: include the occupation and if possible the name of the workplace, for example company, institution, etc.)

113. In this first job, please tell me what you did. What were your jobs and responsibilities? (*Turn on the recorder and take as many notes as you can.*)

114. Was the place you worked owned by a foreigner or an ex-migrant?
    a. Yes
    b. No

115. How long did it take you to find this job?
    a. Years:
    b. Months:
    c. Days:

116. Where was the job located?
    a. State:
    b. Municipality:

117. How did you get this last job?
    a. Friends or relatives recommended you to the employer.
    b. Friends or relatives told you about the job.
    c. You were hired by a friend or relative.
    d. You approached the employer.
    e. The employer approached you.
    f. Classified advertisements
    g. Other

118. How much did you earn in Mexican pesos? (Frequency code: 1=Day, 2=Week, 3=Month, 4=Year)
    a. Salary when you started:
    b. Specify if this salary was per day, week, month, or year:
    c. Salary when you ended:
    d. Specify if this salary was per day, week, month, or year:

119. From what date to what date were you in this first job?
    a. From: _____ Month _____ Year
    b. Until: _____ Month _____ Year

Interviewer: If the interviewee has only had one job since returning from the U.S., continue to #131.

CURRENT JOB

120. What is your current job?

121. What do you do in your current job? What are your tasks, activities, and work responsibilities in this job?

122. Do you think the skills and experience you gained in your first job since returning transfer to your current job?

    a. Yes

    b. No

    c. If yes, how much did the skills transfer? (1=No transfer. 2=Some transfer. 3=High transfer.)

123. Is your current workplace owned by a foreigner or ex-migrant?

    a. Yes

    b. No

If no, go to #125.

124. To whom does it belong?

    a. A Mexican ex-migrant

    b. A foreigner. Nationality:

125. How long did it take you to find this job?

    a. Years:

    b. Months:

    c. Days:

126. Where is your job located?

    a. State:

    b. Municipality:

127. How did you get this last job?

    a. Friends or relatives recommended you to the employer.

    b. Friends or relatives told you about the job.

    c. You were hired by a friend or relative.

    d. You approached the employer.

    e. The employer approached you.

    f. Classified advertisements

    g. Other

128. How much did you earn in Mexican pesos? (Frequency code: 1=Day, 2=Week, 3=Month, 4=Year)

    a. Salary when you started:

    b. Specify if this salary was per day, week, month, or year:

    c. Salary when you ended:

    d. Specify if this salary was per day, week, month, or year:

129. Do you think your work experience in the U.S. helped you get this job?

    a. Yes

    b. No

130. Do you think your work experience in the U.S. helps you in this job?

    a. Yes

    b. No

132. Does your boss know you worked in the U.S.?

    a. Yes

    b. No

133. Do you think that your current boss values your knowledge, skills, new ways of doing things, etc. that you learned in the U.S. and brought with you back to Mexico?

    a. Yes

    b. No

If no, go to #135.

134. Explain how he / she shows that he / she values these things. Choose all that apply.

    a. You got a raise.

    b. You got a promotion or more responsibilities at work.

    c. Your boss asked you to teach other workers.

    d. You boss gave you more liberty in your work (he / she didn't supervise you as frequently anymore).

    e. Your boss adopted or copied your way of completing tasks. If yes, could you give an example? (*Turn on recorder and take brief notes.*)

    f. Other

135. Of the following, which are the most important in your current job? Choose all that apply.

a. Punctuality

b. Quality of service

c. Teamwork

d. Taking initiative

e. Commitment to finish the job (even if you had to work extra hours without pay)

f. Management of assignments and responsibilities assigned by the boss

g. Safety of workers (knowing how to operate machinery, knowing what to do in case of emergency)

h. Importance of competition

i. Other. Please Specify:

136. Do you think that your skills and work experience gained in your first job back in Mexico transfer to your current job?

a. Yes

b. No

c. If yes, how much did the skills transfer? (1=No transfer. 2=Some transfer. 3=High transfer.)

137. Which of the following best describes your level of satisfaction with your current job?

a. Satisfied

b. Indifferent

c. Unsatisfied

138. *(Interviewer: Fill in the blank with the answer to the above.)* Why do you say that you feel _____ in this job?

139. Do you own a business? Did you start your own business?

a. Yes

b. No

If no, go to #145.

140. What type of business is it?

141. Where did you get the money you used to start your business?

a. With my own money, belongings, or savings

b. My family in Mexico helped me. If so, who:

c. My family in the U.S. helped me. If so, who:

d. I got a loan from someone outside of my family. If so, from where? (bank, loan company, friend, etc.)

e. Other

142. How much money did you use to start your business?

143. In this business, how many people do you employ?

144. How many of these employees are ex-migrants?

F. Political and Socioeconomic Situation in Mexico

Now, I would like to ask you about return migrants in general.

145. In your opinion, do you think the Mexican government helps return migrants?

    a. Yes

    b. No

    c. Why?

146. Have you participated in or do you know someone who has participated in any of the following programs? Indicate yes / no.

    a. Paisano Bienvenido a Casa (Welcome Home Countryman)

    b. Programa 3 X 1 (3 for 1 Program)

    c. Programa Directo a México (Straight to Mexico Program)

147. With your migration experience, you now know all of the problems involved in going and coming. In your opinion, what do you think the Mexican government could do to help ex-migrants?

G. English

149. In your opinion, what is your level of English?

    a. I speak fluent English (I am capable of communicating orally with Americans in English in every situation and I understand almost everything).

    b. I speak some English (I can complete daily activities without help, like going to the store and reading signs).

    c. I speak a little English (I know simple phrases like how to say my name and my age, ask for directions, read a map, etc.).

    d. I don't speak English.

150. In your opinion, what is your English writing level?

    a. I can write formal documents in English without much trouble (I can communicate in writing in English in any situation, like school essays, etc.).

b. I write some English (I can write simple texts and fill out forms).

c. I write little English (I can write basic phrases like my name and age).

d. I can't write in English.

Interviewer: If he / she doesn't speak or write English, go to #152.

151. How did you learn English?

a. At work

b. At school before migrating

c. At school in the U.S.

d. Other

152. How important was English in your last job in the U.S.?

a. Important

b. Somewhat important

c. Not important

153. What was your legal status in the U.S.?

a. American Citizen

b. Permanent Resident / Green Card

c. Temporary work visa

d. Undocumented

e. If other, specify:

154. What is your grade and level of schooling? (Example: Grade=1, Level=Primary) (Codes: 00. None / Didn't go to school, 01. Preschool, 02. Incomplete primary, 03. Complete primary, 04. Secondary, 05. High school / Technical school, 06. Higher education)

a. Grade:

b. Level:

155. Do you think your schooling helped you in the U.S.?

156. Last, we want to know a little about your neighborhood. How many adults do you know who live on this block?

157. Can you tell me how many ex-migrants live on this block?

158. Can you give me their names and addresses?

a. Yes

b. No

c. If yes, list here:

159. Could you introduce me to them? (*Interviewer: Offer to pay if necessary.*)

a. Yes

b. No

160. Interviewer: If you think that the interviewee has an interesting story about skill transfer, turn on your recorder and ask them questions freely. Try to get as many details about what they learned as possible, both in Mexico and in the U.S., and how the skills are used.

H. Household Composition

Interviewer, say: Last, I would like to ask a few questions about your family.

161. Please tell me the name of each of the people who normally live in your home, beginning with the head of household, his or her spouse who live in the home, and others who normally reside here. Don't forget to include small children and older adults. *For each individual, acquire the following information:*

a. Name

b. Sex

c. Kinship

d. Age

e. Education Level

f. Was he / she studying in 2009–2010?

g. In the last 12 months, how many months did he / she live in the house?

h. If less than 12 months, where did he / she live during the absences?

162. What is your family's religion?

a. Catholic

b. Evangelical

c. Jehovah's Witness

d. No Religion

e. Other

163. Where was the head of household born?

a. State:

b. City:

164. *If the head of household is not from the same area where being interviewed:* How long has the head of household been living here?

a. Years:

165. What is the marital status of the head of household?
    a. Single
    b. Married or Civil Union
    c. Divorced
    d. Widowed

166. *If the head of household is not single:* Where is the head of household's spouse from?
    a. From the same place as head of household
    b. From other municipality in Guanajuato
    c. Another state

I. Sources of Household Income

167. In the last 12 months, what were the main sources of income for your family, in order of importance? (Pensions, remittances, etc.)
    a. 1st activity and name of people involved:
    b. 2nd activity and name of people involved:
    c. 3rd activity and name of people involved:
    d. 4th activity and name of people involved:
    e. 5th activity and name of people involved:

REMITTANCES RECEIVED OR SENT

Now I would like to ask you about the money or goods that you may have received from friends or family living outside of this area. I would also like to know about the money or goods that you send to other people.

168. In the last 12 months, have you or someone in your household received money or goods that come from someone living abroad or in other parts of Mexico?
    a. Yes
    b. No

If no, go to #171.

169. Who sent or brought you money or goods from abroad or other parts of Mexico? For each individual, please provide the following information.
    a. Name

    b. Kinship

    c. Where does he / she live? 1=Mexico. 2=U.S. 3=Other.

    d. Does he / she send regularly? 1=Yes 2=No

    e. In total, how much have you received in the last 12 months?

    f. Please specify in pesos or dollars.

170. In general, how do you receive the money?

    a. I don't receive money, only goods.

    b. They bring it to me personally.

    c. They send it with someone.

    d. The money is wired to me.

    e. In a bank account of a household member

    f. Through a specialized company (e.g., Western Union)

    f. If other, please specify:

171. In the last 12 months, have you or someone in your household sent money or goods to a friend or family member living abroad or in other parts of Mexico?

    a. Yes

    b. No

If no, go to #174.

172. Who did you or someone in your household send money or goods to? For each individual, please provide the following information.

    a. Name

    b. Kinship

    c. Where does he / she live? 1=Mexico. 2=U.S. 3=Other.

    d. Does you send to him / her regularly? 1=Yes 2=No

    e. In total, how much have you sent in the last 12 months?

    f. Please specify in pesos or dollars.

173. In general, how do you send the money?

    a. I don't send money, only goods.

    b. I take it personally.

    c. I send it with someone.

    d. By mail

    e. In a bank account of a household member

    f. Through a specialized company (e.g., Western Union)

    g. If other, please specify:

GOVERNMENT PROGRAMS

174. In the last 12 months, have you or someone in your household received government assistance or payments through any of the following programs?

    a. Oportunidades / Jovenes con Oportunidades(Opportunities / Youth with Opportunities)

        i. Who receives this support?

        ii. How many times per year?

        iii. The support is (1) All in cash, (2) Cash and goods, or (3) All in goods

        iv. How much does the household member receive each time they receive payment / goods?

    b. 70 y mas (70 and older)

        i. Who receives this support?

        ii. How many times per year?

        iii. The support is (1) All in cash, (2) Cash and goods, or (3) All in goods

        iv. How much does the household member receive each time they receive payment / goods?

    c. Retirement or Pensions

        i. Who receives this support?

        ii. How many times per year?

        iii. The support is (1) All in cash, (2) Cash and goods, or (3) All in goods

        iv. How much does the household member receive each time they receive payment / goods?

    d. Severance Pay, for example payment for being laid off or for an accident

        i. Who receives this support?

        ii. How many times per year?

        iii. The support is (1) All in cash, (2) Cash and goods, or (3) All in goods

        iv. How much does the household member receive each time they receive payment / goods?

    e. Seguro Popular

        i. Who receives this support?

        ii. How many times per year?

    iii. The support is (1) All in cash, (2) Cash and goods, or (3) All in goods

    iv. How much does the household member receive each time they receive payment / goods?

  f. Contigo Vamos a la Escuela (Education Program)

    i. Who receives this support?

    ii. How many times per year?

    iii. The support is (1) All in cash, (2) Cash and goods, or (3) All in goods

    iv. How much does the household member receive each time they receive payment / goods?

  g. Adultos Mayores (Program for Older Adults)

    i. Who receives this support?

    ii. How many times per year?

    iii. The support is (1) All in cash, (2) Cash and goods, or (3) All in goods

    iv. How much does the household member receive each time they receive payment / goods?

  h. If other, please specify:

    i. Who receives this support?

    ii. How many times per year?

    iii. The support is (1) All in cash, (2) Cash and goods, or (3) All in goods

    iv. How much does the household member receive each time they receive payment / goods?

EXPENSES

175. Please tell me about household expenses over the last 12 months, including the approximate amount spent on each.

  a. Weekly food expenses on average:

  b. School expenses combined (fees, uniforms, etc.) for all students residing in your household:

  c. Health/Death total:

  d. Celebrations, social events:

  e. Family leisure (big expenses like vacations, etc.):

  f. If other, please specify:

QUESTIONS TO GUIDE INDIVIDUAL
NARRATIVE

Interviewer: Two important things.

    1. *Please include the job or post name from the survey when you talk about a specific job.*

    2. *Specify how new skills or techniques are carried out. For example, if an ex-migrant learned to pack vegetables, ask how. How is it different to pack vegetables in the U.S. and Mexico?*

Turn on the recorder.

Now I would like to talk to you more informally about the tasks, skills, and knowledge you learned in Mexico and the United States, and I would like to know which ones you think are or have been useful to you.

    I. Which tasks and activities did you learn in your jobs before migrating to the U.S. (referring to the jobs we already discussed in the survey)? How did you learn them?

    II. What techniques, knowledge, and skills or ways of working did you learn in Mexico and were able to use in jobs in the U.S.? Do you remember any one in particular?

    III. Did you learn new techniques, tasks, or activities in your U.S. jobs? How did you learn them? What did you learn, in which job, and how did you use them there?

    IV. What knowledge, techniques, activities, or ways of working did you learn in the U.S. and apply here in Mexico, either in your jobs or outside of work? Explain what they were, in which job, and how you used them. Do you remember any in particular?

    V. What do you think you learned in the U.S. that isn't useful in Mexico? Why isn't it useful?

    VI. Some migrants say that the skills and knowledge they gained in the U.S. have changed the way things are done and the way people work in Mexico. What do you think? Do you agree or disagree? Why? Give an example.

    VII. What are your work plans for the future? Where do you see yourself in 5 years, professionally?

NOTES

CHAPTER 1: WHO ARE THE "UNSKILLED," REALLY?

1. Pseudonyms are used for the names of all migrants as well as all small towns in the book.

2. Cerase 1974.

3. Lopez 2010.

4. Chiswick 1986, 2005; Borjas 2000; Dustmann and Fabbri 2003; Dustmann, Fabbri, Preston, and Wadsworth 2003; among others.

5. Manwaring 1984: 184–85.

6. See Todaro 1969 for neoclassical explanations and Stark 1991 and Stark and Bloom 1995 for the new economics of labor migration theory.

7. See Star and Strauss 1999.

8. For a lifelong human capital approach, also see Hagan, Demonsant, and Chavez 2014.

9. This approach resembles the human capabilities perspective developed in Nussbaum 2011.

10. Sjastaad 1962; Harris and Todaro 1970.

11. Chiswick 1986; Borjas 1990; among others.

12. Williams 2006; Williams and Baláž 2005; Dustmann and Fabbri 2003.

13. Instead of criticizing and revamping this notion of human capital, as developed by Gary Becker in 1964, economic sociologists and migration scholars have left the concept untouched, thereby often unintentionally reproducing the rigid ways in which it is measured. Eschewing the study of immigrants as individuals with a potentially large and diverse bundle of hard-to-measure human capital skills, they have opted to limit their understanding to the social contexts and structures of labor market incorporation through their development of other forms of capital (e.g., social capital, cultural capital, symbolic capital). For a discussion of these other forms of capital, see Portes 2010.

14. Waldinger and Lichter 2003:36.

15. Light 1972; Valenzuela 2001; Waldinger and Lichter 2003; Pisani and Yoskowitz 2006; Ramirez and Hondagneu-Sotelo 2009; Hagan, Lowe and Quingla 2011; Lowe, Hagan, and Iskander 2010; Bailey and Waldinger 1991.

16. See Beckett 2000; Williams and Baláž 2005.

17. See Polanyi 1958.

18. See Polanyi 1966.

19. See Polanyi and Prosch 1975.

20. Polanyi and Prosch 1975: 36–37. Cited in Manwaring and Wood 1984: 60.

21. Kusturer 1978; Waldinger and Lichter 2003; Moss and Tilly 1996; Evans 2002; Donato and Bankston 2008.

22. In his influential book *Labor and Monopoly Capital* (1974), Harry Braverman extended Marx's original argument that in the context of capitalist production, management strives to control the labor process, constantly monitoring workers, fragmenting tasks, and ultimately dispossessing individuals of their skills. A critique of Braverman's thesis can be found in Waldinger and Lichter 2003: 34–36.

23. Manwaring and Wood 1984.

24. In a similar vein, Kusturer divides working knowledge into five subject areas: (1) knowledge of routine procedures, that is, basic working knowledge in constant use during performance of activities and tasks, which is thoroughly assimilated and guides habitualized work without conscious effort; (2) supplementary working knowledge about the materials handled and (3) the machines used. Supplementary working knowl-

edge is used to overcome obstacles to routine activities, to avoid potential disruptions, or to solve problems that interfere with work. Supplementary working knowledge is also used periodically to deal with (4) expected patterns of customer or client behavior and (5) expected work-role behavior of others in the organization. See Kusturer 1978.

25. Manwaring and Wood 1984.

26. See Reich 1992 and Evans 2002.

27. Manwaring 1984: 161. Italics in the original.

28. Manwaring acknowledges that under certain conditions, strong mutual obligations can be used by workers to challenge managerial social control within the firm.

29. Manwaring and Wood 1984: 68.

30. Ibid., 58.

31. On the sources of a migrant worker's relative power in the labor process, see Waldinger and Lichter 2003: 64–65; also see Hagan 1994.

32. Piore 2002.

33. Doeringer and Piore 1985: xi.

34. Piore 1979; Waldinger and Lichter 2003.

35. Waldinger and Lichter 2003.

36. Phillips and Massey 2000.

37. We purposefully paraphrase the concept of the external internal labor market (EILM), developed by Manwaring (1984). According to this author, employers recruit particular groups of workers through the EILM, using the networks of existing workers. The purpose of this recruitment mechanism is to attract new employees who share the tacit skills and social characteristics of the current labor force.

38. Waldinger 1996.

39. Chiswick 1986; Borjas 2000; Chiswick and Miller 2002; Dustmann, Fabbri, Preston, and Wadsworth 2003.

40. Borjas 1990. This critique has been made by other labor sociologists, including Waldinger and Lichter 2003.

41. There are a few exceptions, such as Akresh 2006; Hagan, Lowe, and Quingla 2011; Hernández-León 2004; Sanderson and Painter 2011.

42. Duleep and Regets 2002.

43. Ibid., 4–5.

44. Hernández-León 2004.

45. Waldinger 1996.

46. Hagan, Lowe, and Quingla 2011; Hagan, Demonsant, and Chavez 2014.

47. Hagan, Lowe, and Quingla 2011; Saxenian 1996; Shih 2006. Similar strategies have been used historically. In search of better economic opportunities, Mexican workers in the 1920s frequently jumped or deserted their contracts en route to sugar beet fields in Minnesota and railroad jobs in the Southeast and East. See Peck 1996.

48. Williams and Baláž 2005.

49. Williams 2006, 2007a, 2007b.

50. Dustmann 1999: Williams and Baláž 2005.

51. Salt 1998; Williams 2006.

52. Markovitic and Manderson 2000.

53. Ramirez and Hondagneu-Sotelo 2009.

54. Chiswick 1986, 2005; Borjas 2000; Chiswick and Miller 2002; Dustmann, Preston, and Wadsworth 2003 ; Zahniser and Greenwood 1998; Lacuesta 2006; Dustmann and Kirkchamp 2002; Reinhold and Thom 2011.

55. Lowe, Hagan, and Iskander 2010; Hagan, Lowe, and Quingla 2011. See the Methodological Appendix in this book for a detailed description of the research design of this exploratory phase.

56. Craver 2006; Kasarda and Johnson 2006.

57. See the Methodological Appendix in this book for a description of the sampling method and interview schedules.

58. In Leon, almost 90 percent of the tanneries and small shoe manufacturing shops employ fewer than 20 workers each. About one-quarter of all firms are unregistered. See Brown Grossman and Villalobos 1997.

59. Calleja Pinedo 1994.

60. Hernández Águila 2007.

61. Ibid.

62. Ibid.

63. The Italian industrial districts, located in the northeast and central sections of Italy, are formed by networks of small and medium-size producers that specialize in craft manufacturing. These producers took advantage of artisan work, kinship social structures, merchant networks, and support from local governments to gain a competitive

edge in the global economy. On the Italian industrial districts, see Piore and Sabel 1984.

64. Ortiz 2009; Brown Grossman and Domínguez Villalobos 1997; Martínez 2007.

65. Fernandez, Jilberto, and Hogenboom 1996.

66. Hernández Águila 2006.

67. Lowder 1999.

68. Hernández-León 2008.

69. Fussell 2004; Durand, Massey, and Zenteno 2001; Roberts, Frank, and Lozano-Ascencio 1999; Hernández-León 2008.

70. Masferrer and Roberts 2012; Hernández-León 2008.

71. See the Methodological Appendix for the sampling strategy.

72. Hondagneu-Sotelo 1994; Reyes 1997; Ruiz-Tagle and Wong 2009.

73. We did not ask respondents about the number of children in Mexico. This figure was extrapolated from the household composition section of the questionnaire, the number and age of the children to year of first migration. For this reason this figure underestimates the actual number of children as some may have already left the household at the time of the survey and hence we have no information on them in our quantitative database.

74. Ruiz-Tagle and Wong 2009.

75. The purpose of this book is to examine the labor market experiences of individuals before and after migration. In a paper in progress, we conduct a comparative analysis of the labor market pathways of return migrants and nonmigrants.

76. INEGI 2010; Zenteno 2011.

CHAPTER 2: LEARNING SKILLS
IN COMMUNITIES OF ORIGIN

1. These memories come from a trip one of the authors made with a historian to the tenement museum in New York City. During the visit, we poured over collections of old photographs and archival data of the tenement district, after which we toured several refurbished tenements, one of which was home to the Rosenberg household. The tenement included two rooms: one for sleeping and cooking; the other

a small in-home garment factory that housed several sewing machines and work benches.

2. Massey et al. 1987; Hagan 1998; Menjivar 2000; Ramírez and Hondagneu-Sotelo 2009; Waldinger and Lichter 2003.

3. Milkman 2000, 2006; Waldinger et al. 1996.

4. Wilson and Portes 1980; Bonacich and Light 1998; Waldinger and Lichter 2003; Valdez 2008; Hagan 1994, 1998.

5. Mouw and Chavez 2012; Ramírez and Hondagneu-Sotelo 2009; Hagan et al. 2011.

6. In *Life, Work and Learning* David Beckett and Hagar (2002) also challenge conventional measures of education, arguing that learning develops in both paid and unpaid work contexts.

7. See Misko (2008) for a more developed discussion of the differences between formal and informal learning and the implications of these distinctions.

8. Evans and Rainbird 2002; Misko 2008.

9. Gerlter 2004.

10. Waldinger 1996: 276.

11. This method would soon be banned from many towns and cities in Guanajuato because of the toxic fumes released. Increasingly, production has switched from red to blond bricks because of the effects of the former method on the environment.

12. Calleja Pinedo 1994.

CHAPTER 3: MOBILIZING SKILLS AND MIGRATING

1. Massey et al. 1987; Massey et al. 1993; Stark and Bloom 1985.

2. Former participants of the Bracero Program (1942–64). The Bracero Program was a guest worker agreement established by the governments of the United States and Mexico. The program recruited men from rural areas in Mexico to work in U.S. agriculture. On the Bracero Program, see Durand 1998.

3. Among others, these international agreements included the General Agreement on Tariffs and Trade (GATT), the North Ameri-

can Free Trade Agreement (NAFTA), and the World Trade Organization (WTO).

4. Arias and Peña 2004.

5. Arias and Durand 2008; Gamio 1991 [1930].

6. Durand and Massey 2003.

7. Leite, Ramos, and Gaspar 2003; Fundación BBVA Bancomer 2012.

8. Terrazas 2010.

9. Hernández-León 2008.

10. Durand, Massey, and Capoferro 2005.

11. Hanson and MacIntosh 2010.

12. Zúñiga and Hernández-León 2005; Massey 2008.

13. Hernández-León 2008; Chavez 2012.

14. One of our male interviewees in a small town in central-southern Guanajuato clearly articulated this culture of migration: "Given that the majority of people in my town go to the United States, I joined in. In other words, there was already a pattern of behavior of going to the United States to chase the dream. So when I left the army, I went to Chicago, Illinois, where I have family." For some of the scholarship that has analyzed the culture of migration in rural Mexico, see Kandel and Massey 2002; López Castro 1986; Díaz Gómez 2002; Zúñiga 1992; Cohen 2004.

15. The final document of the *Binational Dialogue on Mexican Migrants in the U.S. and in Mexico* reports that the education levels of Mexican workers in the United States has increased significantly, although most of them have not completed high school. See Latapí et al. 2013.

16. Massey, Durand, and Malone 2003.

17. For example, in Monterrey, Mexico's third largest metropolitan area, decades of stable, formal employment allowed would-be migrants to access tourist and border-crossing visas to enter the United States legally. Working in the country violated the terms of the visa. Still, access to tourist visas afforded these migrants the possibility of moving back and forth across the border numerous times during a given year. Being able to cross the border legally, workers from Monterrey saw their sojourning experience as different from other undocumented Mexican immigrants. See Hernández-León 2008.

18. Massey and Espinosa 1997.

19. We also interviewed H2 workers in Guanajuato City and San Miguel de Allende.

20. Additional details on the H2 visa program can be found at http://monterrey.usconsulate.gov/h2_visa.html.

21. U.S. Visas, U.S. Department of State, Bureau of Consular Affairs, Nonimmigrant visa statistics. Available at http://travel.state.gov/content/dam/visas/Statistics/AnnualReports/FY2013AnnualReport/FY13AnnualReport-TableXVIB.pdf

22. Bruno 2012.

23. See, for example, Griffith 2007. The state of Guanajuato is also home to a developed migration industry. *Coyotes,* migrant-owned transportation operations, remittance companies, and formal and informal recruiters stimulate and facilitate migration to the United States. Even though migration entrepreneurs may not play a direct causal role in international sojourning, they are co-participants in the creation of opportunities and infrastructures that encourage migration. In Guanajuato, U.S. firms formally recruit workers under the auspices of the H2 visa program. For more on the conceptualization of the migration industry, see Castles and Miller 1993; Hernández-León 2008, 2013.

24. This practice is reminiscent of the Bracero-era practice by U.S. authorities, who apprehended undocumented workers from the interior of the United States and returned them to the border, provided them with work documents, and then sent them back to the farms where they were originally employed. On such practices, see Martin 2014.

25. We revisit Herculano's history of skill acquisition and mobilization across the migratory circuit in the context of his return migration to San Miguel de Allende in chapter 5.

26. The survey instrument only included a question about reasons for migration for last trip abroad. Fifty-seven percent migrated only once to the United States.

27. A deep crisis in Mexico and economic expansion in the United States overlapped during the second half of the 1990s, creating simultaneous push and pull pressures for migration. While chapter 3 stresses the causal forces and mechanisms of outmigration, chapter 4 analyzes in detail the demand for migrant labor in distinct sectors of the U.S. economy.

28. See Stark and Bloom 1985.

29. See Donato 1993; Hondagneu-Sotelo 1994; Dreby 2010.

30. Studies show that Guanajuato has become a major source of Mexican women entering these types of occupations in the U.S. labor market. See Arias and Peña 2004.

31. In chapter 4 we revisit Carmen in the United States, where she was able to transfer her cooking skills acquired in Mexico to a job as a cook in a Mexican restaurant.

32. This program of Mexico's Ministry for Social Development encourages migrants to contribute to the social development of their communities of origin. For every peso a club or migrant association invests in a given project, the Mexican government contributes three pesos, hence its name, 3x1. More information about this program can be found at www.sedesol.gob.mx/es/SEDESOL/Programa_3x1_para_Migrantes.

33. Hernández-León 2008; Phillips and Massey 2000; Hagan 1998.

34. Percentage not shown in table.

35. The extent to which this matching of skills takes place also depends on the level of development of the settled migrant community at the destination. For example, Piore (1979: 67) argues that "Migrants to settled communities often have not only a predetermined family role there, but often an assignment in the labor market as well." This process has been subsequently developed and explained by Douglas Massey and his colleagues as a function of a migrant community's social capital. See Massey et al. 1987.

CHAPTER 4: TRANSFERRING SKILLS,
RESKILLING, AND LABORING
IN THE UNITED STATES

1. There is a substantial literature on the role of migrant social networks in migrants' labor market outcomes in countries of destination. These networks, which are shared by newcomers from similar areas of origin or ethnic ties, explain how migrants with low levels of financial and formal human capital gain access to jobs in areas of destination. For studies in the U.S. labor market, see, for example, Waldinger 1996;

Hagan 1998; Light and Gold 2000; Waldinger and Lichter 2003; Massey et al. 1987; Bonacich 1973; Boyd 1989.

2. In contrast, the primary labor market consists of well-paying secure jobs that offer workers with formal human capital opportunities for economic mobility and social welfare benefits. See Michael Piore's seminal work, *Birds of Passage* (1979), for a discussion of Dual Labor Market Theory.

3. Catanzarite 2000; Catanzarite and Aguilera 2002; Kmec 2003; Flippen 2012.

4. Griffith 1993; Mahler 1995; Hernández-León 2008.

5. Sassen 1989; Zlolniski 1994; Light 2006; Valenzuela et al. 2006; Castells and Portes 1989.

6. Wiley 1967.

7. Wilson and Portes 1980; Bailey and Waldinger 1991; Hagan, Lowe, and Quingla 2011; Ramírez and Hondagneu-Sotelo 2009; Mouw and Chavez 2012; Hagan, Demonsant, and Chavez 2014.

8. Alvarez Jr. 1990; Oberle 2006; Ramírez and Hondagneu-Sotelo 2009.

9. Bean and Stevens 2003; Bean and Bell-Rose 1999; Hernández-León 2008; Hagan, Lowe, and Quingla 2011; Hagan, Demonsant, and Chavez 2014.

10. Bean, Leach, and Lowell 2004; Capps, Fix, and Lin 2010; Bean and Stevens 2003; Bean and Bell-Rose 1999.

11. Hernández-León 2008; Fussell 2004.

12. Harris 1995; Sassen 1988, 1993.

13. Zúñiga and Hernández-León 2005; Massey 2008; Singer 2004; Marrow 2011.

14. Kasarda and Johnson 2006; Pew Hispanic Center 2007; Dever 2009; Capps, Fix, and Lin 2010.

15. Portes, Castells, and Benton 1989; Erlich and Grabelsky 2005; Hagan, Lowe, and Quingla 2011.

16. Arias and Peña 2004.

17. Romero 2012. See, for example, Fisher 1953; Taylor, Martin, and Fix 1997; Adams 1937; Martin 2002.

18. Romero 2012:77.

19. Kandel 2008; Griffith 2007.

20. Du Bry 2006; Wells 1996.

21. Krissman 2000; Romero 2012.

22. Hagan, Lowe, and Quingla 2011.

23. Ortiz 2002; Romero 2012.

24. Griffith 2007.

25. Kasarda and Johnson 2006; Pew Hispanic Center 2007; Dever 2009; Capps, Fix, and Lin 2010.

26. Portes, Castells, and Benton 1989; Erlich and Grabelsky 2005.

27. For the most comprehensive and systematic national study on labor violation in construction and other migrant-heavy industries, see Bernhardt et al. 2010.

28. Ibid.

29. David Griffith has conducted the most systematic research on the labor conditions of guestworkers in the United States. See, for example, Griffith 1993, 2006, 2007.

30. Pedraza 1991; Powers and Seltzer 1998; Hochschild 2002; Donato et al. 2008.

31. Pedraza 1991; Hagan 1998; Powers and Seltzer 1998; Hondagneu-Sotelo 2001; Hochschild 2002; Donato et al. 2008; Cobb-Clark and Kossoudji 2000.

32. There is a sizeable literature on live-in and day migrant domestic workers in the U.S. labor market. See, for example, Hondagneu-Sotelo 2001; Parrenas 2001; Romero 2002, 2011; Hagan 1994, 1998.

33. Hagan, Lowe, and Quingla 2011.

34. Lowe, Hagan, and Iskander 2010; Waldinger 1996.

35. Bean, Leach, and Lowell 2004; Hagan, Lowe, and Quingla 2011.

36. In Miryam Hazan's 2013 study on return migration in Mexico, respondents also reported high levels of satisfaction in their U.S. jobs.

37. Waldinger and Lichter 2003. See also Fine 1996; Moss and Tilly 1995; Newman 1999; Donato and Bankston 2008; and Osterman 2001 for further examples and discussion of the soft skills employers expect of their workers, especially in the service sector.

38. Hagan, Lowe, and Quingla 2011; Hagan, Demonsant, and Chavez 2014.

39. Granovetter 1981; Sorenson and Kalleberg 1981.

40. Saxenian 1996; Shih 2006.

41. Fussell 2009.

CHAPTER 5: RETURNING HOME AND REINTEGRATING INTO THE LOCAL LABOR MARKET

1. The stigma faced by deportees who return with tattoos is experienced in many societies in Latin America and elsewhere. Hagan, Eschbach, and Rodriguez 2008; Golash-Boza 2011; Brown 2011.

2. For the following reasons we are analyzing return migration as a fairly permanent process, though we clearly recognize that some in our sample may remigrate to the United States. First, half the sample has been back in Mexico for more than ten years. Second, less than half of the sample stated that they would consider remigration. Moreover, 57 percent of the Leon survey respondents have conducted only one migratory trip to the United States, while 43 percent of them have migrated two or more times. The repeated short-term trips characteristic of Mexican rural streams are absent in Leon.

3. Hagan 1994.

4. Carese 1974; Gmelch 1980; King, Strachan, and Mortimer 1983; Ghosh 1997.

5. Several studies have shown how economic downturns in the immigration country can trigger mass emigration. Levi (1948) writes about the streams of Italians who returned home following the 1929 Depression, and Saloutos (1956) points to the mass return of Greeks in the wake of the depression years in the United States in the 1980s.

6. Hernández-Alvarez 1967: 69; Taylor et al. 2003; Dustmann and Kirckchamp 2002; Woodruff and Zenteno 2007; Gonzalez-Lozano 2012; Mesnard 2004; Massey et al. 1987; Lindstrom 1996.

7. Toren 1976; Appleyard 1962; Richmond 1968.

8. Espinosa 1998.

9. Perez-Armendariz and Crow 2010; Smith 2005.

10. Form and Rivera 1958; Lopreato 1967.

11. Guarnizo 2010.

12. The question as to whether migration abroad is a liberating experience for women is an issue that continues to garner historical and contemporary attention in the literature. See, for example, Abadan-Unat 1976; Tienda and Booth 1991; Buijs 1993; Hondagneu-Sotelo 1994; Smith 2005.

13. Van Hook and Bean 1998: 538–40; and Table 1.

14. Ibid. An estimated 1.4 million out of 2.8 million foreign-born Mexicans in the United States were unauthorized in 1979, and an estimated 6.7 million out of 11.5 million Mexicans in the United States were unauthorized in 2009.

15. See Passel, Cohn, and Gonzalez-Barrera 2012 for a full discussion of these findings.

16. Passel, Cohn, and Gonzalez-Barrera 2012; FitzGerald, Alarcón, and Muse-Orlinoff 2011.

17. Passel, Cohn, and Gonzalez-Barrera 2012.

18. U.S. Department of Homeland Security 2009.

19. The disappointment theory of return migration posits that people return home because they "failed" (that is, could not find employment or could earn only low wages) at the target location (Herzog and Schlottmann 1982). In other words, people move with the intention of settling permanently in the new location, but with limited or no information about the labor market in place of destination, they miscalculate the benefits of migration and are forced to return home.

20. It is probably that the number of deportations in the sample is actually higher than we report since some respondents may have been reluctant to tell us that they had been deported.

21. See Passel, Cohn, and Gonzalez-Barrera 2012 for a full discussion of these findings. In a survey of return migrants conducted by Mexicans and Americans Thinking Together (MATT) in 2014, 11 percent of the respondents cited deportation as the reason for their most recent return, a figure slightly higher than the 10 percent reported in our survey. See Hazan 2014.

22. These findings are consistent with the historical and contemporary evidence on return migration. See, for example, King 2000; Hazan 2014; Sandoval 2014.

23. According to the target income theory, people migrate to accumulate savings to invest in better technologies, to buy more land in their home community, or to start a business (Hill 1987; Borjas 1991; Massey et al. 1993; Lindstrom 1996). This theory assumes that migrants have a strong preference for returning and staying in their home community rather than relocating abroad but must resort to international migration because of limited wage opportunities at home (Berg 1961).

24. FitzGerald and Alarcon 2013.

25. Ibid.; Hazan 2014; Dreby 2010.

26. Villarreal 2010.

27. Consejo Nacional de Evaluación de la Política de Desarrollo Social 2011; Fundación BBVA Bancomer 2012.

28. Percent of exports from January to October 2007; Cenejas Ortiz 2009.

29. *El Economista* 2009; Ajuaa Noticias 2009.

30. Hernández Águila 2007; Martínez Martínez 2007.

31. In contrast, in 2010 Guanajuato's GDP per capita was 18th in the country (out of 32 states). See Instituto Nacional de Estadística y Geografía 2012.

32. Ibid.

33. *El Economista* 2012, 2014.

34. Waldinger and Lichter 2003; Hagan, Eschbach, and Rodriguez 2008.

35. For example, in their study of return migrants in Ireland, Alan Barrett and P.J. O'Connell (2000) found that female return migrants earned more than their male counterparts. The gender difference resulted from differences in the industries where men and women worked while abroad; while the men were concentrated in "low-skilled professions" that did not offer a wage premium (construction and heavy industries), women were clustered in those industries where foreign experience mattered (e.g., financial services). These findings were corroborated by Maria Enchautegui (1993), who found that Puerto Rican return migrants did not benefit economically from the jobs they held in the United States because they had worked in low-wage, low-skill, dead-end service jobs.

36. Zahniser and Greenwood (1998) and Steffen Reinhold and Kevin Thom (2011), in their studies of return migration to Mexico, found that occupation-specific experience in the United States can and does have a positive impact on wages upon return if migrants can channel this experience into comparable industries and occupations upon return.

37. King 1986.

38. Using data from the Mexican Migration Project (MMP), Steven Zahniser and Michael Greenwood (1998) find that additional time in the United States increases the earnings of Mexican return migrants. In contrast, using the Mexican census, Aitor Lacuesta (2006) does not find any wage premium associated with time in the United States.

39. See Dustman 2003. Jackline Wahba and Yves Zenou (2012) found that the decision to launch an entrepreneurial activity upon return was influenced by access to social capital in the home country. That is, entrepreneurs rely on contacts for information and services, a resource that may be lost through migration.

40. Williams and Baláž 2005.

41. Ibid.

42. In his study of migration in Jalisco, David FitzGerald (2009) also found that while some employers valued the disciplined work ethic of return migrants, others were critical of their wage expectations.

43. There are several interpretations of this saying. See www .aaanet.org/sections/alla/awards/.

44. For example, in their study of Turkish emigrants returning from Germany, Christian Dustmann and Oliver Kirchamp (2002) found that 50 percent of their sample started a microenterprise within four years of resettling in Turkey. In their study of return migrants in Tunisia, Alice Mesnard and Martin Ravallion (2006) found that opportunities for return migrants in Tunisia to launch an entrepreneurial venture depended largely on the amount of money saved abroad and the duration of foreign work experience, findings corroborated by Nadeem Ilahi and Sagib Jafarey (1999) in their study of return migrants in Pakistan. In their study of rural-urban migration and return migration in China, Sylvie Démurger and Hui Xu (2011) argue that the migration experience may enhance entrepreneurial skills. However, their study relies on migration duration and number of jobs as proxies for

skill development and lacks detailed occupational analysis to rule out exogenous factors such as risk aversion and innate entrepreneurial proclivity. Other studies focus on the relationship between remittances and self-employment, finding that the remitted savings of emigrants are an important source of start-up capital for microenterprises.

45. Dustmann and Kirkchamp 2002; Papail 2002.

46. Mesnard 2004; Mesnard and Ravallion 2006.

47. Cerase 1974; Gmelch 1980; Earle and Sakova 2000.

48. Santiago Levy (2008) and Gary Fields (2013) also document self-employment as a limited goal, employed to buy time to enter salaried employment.

49. Hagan and Wassink 2014.

50. Ibid.

CHAPTER 6: CONCLUSION

1. Star and Strauss 1999.

2. For a full critique of methodological nationalism, see Wimmer and Glick Schiller 2002.

3. Duleep and Regets 2002:4–5.

4. Díaz-Serrano and Cabral Vieira 2005.

5. Job satisfaction is also a good predictor of intentions or decisions of workers to leave a job. See Gazioglu and Tansel 2002.

6. Our survey did not directly ask the Leon returnees about the labor violations we know migrant workers often face in the United States, such as wage theft, but in response to a follow-up question about job satisfaction in their last jobs, 15 return migrants volunteered information about past exploitation during their last job abroad. We suspect that this figure underestimates the prevalence of work violations experienced for several reasons. First, because the survey only asked about conditions in the last job, it did not capture violations or discrimination experiences in previous jobs. Second, because the return migrants were asked retrospectively about job satisfaction years after returning to Mexico, it is probable that they idealized some of their past U.S. experiences, highlighting the satisfactory dimensions of work in the United States, including learning new skills and sufficient wages to remit home.

7. Sassen 1989; Zlolniski 1994; Valenzuela, Theodore, Melendez, and Gonzalez 2006; Light 2006.

8. On the different attitudes men and women have toward the possibility and experience of return, see Hagan 1994 and Espinosa 1998.

9. Chavez 2012; Hernández-León 2008.

10. Balan, Browning, and Jelin 1973.

11. On the ascription of lack of skill to certain jobs and categories of workers as part of the social construction of skill, see Warhurst, Tilly, and Gatta 2014.

12. Masferrer and Roberts 2012.

13. Interestingly, the Mexican press is already reporting on the current relationship between international and internal migration. In a series of articles published in the spring of 2014, a Mexican newspaper reported how migrants from Zacatecas who had developed skills in construction in the United States were now using those skills in Monterrey, a large and economically dynamic urban center in the northern part of the country. The articles noted the fact that, in light of more stringent border enforcement, these migrants were moving in sizeable numbers to Monterrey where they were earning higher wages by virtue of the skills learned in the United States, and enjoying occupational mobility in the local labor market. These migrants had formed a hometown association to support their less-developed rural communities of origin in Zacatecas. See Romo 2014.

14. Gender and age discrimination are not only experienced by return migrants but also by nonmigrants. At the same time, some forms of discrimination in local labor markets in Mexico prompt workers to migrate to the United States. On this topic, see Hernández-León 2008.

15. Needless to say, the large return flows that took place during the 2005–10 period, resulting from mass deportations, the economic recession in the United States, and Mexico's own recession, also played a role in the experiences of reintegration of our respondents.

16. A rare exception in the Mexican private sector is AHMSA (a large steel corporation privatized in the 1990s) located in the northern city of Monclova, Coahuila, a company that has developed programs

to recruit returning migrants with skills in welding. See Gascón 2013.

17. The full document that describes the Migrant Support Fund can be found at http://dof.gob.mx/nota_detalle.php?codigo = 5334588&fecha = 04/03/2014.

18. Gamio 1991; Vélez Storey 2002; Alanís Enciso 2001; FitzGerald 2009.

19. The Partido Revolucionario Institucional (PRI) governed Mexico from 1929 to 2000. The Partido Acción Nacional (PAN) governed from 2000 to 2012, after which the PRI returned to power.

20. Consejo Nacional de Normalización y Certificación de Competencias Laborales (National Council for the Normalization and Certification of Labor Competences).

21. Hagan interview with Javier Díaz de León, Consul General of Mexico in Raleigh, North Carolina, and former executive director of the Institute for Mexicans Abroad (IME). Consulate of Mexico in Raleigh, 2014.

22. These institutional resources include Mexico's SEP (Secretaria de Educación Pública or Ministry of Public Education) and its large network of vocational high schools, known for its initials in Spanish as CONALEP, the network of Mexican consulates in the United States, the Plazas Comunitarias, local community colleges, trade associations, and universities, such as the City University of New York (CUNY).

23. Authors' translation. Certificación de Competencias Laborales. Instituto de los Mexicanos en el Exterior.

24. The program of Plazas Comunitarias was originally created by Mexico's Instituto Nacional para la Educación de Adultos (National Institute for Adult Education or INEA) and exported through IME and the network of Mexican consulates to the United States and other countries. Plazas in the United States generally focus on English language classes and GED certification.

25. Personal interview with Díaz de León.

26. Hernández-León 2008.

27. Sandoval-Hernández and Hernández-León 2013.

28. These information centers could also connect individuals with credit unions and other lending institutions to help entrepreneurial

migrants develop plans and obtain capital to start a business. Although a number of state migrant affairs offices in Mexico lend money to U.S.-based migrant associations (hometown associations and other types of organizations), these institutions can also include in their agendas return migrants interested in launching entrepreneurial ventures.

29. This is in fact the case of several cities in the state of Guanajuato, especially those where export-oriented firms have established advanced manufacturing centers. For an interesting journalistic account of this phenomenon, see Cave 2013.

30. Latapí, Lowell, and Martin 2013: 21.

31. Ibid.

APPENDIX NOTES

1. Lowe et al. 2010; Hagan, Lowe, and Quingla 2011.

2. U.S. Census Bureau 2001, 2006, 2009.

3. Craver 2006; Kasarda and Johnson 2006; Dever 2009; Pew Hispanic Center 2007.

4. Kasarda and Johnson, 2006; Craver 2006.

5. U.S. Bureau of Labor Statistics 2009.

6. Chavez 1992; Mckenzie and Mistiaen 2009; Hagan 1998, 2008, 2011.

7. The remaining 18 percent were from urban areas in Honduras and the highland region of Guatemala.

REFERENCES

Abadan-Unat, Nermin. 1976. *Turkish Workers in Europe 1960–1975.* Leiden: EJ Brill.

Adams, R. L. 1937. "Farm Labor." *Journal of Farm Economics* 19(4): 913–25.

Ajuaa Noticias. 2009. "Paro de GM en Silao arrastra a proveedores." Available at www.ajuaa.com/news/finanzas/12051-Paro-Silao-arrastra-proveedores.html.

Akresh, Ilana Redstone. 2006. "Occupational Mobility among Legal Immigrants to the United States." *International Migration Review* 40: 854–84.

Alanís Enciso, Fernando S. 2001. "La Constitución de 1917 y la emigración de trabajadores mexicanos a Estados Unidos." *Relaciones* 87: 205–27.

Alarcon, Rafael. 1999. "Recruitment Processes among Foreign-born Engineers and Scientists in Silicon Valley." *American Behavioral Scientist* 42(9): 1381–97.

Alvarez Jr., Robert M. 1990. "Mexican Entrepreneurs and Markets in the City of Los Angeles: A Case of an Immigrant Enclave." *Urban Anthropology and Studies of Cultural Systems and World Economic Development* 19(1 / 2): 99–124.

Appleyard, Reginald Thomas. 1962. "Determinants of Return Migration: A Socio-economic Study of United Kingdom Migrants Who Returned from Australia." *Economic Record* 38(83): 352–68.

Arias, Patricia, and Jorge Durand. 2008. *Mexicanos en Chicago: Diario de campo de Robert Redfield, 1924–1925.* México: Porrúa.

Arias, Patricia, and Emma Peña. 2004. *Las Mujeres de Guanajuato: Ayer y Hoy 1970–2000.* Guanajuato, México: Universidad de Guanajuato / Instituto de la Mujer Guanajuatense.

Bacon, David. 2012. "How US Policies Fueled Mexico's Great Migration." *Nation* 294(4): 11–18.

Bailey, Thomas, and Roger Waldinger. 1991. "Primary, Secondary, and Enclave Labor Markets: A Training Systems Approach." *American Sociological Review* 56(4): 432–45.

Balan, Jorge, Harley Browning, and Elizabeth Jelin. 1973. *Men in a Developing Society: Geographic and Social Mobility in Monterrey, Mexico.* Austin: University of Texas Press.

Barrett, Alan, and Philip O'Connell. 2000. "Is There a Wage Premium for Returning Irish Migrants?" IZA Working Paper no. 135. Bonn: Institute for the Study of Labor.

Bean, Frank, and Stephanie Bell-Rose. 1999. *Immigration and Opportunity: Race, Ethnicity, and Employment in the United States.* New York: Russell Sage Foundation.

Bean, Frank D., Mark Leach, and B. Lindsay Lowell. 2004. "Immigrant Job Quality and Mobility in the United States." *Work and Occupations* 31(4): 499–518.

Bean, Frank, and Gillian Stevens. 2003. *America's Newcomers and the Dynamics of Diversity.* New York: Russell Sage Foundation.

Becker, Gary S. 1964. *Human Capital: A Theoretical and Empirical Analysis, with Special Reference to Education.* Chicago: University of Chicago Press.

Beckett, David. 2000. "Making Workplace Learning Explicit: An Epistemology of Practice for the Whole Person." *Westminster Studies in Education* 23: 41–53.

Beckett, David, and Paul Hager. 2001. *Life, Work and Learning: Practices in Postmodernity.* London and New York: Routledge.

Berg, Elliot J. 1961. "Backward-sloping Labor Supply Functions in Dual Economies: The Africa Case." *Quarterly Journal of Economics* 75(3): 468–92.

Bernhardt, Annette, Ruth Milkman, Nik Theodore, Douglas Heckathorn, Mirabai Auer, James DeFilippis, Ana Luz Gonzalez, Victor

Narro, Jason Perelshteyn, Diana Polson, and Michael Spiller. 2010. *Broken Laws, Unprotected Workers.* New York: National Employment Law Project.

Blackler, Frank. 2002. "Knowledge, Knowledge Work and Organizations." In *The Strategic Management of Intellectual Capital and Organizational Knowledge,* ed. Chun Wei Choo and Nick Bontis, 47–72. New York: Oxford University Press.

Blackman, Allen. 2012. *Small Firms and the Environment in Developing Countries.* Washington, DC: Resources for the Future Press.

Bonacich, Edna. 1973. "A Theory of Middleman Minorities." *American Sociological Review* 38(5): 583–94.

Bonacich, Edna, and Ivan H. Light. 1988. *Immigrant Entrepreneurs: Koreans in Los Angeles, 1965–1982.* Berkeley: University of California Press.

Borjas, George J. 1991. "Self-Selection and the Earnings of Immigrants: Reply." *American Economic Review* 80: 305–8.

———. 2000. "Introduction." In *Issues in the Economics of Immigration,* ed. George Borjas. Chicago: University of Chicago Press.

Boyd, Monica. 1989. "Family and Personal Networks in International Migration: Recent Development and New Agendas." *International Migration Review* 23(3): 638–71.

Braverman, Harry. 1974. *Labor and Monopoly Capital.* New York: Monthly Review Press.

Brown Grossman, Flor, and Lilia Domínguez Villalobos. 1997. "¿Es posible conformar distritos industriales? La experiencia del calzado en León, Gto." In *Pensar globalmente y actuar regionalmente,* ed. Enrique Dussel Peters, Michael Piore, and Clemente Ruiz Durán, 155–84. México: JUS / UNAM / Fundación Friedrich Ebert.

Bruno, Andorra. 2012. *Immigration of Temporary Lower-skilled Workers: Current Policy and Related Issues.* Washington, DC: Congressional Research Service.

Buijs, Gina, ed. 1993. *Migrant Women: Crossing Boundaries and Changing Identities,* vol. 7. Providence, RI: Berg.

Burawoy, Michael. 1976. "The Functions and Reproduction of Migrant Labor: Comparative Material from Southern Africa and the United States." *American Journal of Sociology* 81(5): 1050–87.

Bustamante, Jorge A., and Gerónimo G. Martínez. 1979. "Undocumented Immigration from Mexico: Beyond Borders but within Systems." *Journal of International Affairs* 33(2): 265–84.

Calleja Pinedo, Margarita. 1994. *Microindustria: Principio y soporte de la gran empresa: La producción de calzado en León, Guanajuato.* Guadalajara, México: Universidad de Guadalajara.

Capps, Randy, Michael Fix, and Serena Y.Y. Lin. 2010. *Still an Hourglass?: Immigrant Workers in Middle-skilled Jobs.* Washington, DC: Migration Policy Institute.

Card, David. 2005. "Is the New Immigration Really So Bad?" *Economic Journal* 115(507): F300–23.

Castells, Manuel, and Alejandro Portes. 1989. "World Underneath: The Origins, Dynamics, and Effects of the World Economy." In *The Informal Economy: Studies in Advanced and Less Developed Countries,* ed. Alejandro Portes, Manuel Castells, and Lauren Benton, 11–41. Baltimore: John Hopkins University Press.

Castles, Stephen, and Mark J. Miller. 2003. *Age of Migration: International Population Movements in the Modern World.* Basingstoke, UK: Palgrave.

Catanzarite, Lisa. 2000. "Brown-collar Jobs: Occupational Segregation and Earnings of Recent-immigrant Latinos." *Sociological Perspectives* 43(1): 45–75.

Catanzarite, Lisa, and Michael B. Aguilera. 2002. "Working with Co-ethnics: Earnings Penalities for Latino Immigrants at Latino Job Sites." *Social Problems* 49(1): 101–27.

Cave, Damien. 2013. "In the Middle of Mexico, a Middle Class Rises." *New York Times,* November 19. Retrieved December 28, 2013, from www.nytimes.com/2013/11/19/world/americas/in-the-middle-of-mexico-a-middle-class-is-rising.html?_r = 0.

Cenejas Ortiz, Kenia Nairobi. 2009. *La Industria Maquiladora de Exportación (IME) Textil: Impacto y Tendencia en el Estado de Guanajuato; el Caso de la Empresa Carhartt en el Muncipio de Pénjamo, Guanajuato, 1994–2006.* Undergraduate Thesis in Economics. Universidad Michoacana de San Nicolás de Hidalgo.

Cerase, Francesco P. 1974. "Expectations and Reality: A Case Study of Return Migration from the United States to Southern Italy." *International Migration Review* 8: 245–62.

Chavez, Leo R. 1992. *Shadowed Lives: Undocumented Immigrants in American Society.* Fort Worth, TX: Harcourt, Brace, Jovanovich.

Chávez, Sergio. 2012. "The Sonoran Desert's Domestic Bracero Programme: Institutional Actors and the Creation of Labour Migration Streams." *International Migration* 50(2): 20–40.

Chiswick, Barry R. 1986. "Is the New Immigration Less Skilled than the Old?" *Journal of Labor Economics* 4: 168–92.

Chiswick, Barry R., and Paul W. Miller. 2009. "The International Transferability of Human Capital." *Economics of Education Review* 28(2): 162–69.

Cobb-Clark, Deborah A., and Sherrie A. Kossoudji. 2000. "Mobility in El Norte: The Employment and Occupational Changes of Unauthorized Latin American Women." *Social Science Quarterly* 81(1): 311–24.

Cohen, Jeffrey, H. 2004. *The Culture of Migration in Southern Mexico.* Austin: University of Texas Press.

Consejo Nacional de Evaluación de la Política de Desarrollo Social. 2011. *Informe de Evaluación de la Política de Desarrollo Social de México.* México City: CONEVAL.

Craver, R. 2006. "Building Lives: Hispanics Keep Costs of Construction Down." *Winston-Salem Journal,* January 10.

Démurger, Sylvie, and Hui Xu. 2011. "Return Migrants: The Rise of New Entrepreneurs in Rural China." *World Development* 39(10): 1847–61.

Department of Homeland Security. 2009. "Immigration and Enforcement Actions: 2009." Retrieved January 12, 2014, from www.dhs.gov/xlibrary/assets/statistics/publications/enforcement_ar_2009.pdf.

Dever, A. 2009. "Tennessee: A New Destination for Latino and Latino Immigrants." In *Global Connection and Local Receptions: New Latinos to the Southeastern United States,* ed. F. Ansley and J. Shefner, 65–87. Nashville: University of Tennessee Press.

Díaz Gómez, Leticia. 2002. "Siguiendo los pasos hacia Estados Unidos: Interacción infantil con videos, cartas y fotografías." In *Migración internacionale identidades cambiantes,* ed. Eugenia Anguiano Téllez and Miguel Hernández Madrid, 229–50. Zamora, Michoacán: El Colegio de Michoacán.

Díaz-Serrano, Luís, and José António Cabral Vieira. 2005. "Low Pay, Higher Pay and Job Satisfaction within the European Union:

Empirical Evidence from Fourteen Countries." IZA Discussion Paper no. 1558. Bonn: Institute for the Study of Labor.

Doeringer, Peter B., and Michael J. Piore. 1985. "Internal Labor Markets and Manpower Analysis: A Second Look." In *Internal Labor Markets and Manpower Analysis,* ix–xxxv. Armonk, NY and London: Sharpe.

Donato, Katharine M. 1993 "Current Trends and Patterns in Female Migration: Evidence from México." *International Migration Review* 27(4): 748–71.

———. 2010. "US Migration from Latin America: Gendered Patterns and Shifts." *Annals of the American Academy of Political and Social Science* 630: 78–92.

Donato, Katherine M., and Carl L. Bankston III. 2008. "The Origins of Employer Demand for Immigrants in a New Destination: The Salience of Soft Skills in a Volatile Economy." In *New Faces in New Places: The Changing Geography of American Immigration,* ed. Douglas S. Massey, 124–48. New York: Russell Sage Foundation.

Donato, Katharine M., Chizuko Wakabayashi, Shirin Hakimzadeh, and Amada Armenta. 2008. "Shifts in the Employment Conditions of Mexican Migrant Men and Women: The Effect of US Immigration Policy." *Work and Occupations* 35(4): 462–95.

Dreby, Joanna. 2010. *Divided by Borders: Mexican Migrants and Their Children.* Berkeley: University of California Press.

Du Bry, Travis. 2006. *Immigrants, Settlers and Laborers: The Socioeconomic Transformation of a Farming Community.* El Paso, TX: LFB Scholarly Publishing.

Duleep, Harriet O., and Mark C. Regets. 1999. "Immigrants and Human-Capital Investment." *American Economic Review* 89(2): 186–91.

———. 2002. "The Elusive Concept of Immigrant Quality: Evidence from 1970–1990." IZA Discussion Paper no. 631. Bonn: Institute for the Study of Labor.

Durand, Jorge. 1998. *Política, modelos y patrón migratorios: El trabajo y los trabajadores mexicanos en Estados Unidos.* San Luis Potosí, México: El Colegio de San Luis.

Durand, Jorge, and Douglas S. Massey. 2003. *Clandestinos: Migración México-Estados Unidos en los albores del siglo XXI.* México: Porrúa and Universidad Autónoma de Zacatecas.

Durand, Jorge, Douglas Massey, and Chiara Capoferro. 2005. "The New Geography of Mexican Immigration." In *New Destinations: Mexican Immigration in the United States*, 1–20. New York: Rusell Sage Foundation.

Durand, Jorge, Douglas S. Massey, and Emilio Parrado. 1999. "The New Era of Mexican Migration to the United States." *Journal of American History* 86: 518–36.

Durand, Jorge, Douglas S. Massey, and Rene M. Zenteno. 2001. "Mexican Immigration to the United States: Continuities and Changes." *Latin American Research Review* 36(1): 107–27.

Dustmann, Christian. 2003. "Return Migration, Wage Differentials, and the Optimal Migration Duration." *European Economic Review* 47(2): 353–69.

Dustmann, Christian, and Francesca Fabbri. 2003. "Language Proficiency and Labor Market Performance of Immigrants in the UK." *Economic Journal* 113: 695–717.

Dustmann, Christian, Francesca Fabbri, Ian Preston, and Jonathan Wadsworth. 2003. *The Local Labour Market Effects of Immigration in the UK*. Retrieved June 2010 from www.ucl.ac.uk/~uctpb21/reports /HomeOffice06_03.

Dustmann, Christian, and Oliver Kirkchamp. 2002. "The Optimal Migration Duration and Activity Choice after Re-migration." *Journal of Development Economics* 67: 351–72.

Dustmann, Christian, and Yoram Weiss. 2006. "Return Migration: Theory and Emperical Evidence from the UK." *British Journal of Industrial Relations* 45(2): 236–56.

Earle, John S., and Zuzana Sakova. 2000. "Business Start-Ups or Disguised Unemployment? Evidence on the Character of Self-Employment from Transition Economies." *Labour Economics* 7(5): 575–601.

El Economista. 2009. "GM prolonga paro técnico en planta de Silao." Available at http://eleconomista.com.mx/notas-online/negocios /2009/04/23/gm-prolonga-paro-tecnico-planta-silao.

———. 2012. "Prefieren surtir piel a armadoras que al sector zapatero." Available at http://eleconomista.com.mx/estados/2012/05/03 /prefieren-surtir-piel-armadoras-que-sector-zapatero.

———. 2014. "Récord exportador por quinto año consecutivo." Available at http://eleconomista.com.mx/industrias/2014/05/07/produccion-automotriz-mexico-crece-39-abril.

Enchautegui, Maria E. 1993. "The Value of US Labor Market Experience in the Home Country: The Case of Puerto Rican Return Migrants." *Economic Development and Cultural Change* 42(1): 169–91.

Erlich, Mark, and Jeff Grabelsky. 2005. "Standing at a Crossroads: The Building Trades in the Twenty-first Century." *Labor History* 46(4): 421–45.

Espinosa, Victor M. 1998. *El Dilema del Retorno: Migracion, Genero y Pertenenecia en un Contexto Transnacional.* Zamora, Mexico: El Colegio de Michoacán.

Evans, Karen. 2002. "The Challenge of 'Making Learning Visible': Problems and Issues in Recognizing Tacit Skills and Key Competences." In *Working to Learn: Transforming Learning in the Workplace,* ed. Karen Evans, Phil Hodkinson, and Lorna Unwin, 7–28. London: Kogan.

Evans, Karen, and Helen Rainbird. 2002. "The Significance of Workplace Learning for a 'Learning Society.'" In *Working to Learn: Transformative Learning in the Workplace,* ed. Karen Evans, Phil Hodkinson, and Lorna Unwin, 79–94. London: Kogan.

Fernández Jilberto, Alex E., and Barbara Hogenboom. 1996. "Mexico's Integration in NAFTA: Neoliberal Restructuring and Changing Political Alliances." In *Liberalizing in the Developing World: Institutional and Economic Changes in Latin America, Africa and Asia,* ed. Alex E. Fernández Jilberto and André Mommen, 138–61. London and New York: Routledge.

Fields, Gary. 2013. *Self-Employment in the Developing World.* Submitted to the High Level Panel on the Post-2015 Development Agenda, United Nations.

Fine, Gary A. 1996. *Kitchens.* Berkeley: University of California Press.

Fisher, Lloyd H. 1953. *The Harvest Labor Market in California.* Cambridge, MA: Harvard University Press.

FitzGerald, David. 2009. *A Nation of Emigrants: How Mexico Manages Its Migration.* Berkeley: University of California Press.

FitzGerald, David, and Rafael Alarcon. 2013. "Migration: Policies and Politics." In *Mexico and the United States: The Politics of Partnership,* ed. Peter H. Smith and Andrew Selee. London: Lynne Rienner.

FitzGerald, David, Rafael Alarcón, and Leah Muse-Orlinoff, eds. 2011. *Recession without Borders: Mexican Migrants Confront the Economic Downturn.* La Jolla: Center for Comparative Immigration Studies, University of California.

Flippen, Chenoa. 2012. "Laboring Underground: The Employment Patterns of Hispanic Immigrants Men in Durham, NC." *Social Problems* 59: 21–42.

Form, William Humbert, and Julius Rivera. 1958. *The Place of Returning Migrants in a Stratification System.* East Lansing: Labor and Industrial Relations Center, Michigan State University.

Fundacion BBVA Bancomer. 2012. *Situación Migración México.* Available at www.bbvaresearch.com.

Fussell, Elizabeth. 2004. "Sources of Mexico's Migration Stream: Rural, Urban, and Border Migrants to the United States." *Social Forces* 82(3): 937–67.

———. 2009. "Hurricane Chasers in New Orleans Latino Immigrants as a Source of a Rapid Response Labor Force." *Hispanic Journal of Behavioral Sciences* 31(3): 375–94.

Gamio, Manuel. 1991. [1930]. "Número, procedencia y distribución geográfica de los inmigrantes mexicanos en Estados Unidos." In *Migración México-Estados Unidos: Años veinte.* México: Consejo Nacional para la Cultura y las Artes.

Gascón, Verónica. 2013. "Implican repatriados reto laboral." Retrieved May 14, 2014, from www.reforma.com.

Gazioglu, Saziye, and Aysit Tansel. 2002. "Job Satisfaction in Britain: Individual and Job Related Factors." ERC Working Paper in Economics. Ankara: Economic Research Center.

Gertler, Meric S. 2004, *Manufacturing Culture: The Institutional Geography of Industrial Practice.* Oxford: Oxford University Press.

Ghosh, Bimal. 1997. "Migration and Development: Some Selected Issues." Paper prepared for the International Organization for Migration and presented at the Second Regional Conference on Migration, Panama.

Gmelch, George. 1980. "Return Migration." *Annual Review of Anthropology* 9: 135–59.

Golash-Boza, Tanya. 2011. "Paying Attention to Whiteness and Class." *Du Bois Review: Social Science Research on Race* 8(2): 517–21.

Gonzalez-Lozano, Heriberto. 2012. "Return Migration and Self-Employment in Mexico." Retrieved January 12, 2014, from http://sole-jole.org/13316.pdf.

Granovetter, Mark. 1981. "Toward of Sociological Theory of Income Differences." In *Sociological Perspectives on Labor Markets*, ed. I. Berg, 11–47. New York: Academic Press.

Griffith, David. 1993. *Jones's Minimal: Low-wage Labor in the United States.* Albany, NY: SUNY Press.

———. 2007. *American Guestworkers: Jamaicans and Mexicans in the U.S. Labor Market.* University Park: Pennsylvania State University Press.

Guarnizo, Luis Eduardo. 2010. "The Emergence of a Transnational Social Formation and the Mirage of Return Migration Among Dominican Transmigrants." *Identities: Global Studies in Culture and Power* 4(2): 281–322.

Hagan, Jacqueline M. 1994. *Deciding to Be Legal: A Maya Community in Houston.* Philadelphia: Temple University Press.

———. 1998. "Social Networks, Gender and Immigrant Settlement: Resource and Constraint." *American Sociological Review* 63(1): 55–67.

———. 2008. *Migration Miracle: Faith, Hope, and Meaning on the Undocumented Journey.* Cambridge, MA: Harvard University Press.

Hagan, Jacqueline, Jean Luc Demonsant, and Sergio Chavez, 2014. "Identifying and Measuring the Lifelong Human Capital of 'Unskilled' Migrants in the Mexico-US Migratory Circuit." *Journal on Migration and Human Security* 2(2): 76–100.

Hagan, Jacqueline, Karl Eschbach, and Nestor Rodriguez. 2008. "US Deportation Policy, Family Separation, and Circular Migration." *International Migration Review* 42(1): 64–88.

Hagan, Jacqueline M., Nichola Lowe, and Christian Quingla. 2011. "Skills on the Move: Rethinking the Relationship between Human Capital and Immigrant Economic Mobility." *Work and Occupations* 38: 149–78.

Hagan, Jacqueline, and Joshua Wassink. 2014. "Return Migration, Skill Transfers, and Entrepreneurship: Implications for Development." Paper presented at the annual meetings of the American Sociological Association, San Francisco, August 16–19.

Hanson, Gordon H., and Craig McIntosh. 2010. "The Great Mexican Emigration." *Review of Economics and Statistics* 92(4): 798–810.

Harris, John R., and Michael P. Todaro. 1970. "Migration, Unemployment and Development: A Two-Sector Analysis." *American Economic Review* 60: 126–42.

Harris, Nigel. 1995. *The New Untouchables: Immigration and the New World Worker.* London: Penguin.

Hazan, Miryam. 2014. "Understanding Return Migration to Mexico: Towards a Comprehensive Policy for the Reintegration of Returning Migrants." Paper presented at the Center for U.S.-Mexican Studies, University of California, San Diego, March 5.

Hernández Águila, Elena de la Paz. 2007. "Retos y perspectivas de la industria mexicana ante la apertura comercial." *Espiral* 14(40): 95–121.

Hernández-Alvarez, José. 1967. *Return Migration to Puerto Rico.* Berkeley: Institute of International Studies, University of California.

Hernández-León, Rubén. 2004. "Restructuring at the Source." *Work and Occupations* 31: 424–52.

———. 2008. *Metropolitan Migrants: The Migration of Urban Mexicans to the United States.* Berkeley: University of California Press.

———. 2013. "Conceptualizing the Migration Industry." In *The Migration Industry and the Commercialization of International Migration,* ed. T. Gammeltoft-Hansen and N. Nyberg Sorensen, 25–45. London: Routledge.

Herzog, Henry, and Alan M. Schlottmann. 1982. "Migration Information, Job Search and the Remigration Decision." *Southern Economic Journal* 50(1): 43–56.

Hill, John K. 1987. "Immigrant Decisions Concerning Duration of Stay and Migratory Frequency." *Journal of Development Economics* 25(1): 221–34.

Hochschild, Arlie R. 2002. "Love and Gold." In *Global Woman: Nannies, Maids, and Sex Workers in the New Economy,* ed. Barbara Ehrenreich and Arlie Russell Hochschild, 15–30. New York: Metropolitan Books.

Holzer, Harry J., and Robert I. Lerman. 2007. "America's Forgotten Middle-skill Jobs." Washington, DC: Workforce Alliance.

Hondagneu-Sotelo, Pierrette. 1994. *Gendered Transitions: Mexican Experiences of Immigration.* Berkeley: University of California Press.

———. 2001. *Doméstica: Immigrant Workers Cleaning and Caring in the Shadows of Affluence.* Berkeley: University of California Press.

Ilahi, Nadeem, and Saqib Jafarey. 1999. "Guestworker Migration, Remittances and the Extended Family: Evidence from Pakistan." *Journal of Development Economics* 58(2): 485–512.

Instituto Nacional de Estadística y Geografía (INEGI). 2010. *Encuesta Nacional de Ocupación y Empleo.* Aguascalientes, México.

———. 2012. *Perspectiva estadística Guanajuato.* Diciembre 2012. Mexico City: Instituto Nacional de Estadística, Geografía e Informática.

Kandel, William. 2008. *Profile of US Farmwokers: A 2008 Update.* Economic Research Service. US Department of Agriculture, Washington, DC.

Kandel, William, and Douglas Massey. 2002. "The Culture of Mexican Migration: A Theoretical and Empirical Analysis." *Social Forces* 80(3): 981–1004.

Kasarda, John D., and James H. Johnson. 2006. *The Economic Impact of the Hispanic Population on the State of North Carolina.* Chapel Hill, NC: Frank Hawkins Kenan Institute of Private Enterprise.

King, Russell, ed. 1986. *Return Migration and Regional Economic Problems.* London: Croom Helm.

———. 2000. "Generalizations from the History of Return Migration." In *Return Migration: Journey of Hope or Despair,* ed. Bimal Ghosh. International Organization of Migration. Geneva: United Nations.

King, Russell, Alan Strachan, and Jill Mortimer. 1983. "Return Migration: A Review of the Literature." Oxford: Oxford Polytechnic Discussion Paper in Geography, no. 19.

Kmec, Julie A. 2003. "Minority Job Concentration and Wages." *Social Problems* 50(1): 38–59.

Krissman, Fred. 2000. "Immigrant Labor Recruitment: U.S. Agribusiness and Undocumented Migration from Mexico." In *Immigration*

Research for a New Century: Multidisciplinary Perspectives, ed. Nancy Foner, Rubén G. Rumbaut, and Steven Gold. New York: Russell Sage Foundation.

Kusterer, Kenneth C. 1978. *Know-how on the Job: The Important Working Knowledge of Unskilled Workers.* Boulder, CO: Westview Press.

Lacuesta, Aitor. 2006. "Emigration and Human Capital: Who Leaves, Who Comes Back, and What Difference Does it Make?" Banco de España Working Papers 0620. Madrid: Banco de España.

Latapí, Agustín Escobar, Lindsay Lowell, and Susan Martin. 2013. *Binational Dialogue on Mexican Migrants in the US and in Mexico.* CIE-SAS and Georgetown University.

Latapí, Agustín Escobar, Susan F. Martin, Lindsay L. Lowell, and Rafael Fernández de Castro. 2013. "Estudio binacional sobre migrantes mexicanos en Estados Unidos y en México: Las implicaciones de la emigración cero de México a Estados Unidos." *Foreign Affairs: Latinoamérica* 13(3): 12–17.

Leite, Paula, Luis Felipe Ramos, and Selena Gaspar. 2003. "Tendencias recientes de la migración México-Estados Unidos." In *La situación demográfica de México 2003,* 97–115. Mexico City: CONAPO.

Levi, Carlo. 1948. *Christ Stopped at Eboli.* London: Gassell.

Levy, Santiago. 2008. *Good Intentions, Bad Outcomes: Social Policy, Informality, and Economic Growth in Mexico.* Washington, DC: Brookings Institution Press.

Light, Ivan. 1972. *Ethnic Enterprise in America.* Berkeley: University of California Press.

———. 2006. *Deflecting Immigration: Networks, Markets, and Regulation in Los Angeles.* New York: Russell Sage.

Light, Ivan H., and Steven J. Gold. 2000. *Ethnic Economies.* San Diego: Academic Press.

Lindstrom, David P. 1996. "Economic Opportunity in Mexico and Return Migration from the United States." *Demography* 33(3): 357–74.

Lopez, Sandra Lynn. 2010. "The Remittance House: Architecture of Migration in Rural Mexico." *Buildings & Landscapes: Journal of the Vernacular Architecture Forum* 17(2): 33–52.

López Castro, Gustavo. 1986. *La casa dividida: Un estudio de caso sobre la migración a Estados Unidos en un pueblo michoacano.* México: Asociación Mexicana de Población.

Lopreato, Joseph. 1967. *Peasants No More: Social Class and Social Change in an Underdeveloped Society.* San Francisco: Chandler.

Lowder, Stella. 1999. "Globalisation of the Footwear Industry: A Simple Case of Labour?" *Tijdschrift voor economische en sociale geografie* 90(1): 47–60.

Lowe, Nichola, Jacqueline Hagan, and Natasha Iskander. 2010. "Revealing Talent: Informality and Intermediation as Emergent Pathways to Immigrant Labor Market Incorporation." *Environment and Planning* 42(1): 205–22.

Lowell, B. Lindsay, and Allan Findlay. 2002. *Migration of Highly Skilled Persons from Developing Countries: Impact and Policy Reponses.* Geneva: International Labour Office.

Mahler, Sarah J. 1995. *American Dreaming: Immigrant Life on the Margins.* Princeton, NJ: Princeton University Press.

Manwaring, Tony. 1984. "The Extended Internal Labor Market." *Cambridge Journal of Economics* 8: 161–87.

Manwaring, Tony, and Stephen Wood. 1984. "The Ghost in the Machine: Tacit Skills in the Labor Process." *Socialist Review* 14(2): 55–83.

Markovic, Milica, and Lenore Manderson. 2000. "European Immigrants and the Australian Labour Market: A Case Study of Women from the Former Yugoslavia." *Journal of Ethnic and Migration Studies* 26(1): 127–36.

Marrow, Helen. 2011. *New Destination Dreaming: Immigration, Race, and Legal Status in the Rural American South.* Stanford, CA: Stanford University Press.

Martin, Philip L. 1988. *Harvest of Confusion: Migrant Workers in US Agriculture.* Boulder, CO: Westview Press.

———. 2002. "Mexican Workers and U.S. Agriculture: The Revolving Door." *International Migration Review* 36(4): 1124–42.

———. 2003. *Promise Unfulfilled: Unions, Immigration and Farmworkers.* Ithaca, NY: Cornell University Press.

————. 2014. "The H2-A Program: Evolution, Impacts and Outlook." In *(Mis)managing Migration: Guestworkers' Experiences with North American Labor Markets*, ed. David Griffith, 33–62. Santa Fe, NM: School for Advanced Research Press.

Martínez Martínez, Adriana. 2007. "¿Es factible hablar de un distrito industrial del calzado en León?" *Economía Informa* 345: 144–76.

Masferrer, Claudia, and Bryan R. Roberts. 2012. "Going Back Home: Changing Demography and Geography of Mexican Return Migration." *Population Research Policy Review* 31: 465–96.

Massey, Douglas S. 1987. "Understanding Mexican Migration to the United States." *American Journal of Sociology* 92(6): 1372–1403.

————, ed. 2008. *New Faces in New Places: The Changing Geography of American Immigration*. New York: Russell Sage Foundation.

Massey, Douglas S., Rafael Alarcón, Jorge Durand, and Humberto González. 1987. *Return to Aztlan: The Social Process of International Migration from Western Mexico*. Berkeley: University of California Press.

Massey, Douglas S., Joaquin Arango, Graeme Hugo, Ali Kouaouci, Adela Pellegrino, and J. Edward Taylor. 1993. "Theories of International Migration: A Review and Appraisal." *Population and Development Review* 19(3): 431–66.

Massey, Douglas S., Jorge Durand, and Nolan J. Malone. 2003. *Beyond Smoke and Mirrors: Mexican Immigration in the Area of Economic Integration*. New York: Russell Sage Foundation.

Massey, Douglas S., and Kristin E. Espinosa. 1997. "What's Driving Mexico-US Migration? A Theoretical, Empirical and Policy Analysis." *American Journal of Sociology* 102(4): 939–99.

McKenzie, David J., and Johan Mistiaen. 2009. "Surveying Migrant Households: A Comparison of Census-Based, Snowball and Intercept Point Surveys." *Journal of the Royal Statistical Society: Series A (Statistics in Society)* 172: 339–60.

Menjivar, Cecilia. 2000. *Fragmented Ties: Salvadoran Immigrant Networks in America*. Berkeley: University of California Press.

Mesnard, Alice. 2004a. "Temporary Migration and Capital Market Imperfections." *Oxford Economic Papers* 56(2): 242–62.

————. 2004b. "Temporary Migration and Self-Employment: Evidence from Tunisia." *Brussels Economic Review / Cahiers Economiques de Bruxelles* 47: 119–38.

Mesnard, Alice, and Martin Ravallion. 2006. "The Wealth Effect on New Business Startups in a Developing Economy." *Economica* 73(291): 367–92.

Milkman, Ruth. 2000. "Immigrant Organizing and the New Labor Movement in Los Angeles." *Critical Sociology* 26(1–2): 59–81.

————. 2006. *LA Story: Immigrant Workers and the Future of the US Labor Movement.* New York: Russell Sage Foundation.

Mincer, Jacob. 1958. "Investment in Human Capital and Personal Income Distribution." *Journal of Political Economy* 66: 281–302.

Misko, Josie. 2008. "Combining Formal, Non-Formal, and Informal Learning for Workforce Skill Development." Australian Department of Education, Employment and Workplace Relations (NCVER).

Moss, Philip, and Chris Tilly. 1995. "Skills and Race in Hiring: Quantitative Findings from Face-to-face Interviews." *Eastern Economic Journal* 21(3): 357–74.

————. 1996. " 'Soft Skills' and Race: An Investigation of Black Men's Employment Problems." *Work and Occupations* 23(3): 252–76.

Mouw, Ted, and Sergio Chavez. 2012. "Occupational Linguistic Niches and the Wage Growth of Latino Immigrants." *Social Forces* 91(2): 423–52.

Newman, Katherine. 1999. *No Shame in My Game: The Working Poor in the Inner City.* New York: Knopf.

Nussbaum, Martha C. 2011. *Creating Capabilities: The Human Development Approach.* Cambridge, MA: Belknap Press of Harvard University Press.

Oberle, Alex. 2006. "Latino Business Landscapes and the Hispanic Ethnic Economy." In *Landscapes of the Ethnic Economy,* ed. David H. Kaplan and Wei Li, 149–63. Lanham, MD: Rowman and Littlefield.

Ortiz, Silvia. 2009. "Crisis, oportunidad para sector calzado." Available atwww.cnnexpansion.com/manufactura/2009/04/24/crisis-oportunidad-para-sector-calzado.

Ortiz, Sutti. 2002. "Laboring in the Factories and in the Fields." *Annual Review of Anthropology*. 31: 395–417.

Osterman, Paul. 2001. "Employers in the Low Wage / Low Skill Labor Market." In *Low-Wage Workers in the New Economy*. Washington, DC: Urban Institute.

Papademetriou, Demetrios G., Doris Meissner, and Eleanor Sohnen. 2013. *Thinking Regionally to Compete Globally: Leveraging Migration and Human Capital in the US, Mexico, and Central America*. Washington, DC: Migration Policy Institute.

Papail, Jean. 2002. "De Asalariado a Empresario: La Reinsercion Laboral de los Migrantes Internacionales en la Region Centro-occidente de Mexico." *Migraciones Internacionales* 1: 79–102.

Parrenas, Rhacel. 2001. *Servants of Globalization: Women, Migration , and Domestic Work*. Stanford, CA: Stanford University Press.

Passel, Jeffrey, D'Vera Cohn, and Ana Gonzalez-Barrera. 2012. *Net Migration from Mexico Falls to Zero—and Perhaps Less*. Washington, DC: Pew Hispanic Center.

Peck, Gunther. 1996. "Reinventing Free Labor: Immigrant Padrones and Contract Laborers in North America, 1885–1925." *The Journal of American History*. 83(3): 848–871.

Pedraza, Silvia. 1991. "Women and Migration: The Social Consequences of Gender." *Annual Review of Sociology* 17: 303–25.

Perez-Armendariz, Clarisa, and David Crow. 2010. "Do Migrants Remit Democracy? International Migration, Political Beliefs, and Behavior in Mexico?" *Comparative Political Studies* 43(1): 119–48.

Pessar, Patricia R. 1999. "Engendering Migration Studies: The Case of New Immigrants in the United States." *American Behavioral Scientist* 42: 577–600.

Pew Hispanic Center. 2007. *Construction Jobs Expand for Latinos Despite Slump in Housing Market* (Fact sheet), March 7. Washington, DC: Author.

Phillips, Julie A., and Douglas S. Massey. 2000. "Engines of Immigration: Stocks of Human and Social Capital in Mexico." *Social Science Quarterly* 81(1): 33–48.

Piore, Michael. 1979. *Birds of Passage: Long-Distance Migrants in Industrial Societies.* Cambridge: Cambridge University Press.

———. 2002. "Thirty Years Later: Internal Labor Markets, Flexibility and the New Economy." *Journal of Management and Governance* 6: 271–79.

Piore, Michael, and Charles Sabel. 1984. *The Second Industrial Divide.* New York: Basic Books.

Pisani, Michael J., and David W. Yoskowitz. 2006. "Opportunity Knocks: Entrepreneurship, Informality, and Home Gardening in South Texas." *Journal of Borderland Studies* 21(2): 59–76.

Polanyi, Michael. 1958. *The Study of Man.* Chicago: University of Chicago Press.

———. 1966. *The Tacit Dimension.* London: Routledge & Kegan.

Polanyi, Michael, and Harry Prosch. 1975. *Meaning.* Chicago: University of Chicago Press.

Portes, Alejandro. 2010. *Economic Sociology: A Systematic Inquiry.* Princeton, NJ: Princeton University Press. In *The Informal Economy: Studies in Advanced and Less Developed* Countries, ed. Alejandro Portes, Manuel Castells, and Lauren A. Benton. Baltimore: Johns Hopkins University Press.

Powers, Mary, and William Seltzer. 1998. "Occupational Status and Mobility among Undocumented Immigrants by Gender." *International Migration Review* 32: 21–55.

Ramirez, Hernan, and Pierrette Hondagneu-Sotelo. 2009. "Mexican Immigrant Gardeners: Entrepreneurs or Exploited Workers?" *Social Problems* 56(1): 70–88.

Reich, Robert B. 1992. *The Work of Nations: Preparing Ourselves for 21st-century Capitalism.* London: Simon and Schuster.

Reinhold, Steffen, and Kevin Thom. 2011. "Migration Experience and Earnings in the Mexican Labor Market." Working Paper, Department of Economics, New York University, New York, NY.

Reyes, Belinda I. 1997. *Dynamics of Immigration: Return Migration to Western Mexico.* San Francisco: Public Policy Institute of California.

Richmond, Anthony H. 1968. "Return Migration from Canada to Britain." *Population Studies* 22(2): 263–71.

Roberts, Bryan R., Reanne Frank, and Fernando Lozano-Ascencio. 1999. "Transnational Migrant Communities and Mexican Migration to the US." *Ethnic and Racial Studies* 22(2): 238–66.

Romero, Manuel A. H. 2012. "Nothing to Learn? Labor Learning in California's Farmwork." *Anthropology of Work Review* 33(2): 73–88.

Romero, Mary. 2002. *Made in America*. New York: Routledge.

———. 2011. *The Maid's Daughter: Living Inside and Outside the American Dream*. New York: NYU Press.

Romo, Gerardo. 2014. "Dejan Zacatecas por sueño 'regio'." Retrieved May 14, 2014, from www.elnorte.com/local/articulo/791/1580441/?grcidorigen=1.

Ruiz-Tagle, Juan C., and Rebeca Wong. 2009. "Determinants of Return Migration to Mexico among Mexicans in the United States." Detroit: Population Association of America Annual Meeting.

Saloutos, Theodore. 1956. *They Remember America: The Story of the Repatriated Greek-Americans*. Berkeley: University of California Press.

Sanderson, Matthew, and Matthew Painter II. 2011. "Occupational Channels for Mexican Migration: New Destination Formation in a Binational Context." *Rural Sociology* 76: 461–80.

Sandoval, Cristian. 2014. "The U.S.-Mexico Cycle: The End of an Era." Mexicans and Americans Working Together (MATT). http://research.matt.org/category-research/return-migration/.

Sandoval Hernández, Efrén, and Ruben Hernández-León. 2013. "La Industria de la movilidad migratoria: el programa de visas H2 para trabajadores temporales mexicanos." Paper presented at the conference La Fábrica de las Migraciones. Perspectivas desde México-Centroamérica y Magreb-Machrek, Mexico City, October 21–23, 2013.

Sassen, Saskia. 1988. *The Mobility of Labor and Capital*. Cambridge: Cambridge University Press.

———. 1989. "New York City's Informal Economy." In *The Informal Economy: Studies in Advanced and Less Developed Countries,* ed. Alejandro Portes, Manuel Castells, and Lauren A. Benton, 60–77. Baltimore: Johns Hopkins University Press.

———. 1993. "Rebuilding the Global City: Economy, Ethnicity, and Space." *Social Justice* 20(3/4): 32–50.

Saxenian, Analee. 1996. "Beyond Boundaries: Open Labor Markets and Learning in Silicon Valley." In *Boundaryless Career: A New Employment Principle for a New Organizational Era,* ed. Michael B. Arthur and Denise Rousseau, 23–39. New York: Oxford University Press.

Shih, Johanna. 2006. "Circumventing Discrimination." *Gender and Society* 20: 177–206.

Singer, Audrey. 2004. *The Rise of New Immigrant Gateways.* Brookings Institution Living Cities Census Series. Brookings Institution, Washington, DC.

Sjaastad, Larry A. 1962. "The Costs and Returns of Human Migration." *Journal of Political Economy* 70: 80–93.

Smith, Robert Courtney. 2005. *Mexican New York: Transnational Lives of New Migrants.* Berkeley: University of California Press.

Sorenson, Aage B., and Arne L. Kalleberg. 1981. "An Outline of a Theory of the Matching of Persons to Jobs." In *Sociological Perspectives on Labor Markets,* ed. I. Berg, 49–74. New York: Academic Press.

Star, Susan L., and Anselm Strauss. 1999. "Layers of Silence, Arenas of Voice: The Ecology of Visible and Invisible Work." *Computer-Supported Cooperative Work: Journal of Collaborative Computing* 8: 9–30.

Stark, Oded. 1991. *The Migration of Labor.* Oxford: Blackwell.

Stark, Oded, and David Bloom. 1985. "The New Economics of Labor Migration." *American Economic Review* 75: 173–78.

Taylor, J. Edward, Philip L. Martin, and Michael Fix. 1997. *Poverty amid Prosperity: Immigration and the Changing Face of Rural California.* Washington, DC: Urban Institute.

Taylor, J. Edward, Scott Rozelle, and Alan De Brauw. 2003. "Migration and Incomes in Source Communities: A New Economics of Migration Perspective from China." *Economic Development and Cultural Change* 52(1): 75–101.

Terrazas, Aaron. 2010. *Mexican Immigrants in the United States.* Migration Information Source. Available at www.migrationpolicy.org/article /mexican-immigrants-united-states-0#12.

Theodore, N., A. Valenzuela, Jr., and E. Meléndez. 2006. "*La Esquina* (The Corner): Day Laborers on the Margins of New York's Formal Economy." *Journal of Labor and Society* 9: 407–23.

Tienda, Marta, and Karen Booth. 1991. "Gender, Migration and Social Change." *International Sociology* 6(1): 51–72.

Todaro, Michael P. 1969. "A Model of Labor Migration and Urban Unemployment in Less-developed Countries." *American Economic Review* 59(1): 138–48.

Toren, Nina. 1976. "Return to Zion: Characteristics and Motivations of Returning Emigrants." *Social Forces* 54(3): 546–58.

U.S. Bureau of Labor Statistics. 2009. *North Carolina Wages and Salaries by Industrial Sector.* Available at www.bls.gov/oes/2002/oes_nc.htm#b47–0000.

U.S. Census Bureau. 2001. *Hispanic or Latino Origin: All Races Mapping Census 2000: The Geography of U.S. Diversity.* December 7. Available at www.census.gov/population/www/cen2000/dt_atlas.html.

———. 2006–08. *American Community Survey.* Available at http://factfinder.census.gov.

———. 2007. *The American Community—Hispanics: 2004.* American Community Survey Reports. Available at www.census.gov/prod/2007pubs/acs-03.pdf.

———. 2009. *Hispanic Population by State.* Available at http://quickfacts.census.gov/qfd/states/37000.html.

Valdez, Zulema. 2008. "Latino / A Entrepreneurship in the United States: A Strategy of Survival and Economic Mobility." In *Latinas / os in the United States: Changing the Face of América,* ed. Havidan Rodriguez, Rogelio Saenz, and Cecilia Menjivar, 168–80. New York: Springer.

Valenzuela, Abel Jr. 2001. "Day Laborers as Entrepreneurs?" *Journal of Ethnic and Migration Studies.* 27(2): 335–352.

———. 2003. "Day Labor Work." *Annual Review of Sociology* 29: 307–33.

Valenzuela, Abel Jr., Nik Theodore, Edwin Melendez, and Ana L. Gonzalez. 2006. "On the Corner: Day Labor in the United States." Technical Report. Los Angeles: UCLA Center for the Study of Urban Poverty.

Van Hook, Jennifer, and Frank Bean. 1998. "Estimating Unauthorized Mexican Migration to the United States: Issues and Results." In *Migration between Mexico and the United States, Binational Study, Vol. 2,*

511–50. Washington, DC, and Mexico City: US Commission on Immigration Reform and Mexican Ministry of Foreign Affairs.

Vélez Storey, Jaime. 2002. "Los Braceros y el Fondo de Ahorro Campesino." In *Migración internacional e identidades cambiantes*, ed. Ma. Eugenia Anguiano Téllez and Miguel Hernández Madrid, 19–42. Zamora, Michoacán: El Colegio de Michoacán.

Villarreal, M. Angeles. 2010. *The Mexican Economy after the Global Financial Crisis*. Washington, DC: Congressional Research Service.

Wahba, Jackline, and Yves Zenou. 2012. "Out of Sight, Out of Mind: Migration, Entrepreneurship and Social Capital." *Regional Science and Urban Economics* 42(5): 890–903.

Waldinger, Roger. 1996. *Still the Promised City? African-Americans and New Immigrants in Postindustrial New York*. Cambridge, MA: Harvard University Press.

Waldinger, Roger, C. Erickson, R. Milkman, D. Mitchell, A. Valenzuela, K. Wong, and M. Zeitlin. 1996. *Helots No More: A Case Study of the Justice for Janitors Campaign in Los Angeles* (Working Paper no. 15). Ralph and Goldy Lewis Center for Regional Policy Studies, UCLA, Los Angeles, California.

Waldinger, Roger, and Michael I. Lichter. 2003. *How the Other Half Works: Immigration and the Social Organization of Labor*. Berkeley: University of California Press.

Warhurst, Chris, Chris Tilly, and Mary Gatta. 2014. "A New Social Construction of Skill." Paper presented at the annual meeting of the SASE Annual Conference, University of Milan, Milan, Italy, July 19.

Wells, Miriam J. 1996. *Strawberry Fields: Politics, Class, and Work in California Agriculture*. Ithaca, NY: Cornell University Press.

Wiley, Norbert F. 1967. "The Ethnic Mobility Trap and Stratification Theory." *Social Problems* 15: 147–59.

Williams, Allan M. 2006. "Lost in Translation? International Migration, Learning and Knowledge." *Progress in Human Geography* 30(5): 588–607.

———. 2007a. "Listen to Me, Learn with Me: International Migration and Knowledge Transfers." *British Journal of Industrial Relations* 45(2): 361–82.

————. 2007b. "International Labor Migration and Tacit Knowledge Transactions: A Multi-Level Perspective." *Global Networks* 7(1): 29–47.

Williams, Allan M., and Vladimir Baláž. 2005. "What Human Capital, Which Migrants? Returned Skilled Migration to Slovakia From the UK." *International Migration Review* 39: 439–68.

Wilson, Kenneth L., and Alejandro Portes.1980. "Immigrant Enclaves: An Analysis of the Labor Market Experiences of Cubans in Miami." *American Journal of Sociology* 86(2): 295–319.

Wimmer, Andreas, and Nina Glick Shiller. "Methodological Nationalism and Beyond: Nation-state Building, Migration, and Social Sciences." *Global Networks* 2(4): 301–34.

Woodruff, Christopher, and Rene Zenteno. 2007. "Migration Networks and Microenterprises in Mexico." *Journal of Development Economics* 82(2): 509–28.

Zahniser, Steven S., and Michael J. Greenwood. 1998. "Transferability of Skills and the Economic Rewards to US Employment for Return Migrants in Mexico." *Migration between Mexico and the United States: Binational Study* 3: 1133–52.

Zenteno, Rene. 2011. "Recent Trends in Mexican to the US: The Mexico Perspective." Retrieved June 1, 2012, from www.somede.org /documentos/zenteno-2011.pdf.

Zlolniski, Christian. 1994. "The Informal Economy in an Advanced Industrialized Society: Mexican Immigrant Labor in Silicon Valley." *Yale Law Review* 103: 2305–35.

Zúñiga, Víctor. 1992. "Tradiciones migratorias internacionales y socialización familiar: expectativas migratorias de los alumnos de secundaria de cuatro municipios del norte de Nuevo León." *Frontera Norte* 4(7): 45–74.

Zúñiga, Víctor, and Rubén Hernández-León. 2005. *New Destinations: Mexican Immigration in the United States.* New York: Russell Sage Foundation.

INDEX

295